the better
way to care
for your baby

A Week-by-Week Illustrated Companion

for Parenting and Protecting Your Child

Using the Latest and Safest Techniques

Robin Elise Weiss
L.C.C.E., I.C.C.E.-C.P.E., C.L.C.

FAIR WINDS
PRESS
BEVERLY, MASSACHUSETTS

Text © 2010 Robin Elise Weiss

First published in the USA in 2010 by
Fair Winds Press, a member of
Quayside Publishing Group
100 Cummings Center
Suite 406-L
Beverly, MA 01915-6101
www.fairwindspress.com

14 13 12 11 10   1 2 3 4 5

ISBN-13: 978-1-59233-420-9
ISBN-10: 1-59233-420-2

Library of Congress Cataloging-in-Publication Data available

Cover design: Carol Holtz
Book design: Laura H. Couallier, Laura Herrmann Design
Editor: Andrea Mattei
Technical Edit: Dr. Marcello Pietrantoni, M.D., F.A.C.O.G
Photo Research: Daryl Gammons-Jones
Illustrations: Robert Brandt

Printed and bound in China

Cover images, (left to right): shutterstock.com; iStockphoto.com, (second,
middle, & right); Absodels/gettyimages.com; iStockphoto.com, (bottom, right)

Bambu Productions/gettyimages.com, 1 (bottom, middle)
© Liane Cary/agefotostock.com, 1 (top, middle)
Top, left; second row, middle & right; third row, left & middle; bottom, left &
      right; iStockphtoto.com, 1
shutterstock.com, 1 (top, right)
© Juan Manuel Silva/agefotostock.com, 1 (second row, left)
Camille Tokerud/gettyimages.com, 1 (third row, right)

The information in this book is for educational purposes only. It is not
intended to replace the advice of a physician or medical practitioner. Please
see your health care provider before beginning any new health program.

DEDICATION

To Noa Simone—for sharing your first year with me as I wrote this book. You are one sweet, energetic, and lovely baby girl. Happy first birthday!

ACKNOWLEDGMENTS

They say that raising a child takes a village. Well, writing a book takes a village as well. Many people have helped me along this journey. Marci Yesowitch Hopkins, Teri Shilling, and Pat Predmore were great online cheerleaders as I worked diligently. Many thanks go to Sarah and Ashley Benz, Lucian and Stacie Walker, and Erin and Bella Vest for answering endless questions about the first year of a baby's life. Sharon Muza, Angela Garvin, and Nicole Aldridge were great go-to-gals for those last-minute questions on what should be contained on the pages within this book, as well as tireless cheerleaders. Jill Alexander was a wonderful sounding board at Fair Winds Press. Andrea Mattei helped with gentle and thoughtful editing and her experience as a mother. My agent, Barb Doyen, was always there with a great suggestion and positive attitude. Much love and appreciation also go to my family for helping me run the house while writing: Kevin, Hilary, Benjamin, Isaac, Lilah, Owen, Clara, Ada, and Noa.

Contents

MONTH 5-8

MONTH 9-12

INTRODUCTION

Babies are really great!
They are sweet, adorable, quiet . . .
oh wait, that's a television prop, not a real baby.

Babies can be all of those things at times. The problem is that those cute and cuddly moments might not occur as often as you expected after watching babies on TV or talking to friends who have babies.

In truth, newborn babies can be perplexing— they are helpless little bundles who need to eat and be changed constantly, cannot do anything for themselves, and, yes, cry and fuss . . . sometimes more than you might like. In the early days of parenthood, it might seem daunting to read your baby's signals and decipher what she is trying to tell you. After all, babies don't come with an owner's manual.

Most parents complain that the missing owner's manual is the problem. What do you do when your baby cries? Which cry means what? How do you know what your baby needs? How can you enjoy your baby with everything else going on?

Look at this book as your replacement owner's manual. Here you will find quick tips on the things that matter most in your life: feeding, sleeping, and playing with your baby. You will also find lengthier discussions on what your baby's development will look like at certain points along the way in the first year of life. The photos and drawings within will also give you plenty of visual examples for guidance as you navigate the murky waters of new parenthood.

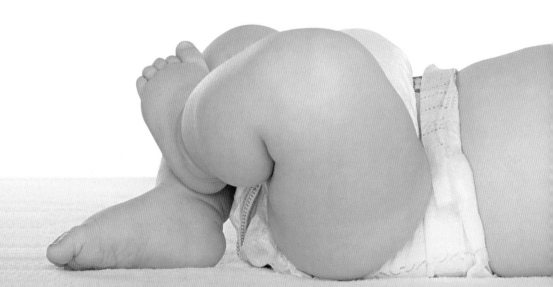

This book is designed to help every parent. Whether this is your first baby or your sixth, there are things you need to remember. The fog of being a new parent is the same for almost all of us. Having everything in one handy location is a huge benefit.

Making all the decisions that need to be made about your baby's health and safety is a big part of baby's first year. Which pediatrician or doctor should you choose? Should you get immunizations? On which time schedule? Do you need to get all of them? What do the top doctors and baby organizations say about hot topics like infant feeding, allergies, developmental play, and more? In these pages, we're certainly not shying away from the tough issues.

Sit down and flip through each chapter. You will get the basics of what you're looking forward to if you scan ahead. Each month will offer you some in-depth looks at various topics, not to mention weekly advice. Each week, you can find a new tip or trick to use when it comes to eating, playing, sleeping, and general advice for your family. As with any advice, some will work perfectly and some will need to be tweaked to fit into your family's lifestyle. Remember, parenting is about compromise, patience, and love. You will be able to make the right choices for your family if you have all the information you need.

Enjoy reading and using this book. But above all, enjoy the first year with your baby. Walk that fine line between enjoying being in the moment and looking forward to the next big thing. Remembering to pause and appreciate each moment as it happens can be one of the hardest things about parenting in general. But with all the excitement and anticipation of things to come during the first year, it becomes even harder. From the moment your baby is born, until you're singing happy birthday and blowing out a single candle, the time flies. Don't miss a thing!

MONTH ONE

Week 1-4

Get to Know Baby

√ **Checklist for Month One**

- ☐ Learn the basics of baby care.
- ☐ Find the proper way to hold an infant.
- ☐ Practice calming a crying baby.
- ☐ Watch for sleeping and waking cycles.
- ☐ Understand breastfeeding basics.
- ☐ Learning basic diapering methods.
- ☐ Learn your baby's feeding cues and the best burping techniques.
- ☐ Know where and when to ask for help.

What to Watch For in the First Month

- ☐ Feeding difficulties including poor weight gain or weight loss
- ☐ Temperature of over 100.1°F (37.8°C)
- ☐ A bluish tinge to the lips
- ☐ Labored breathing

Be Sure to:

- ☐ Protect baby's soft spot (fontanelle).
- ☐ Support baby's head and neck when in an upright position.
- ☐ Avoid loud noises or bright lights that might frighten baby.
- ☐ Watch baby's reactions to shots.

Baby Skills:

In the first month, your baby:

- ☐ Will give you signals to indicate hunger and other needs
- ☐ Can smile without prompting at things such as toys
- ☐ Can also smile when smiled at or smile on purpose when seeing a parent
- ☐ Has improved vision—can see high-contrast images
- ☐ Can make eye contact
- ☐ Can hold his or her head up to a 45-degree angle
- ☐ Can make noises
- ☐ Can suck hands or fingers
- ☐ Prefers objects eight to ten inches (20.3 to 25.4 cm) away
- ☐ Tends to keep hands curled up in fists

BABY DATA

Congratulations! Your baby is finally here! After months and months of waiting you are holding your newborn in your arms.

The average full-term newborn will weigh about 7½ pounds (3 kg). But birth weights can vary widely depending on many factors, including length of pregnancy and any complications. Healthy birth weights can range between 5 pounds 8 ounces (2 kg) and 9 pounds 8 ounces (4 kg). Boys might also be slightly heavier than girls. It is also not uncommon for twins or other multiples to weigh less than their singleton counterparts.

At birth, babies tend to be between 18 and 23 inches (46 to 58 cm) long, with boys being slightly longer. Head circumference for girls usually falls between 12.75 and 15.25 inches (33 and 38 cm), with boys' averaging up to 15.75 inches (40 cm). While it's easy to rattle off all of these newborn stats, don't freak out if your baby doesn't fall into some of these ranges. The truth is, all babies are unique, and there is no "one size fits all" model!

Apart from matters of size and shape, what else can you expect in your first few days of parenthood? In short, lots of eating, followed by just as much diaper changing. In the first few days, your baby's diapers will be full of meconium. Meconium is a thick, tar-like substance that lines the baby's intestines while in utero. After the baby is born, the meconium comes out in the baby's diapers. Stools will change color as baby begins to eat and eliminate on his/her own. This is a good thing.

During the first week, the number of your baby's diapers will differ almost daily. You might see one or two dirty diapers the first day. A dirty diaper is considered to be a teaspoon of solid material or a stain about the size of your baby's clenched hand. Days 2 through 4 you should expect to see three or more dirty diapers, and the rest of the week look for four or more dirty diapers. Normal breastfed stools are yellow, seedy, and not solid but runny.

Wet diapers should happen about six times a day by the end of the first week. The urine should be pale in color or clear. If your baby has fewer than six wet diapers or the urine is dark or red, see your lactation consultant or pediatrician for advice. A wet diaper is a tablespoon of urine. In disposable diapers this small amount can hide from you. Try placing a square of toilet tissue in the diaper. If it's wet, you know baby has urinated.

Hot Mama for Month One

You should plan to take a shower and get dressed nearly every day. Even if it doesn't happen until late afternoon or evening, a shower will lift your spirits. You can wait for someone to be home to hold the baby for you or grab a quick shower during nap time. Many new mothers fear leaving their newborn unattended even for few minutes to take a quick shower, particularly if their child cries or fusses when they aren't present. A good solution if you are nervous is to place your child in a baby car seat, bouncey chair, Moses basket, or the like, and take the baby into the bathroom with you. Place the carrier on the floor in the bathroom. You'll be able to take your shower and keep an eye on your baby.

Getting to know your new baby is a very important job. New parenthood can be a wild ride. In the midst of the craziness, try to take some time to pause and enjoy the quiet moments. Open your eyes to the joy and wonderment of this new life.

MONTH ONE:
Bringing Up Baby

Your three goals this month are simple:

- Learn the basics of baby care.

- Feed your baby.

- Know where to go for help.

LEARN THE BASICS OF BABY CARE

As wonderful as new babies are, they don't come with instructions. In fact, they can be downright perplexing at first. Over time, as you get to know

Remember to sleep while the baby sleeps, but if you can't, try relaxing and watching your baby sleep. Observing all the little things about your baby in this stillness is truly amazing.

your baby and begin to pick up her cues, life will get easier. These first weeks can be particularly difficult if you're not feeling great physically. If you have had a complicated vaginal birth or a cesarean birth, you might really need to have some extra help caring not only for your baby but for yourself as well.

Baby care is not as easy as you might think it is! Babies are small and wiggly. They might not take well to having diapers put on or being bathed. With a new baby, suddenly seemingly simple tasks can become time consuming and challenging. Hang in there, take your time, and you'll get the hang of it.

Umbilical Cord Care

The place where your baby's umbilical cord was is called the cord stump. The first few days your baby will have a clamp or pin on the stump to ensure that it stays closed. Then it will be removed, leaving a hard, dried stub.

Many doctors simply advise parents to leave the umbilical cord stump alone, and just keep it dry. If it gets wet during bathing or because of a diaper accident, do not panic. Simply dry it with a piece of cotton and allow it to air out for a bit.

If your baby's cord area is red, warm to the touch, or foul-smelling, call your baby's doctor. It may be the sign of an infection. Some practitioners might want you to clean the stump area with alcohol and cotton swabs. If so, simply wet a cotton swab with alcohol. Press the area around the cord in, to expose more of the stump. Make a quick swipe with the cotton swab. Finish diapering and dressing your baby as needed, and throw the cotton swab away.

Typically the stump will fall off within the first two weeks. Do not pull at the stump. Simply throw away the stump. If all goes well, there is no need to keep it or to report it to your baby's practitioner.

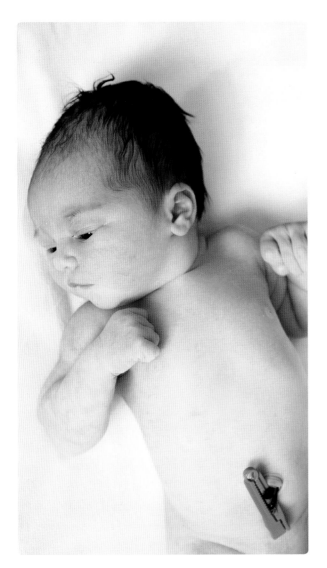

Don't be frightened of your baby's umbilical cord stump. The stump dries up nicely and falls off quickly, without having to do much to it. It's temporary and shouldn't cause much of a fuss.

Bathing Baby

The good news is that babies don't get too dirty, particularly in these early weeks. Good hygiene at diaper changes will help ensure that baby is getting the biggest problem area clean. You can also take a washcloth under baby's neck for another "hot spot" in baby cleanliness.

If you're feeling up for a real bath, try bathing with the baby. Have someone bring you the baby while you sit in the bathtub with your legs up. Cradle baby with your legs while you bathe him in shallow water. You can make sure the water is not too hot by testing it with your elbow, which is quite sensitive. A bath with mom works out really well for a baby who might be frightened of bathing, because it is so comforting. Bath time is also a nice, relaxing time to nurse the baby. When you're done bathing baby you can simply hand him off to your helper and finish your bath. Don't try to get out of the tub with baby in your arms—it's too slippery, and dangerous!

The sink is another great spot for baby's early baths, mainly because it is much more comfortable for you to stand rather than bend over a bathtub. It is also handy for getting water and draining it when you're done.

With all baby bathing activities, there are a few rules. The first is, never leave the baby alone. Ever. Even for a minute. Second, gather your supplies before you get started. Remember the towel, clean clothes and diaper, and any soaps or lotions you will be using. This will help you enforce rule number one.

The Safest Ways to Hold an Infant

Supporting your newborn's head, neck, and spine is important to his safety and well-being. Safe handling is crucial when passing your baby from one person to another, so be sure to review these precautions with anyone who might not be familiar with the proper procedures.

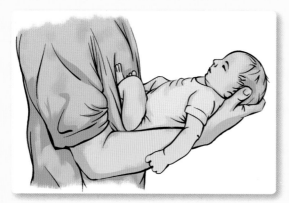

When your baby is tiny, you can effectively support his head, neck, and spine with both hands cradled behind his head and his feet toward your body. Your arms can be supported by your lap, if needed. This gives the baby the opportunity to see your full face and absorb the sound of your voice.

Perhaps the most common practice for holding an infant is to support the spine and buttocks with one arm while wrapping the other arm around the neck to support the head with the elbow area. You will find it more comfortable to use your dominant arm to bear the extra weight of the head. Use extra caution to protect the head when walking through doorways and carrying a baby in this manner.

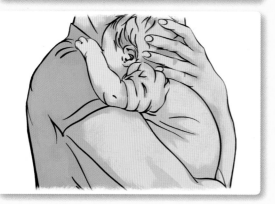

Hold your baby close to your shoulder supporting his head and neck and supporting his bottom with the opposite forearm. Drape his arms toward your shoulders. This is similar to one of the position commonly used for burping—close and comforting for both of you.

Diapering Baby

Choosing which type of diapers to use is not easy these days. There are a lot of baby diapering options. The biggest choice will be whether to use disposable diapers or cloth diapers. Both have advantages and disadvantages.

Cloth diapers come in several categories:

- All-in-one diapers
- Pocket diapers
- Diapers used with covers

Even prefolds, which are what most of us think of as cloth diapers, rarely use pins these days. Most cloth diapers have hook-and-loop fastening strips, like Velcro.

Cloth diapers are typically better for your baby's sensitive skin. They are also better for the environment, even when you factor in washing them. Economically, they can be a real savings. While the initial investment is more, the savings add up, particularly if you use them for more than one child.

The real trick with cloth diapers is figuring out which system works best for you. Try a sampler pack if you are having trouble deciding which diapers would be best for your baby. Talking to other families who use cloth diapers will also help.

Disposable diapers are convenient but expensive. Some parents choose to use disposables for the first week or so due to meconium. Other families find that disposables are just what they need to make their lives easier, particularly if no diaper service or washer and dryer is available to them. No matter what type of diapers you use, you'll want to ensure a safe diaper-changing experience.

During the first week decide where you change the baby most frequently. Since you might not be able to trek up to a diaper-changing table on another floor yet, it is handy to have a few locations well stocked with all of your diaper necessities.

Take a few baskets and fill them with diaper supplies, such as wipes, diapers, creams, and a changing mat. (The plastic-lined kind you find in a diaper bag is perfect and can be found separately for this purpose.) Stash the baskets in different parts of the house so you'll always be prepared to make quick changes.

When changing baby, having a game plan is usually the best tactic. Be prepared to change the diaper before removing the old diaper. Have a couple of wipes and a diaper open and ready. Place your baby on the changing surface, keeping one hand on the baby at all times. Remove the clothing and open the diaper. While the dirty diaper is under your baby, use the wipes to clean baby off. Set the dirty diaper, with the wipes on top, aside. Now fasten the new diaper and return baby's clothing. You can either hand the baby to someone else or sit the baby someplace safe. Dispose of the dirty diaper and wipes and wash your hands.

Tiny babies are wiggly and hard to hold while changing diapers. You are also under "fire" from girls and boys while the diaper area is uncovered. So working quickly and efficiently is in your best interest. (To avoid being a target, a good trick is having the clean diaper ready underneath the dirty one before you remove it.) These skills come with practice—which you will have a lot of very shortly.

The Most Effective Way to Diaper Your Baby

Disposable Diapering

Open the diaper tabs on the soiled diaper, and fasten them back so they do not stick to your baby.

Lift your baby's behind off the changing surface by grasping the ankles and gently lifting up.

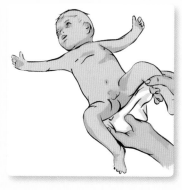

Fold the diaper in half under your baby with the outside of the diaper facing up.

Use a baby wipe or a wet cloth to cleanse your baby's frontal area. If your baby is a girl, be sure to wipe front to back to keep bacteria from the vaginal area.

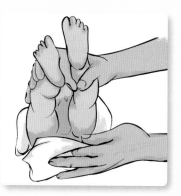

Gently lift your baby's legs and clean his bottom, applying ointment if needed.

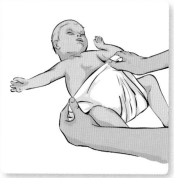

Remove the soiled and folded diaper from under your baby and position the clean diaper under his bottom with the front half between his legs. Pull each side of the diaper securing the tabs until it is wrapped snuggly but comfortably.

Diapering with Cloth (cleanse your baby as described, opposite)

Fold down the front of the cloth diaper to attain the proper length needed to diaper your baby.

Accounting for your baby's individual size, fold the diaper in thirds and fan out the back.

Grasp the ankles as described, at left, and bring the front of the diaper between the legs.

Fasten the diaper to achieve a snug fit. Cover the diapering with a diaper cover.

Diapering Accessory: Diaper Cover

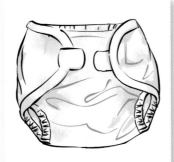

A diaper cover is put over the diaper. All cloth diapers, with the exception of the all-in-ones, need a cover of some sort to be waterproof. There are many styles to choose from including the wrap-style diaper cover, which wraps around from back to front, shown here.

Diapering Alternative: All-in-One Diaper

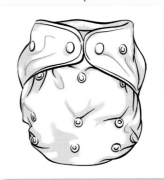

The all-in-one diaper is a convenient choice. It has a soft fleece to keep baby dry and a self-cleaning method that makes washing easier. They are designed to keep waste self-contained and have snaps and closures that fit babies within a broad weight range.

Sleeping

One thing that all parents nearly unanimously ask for is sleep. That only comes when the baby sleeps. In learning to help your little one have a safe sleep cycle, there are a few rules to play by:

- Place your baby on his back to sleep.
- Make sure your baby is sleeping on a firm mattress or surface.
- Swaddle your baby in a lightweight blanket or put him/her in a sleep sack. Do not allow your baby to overheat.
- Do not allow your baby to sleep on the couch, in a chair, or on a water bed.
- Remove all fluffy pillows, stuffed animals, and thick blankets from the sleep area.

Sleep safety is important. Be sure to remove fluffy objects from where your baby sleeps. This means fluffy pillows, comforters, bumper pads, and stuffed animals need to go.

Care of the Penis

If you've had a son and he has an intact penis, you will not need to take special care with his penis. You might want to request that during exams his foreskin is not retracted. This can be painful when forced. The foreskin naturally retracts around the age of two.

If your son was circumcised, you might need to do several special things to clean and care for his penis. After the circumcision you will note that his penis looks red, raw, and bloody. This is normal.

Depending on the type of circumcision, you might have to apply ointments or salves to his penis at every diaper change. You can use some sort of cream or ointment, like Un-Petroleum jelly. Simply use a nonstick medical pad to gently place it over the tip of the penis for protection from urine and feces, and so the diaper won't stick to the open wound.

Some doctors do what's known as a PlastiBell circumcision, which leaves a tiny plastic part on the top of the penis. This will typically fall off after several days, once the foreskin has died and dried off. You will simply throw it away.

You should call the person who performed the circumcision, unless otherwise noted, if your baby has trouble urinating, is bleeding or swollen, has a foul odor, or is warm around the area of the circumcision.

All of this information is valid for circumcisions done as a Brit Milah or bris as well.

Burping Your Baby

It's important to burp your baby whether you are breast- or bottle-feeding. Burping allows any air that your baby has swallowed to come back up. Burping will help to keep your baby more comfortable, better able to hold down food, and less gassy.

To burp your baby, first cover your shoulder or lap with a burp cloth. The classic burping position has the baby up on your shoulder, facing behind you. With one hand, hold the back of his neck and pat with varying degrees of force until he expels the air. The cloth should hold any spit-up that follows.

If you use your lap, you can sit the baby, bent at her waist, leaning forward into the palm of one of your hands. Use your other hand to pat or rub her back until she burps.

The Best Burping Techniques

Burping your baby is an important step in assuring their comfort and contentment. If a baby is not properly burped, it can lead to irritability, sleep disturbances, or spitting up. Be patient with this essential process. It becomes easier as your baby grows stronger.

Hold your baby over your shoulder while supporting his neck. Apply gentle pressure against his abdomen by rubbing and patting his back until he expels the excess gas.

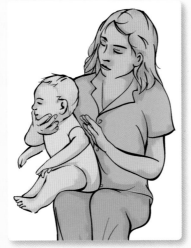

Position your baby in a seated position supporting her head by cupping her chin in your hand, depending on how much neck strength she has achieved. Her legs should be extended forward. Pat and rub her back until she is able to pass the excess gas.

Drape the baby across your lap with your legs crossed or spread so that pressure it applied against his tummy. Support the baby with one hand while you rub his back with the other until the gas is expelled.

As an alternative to the lap position, you can place the baby, feet down, between your legs. Close your legs securely, but not too tightly around his waist, exposing his back for rubbing or patting. Do not forget the cloth to catch any spills.

Some babies burp a lot. Some don't burp very often. You will figure out how much burping your baby needs. If she burps a lot, then be sure to pass this information on to your lactation support or pediatrician. Perhaps her latch is not perfect, which

Burping is important to think about at feeding time. The truth is, some babies burp more readily than others, some are delayed burpers—they burp after the feeding session is over. You'll figure out your baby's burping style soon enough.

is causing her to swallow more air than normal. Excess burping can also be very common with bottle-fed babies, though less so with those using a vented bottle system.

KNOW WHY BABIES CRY

Babies cry. It's a fact. But what might surprise you is that your baby will probably cry for lots of reasons, and those reasons aren't always so easy to figure out. While you know that hunger and pain are on the list of reasons for crying, also consider these:

- Fear
- Overstimulation
- Loneliness
- Understimulation
- Wet/dirty diaper
- Frustration

As parents we need to remember that newborn babies are the neediest they will ever be. Unfortunately, early infancy is also the time that babies have the fewest communication skills. Now, you can miss plenty of things that your newborn baby is trying to communicate, even when you're being the most attentive you can be. For example, until you learn your baby's movements, would you know that a case of the hiccups means that he is bored?

So when baby cries, try to look at it as if he's giving you some much-needed advice. He needs you to help him, and as frustrating as it can be sometimes, he's telling you the only way he knows how. It's not always about food or diapers. Sometimes he wants you or a change of scenery in general.

HOW TO CALM A CRYING BABY

There's no way around it: The cry of a baby is irritating. Just remember, there's a natural method to the madness—it's purposefully designed to make you pay attention. Pay attention you do, when a baby cries—particularly when it is your baby.

While you can already give a good list of reasons your baby is crying, the next step is to be able to deal with a crying infant. The good news is you can do many things to help calm an infant.

As you get to know your baby and learn how to meet her needs, crying spells will be shorter. Meeting your baby's needs is the fastest way to calm her. But sometimes you'll find you have tried everything you can think of, and the baby is still crying. If you have fed and changed your baby and she is still crying, it is time to move on to a different technique.

Start by asking yourself some questions:

- Has he recently slept?
- Have I checked his clothing for tags or annoying seams?
- Is he sitting on something? (Think pacifier under his bottom in a seat.)
- Has he been burped?
- Is he ill?

These types of questions will help you to figure out how best to deal with the cries. For example, if he has not had a recent period of sleep, perhaps he is tired and not sure how to fall asleep. If he has been crying, perhaps he's gulped down too much air and now he needs burping.

Other Comfort Techniques

The swaddle is one of the best comfort techniques (see pages 24–25). It works well with most babies no matter what is causing their fussiness. You can also add other comfort techniques to the swaddle. Or if your baby does not enjoy being swaddled, simply try these other techniques alone.

Babies cry to get our attention so that we can help them find a solution to a problem. Remember, it's not meant to trouble you! It can be frustrating when you have to guess what's wrong, but in time, as you observe, you'll learn to read your baby's cues more easily.

Swaddling

Swaddling is a great trick for babies at this age. It's simple and yet so effective. Swaddling works because it prevents baby from flailing around. For all those months, your baby was snugly nestled in the uterus; once on the outside, baby is a bit shocked to find that she can move all over the place, with no control. Swaddling helps her to feel safe and secure. And the best part is, all you need to swaddle is a baby and an appropriately sized blanket.

Be sure to keep the baby wrapped tightly but not too tightly. A good rule is that your baby should be able to move, but not to break

First lay the blanket out flat. Fold one corner down about a quarter of the way to the center of the blanket. Now place baby's neck even with the edge of the folded side.

Bring either side of the blanket near his arm (right or left) all the way, crossing baby's body. Tuck this side snugly under the baby.

free of the blanket. In other words, wiggling is good, while being able to move her limbs away from her body defeats the purpose.

You can buy special blankets for swaddling, but try the old-fashioned method before running out for a specialty item. It is never a bad idea to know how to swaddle a baby with a basic blanket because you never know when a good swaddle might come in handy when you are nowhere near your favorite swaddling blanket.

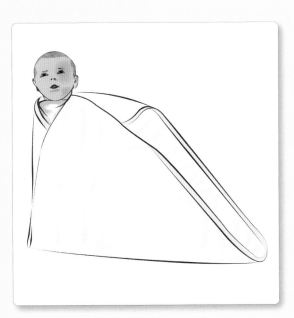

Now bring the bottom of the blanket up and fold down so that your baby's face is not covered.

Bring the second corner over your baby's left arm and tuck it under the back on his right side so it wraps snuggly and securely. As your baby grows he may prefers to have his arms free. If so, you can swaddle him underneath the arms giving him access to his hands and fingers.

White Noise

White noise is basically a signal that contains noise at the same volume on all frequencies. The better way to look at it is background noise. Plenty of premade compact discs contain white noise just for babies. Your baby might also prefer the homemade version. Consider running the vacuum cleaner, tuning your radio to a spot of static, or running the shower. The constant drone of washing machines and dryers has even been known to do the trick.

Your baby might fuss for a few more minutes, so don't give up after the first sixty seconds. Turn the "music" on and try it at different volumes. You can also try it with and without swaddling.

Babies love to hear you talk or sing. Many babies particularly love male voices as a soothing way to calm.

Movement

Babies are used to moving. In utero they moved a lot. Even if they were not moving on their own, you were rocking them. Some babies seem to miss the movement while others are completely oblivious.

The trick here is to try lots of different types of movement. Some babies will respond to side-to-side movements, while others prefer a back-and-forth motion. Even though you might be making what seems like a minor change in the movement, it can make a major difference to your baby.

You might also want to change up where you are moving. By this I mean, try standing in different rooms. You can even try standing on different surfaces. Your baby might really like to go back and forth while you are standing on your bed.

Other alternatives for movement include:

- Baby swing
- Rocking chair
- Glider
- Baby bouncy seat (with or without battery power)
- Car rides (in car seat)

Voices and Music

Sometimes your baby simply wants to hear you sing or talk. Don't panic and worry that your voice isn't good enough. Your baby is already accustomed to your voice and finds it soothing.

Many parents are not sure what to say to a little baby or feel silly doing so. The truth is, you can say anything. "Baby talk" is simply exaggerated speaking to your baby. Sometimes this is actually easier for babies to pay attention to when you are talking. If you can't figure out what to say, try narrating you baby's day. "Boy, you are so cute. I love that outfit you are wearing. Do you need a clean diaper?" Just talk as you go along. If that does not seem to work for you, consider reading out loud to your baby.

No doubt there will be times when you are too tired even to think of something to say. At those moments, music can be really handy, and many babies calm quickly to various musical pieces.

When your baby starts to move into drowsiness, look for ways you can help promote healthy sleep. Waiting too long to get your baby to sleep can prevent her from getting as much sleep as she needs, and can create an agitated, upset baby.

Don't panic; you don't have to go out and buy loads and loads of baby-related music. Any music that calms your baby will do the trick. Yes, classical music is a good candidate because it often works well, but that is not the only thing to try. If your baby prefers jazz, so be it. Baby destined to become a metal fan? Go for it. The only limitations are that you not have the music too loud and that your baby actually calms to it. You will quickly figure out which sounds baby prefers.

WATCH FOR SLEEPING AND WAKING CYCLES

You can look out for several clues to help you read your baby's sleeping and waking signals. It's easier to break them into stages:

Drowsiness

Drowsiness is common in all human beings, but especially in your little one, who sleeps so much more than the average adult. When he is drowsy, you will find your baby's eyes are drooping. He can't really focus on anything very well. He might smile and drop his head a bit, all in preparation to sleep.

Active Sleep

This is a lighter stage of sleep. Here you might note that your baby is just barely asleep. This is also a time of rapid eye movement (or REM) sleep. You will notice that your baby's breathing is still slightly irregular in pattern and maybe not as deep as in a quiet sleep.

It's theorized that during active sleep a baby's brain grows and processes what he has learned during more wakeful periods. You might notice that he is prone to smiling in his sleep, sometimes even letting out an occasional laugh-like sound. Twitches from the arms and legs are also common.

Your baby will spend more time in this type of sleep. During active sleep he is more able to wake up to have his needs met. As he cycles through quiet and active sleep, hunger pains, being cold, or other stimuli might arouse him more easily. The anticipation of such restlessness during these many instances of baby's light, active sleep are what make so many new parents cringe anytime the phone rings or pots clatter in the kitchen!

Quiet Sleep

Now's the time for mom's temporary sigh of relief: In this stage of sleep, your baby is—finally—sleeping soundly. Breathing is deep and regular. You can tell your baby is in quiet sleep when you pick up her arm with the edge of her sleeve and the hand droops down, unencumbered. There is not a lot of movement except for the occasional contented sigh and a startle reflex or two. Get ready to catch some Zs—baby just might be down for the count!

Quiet Alert

The quiet alert state is typically where your baby starts life. Here she is able to take in your voices and faces more easily. Her breathing is relaxed and even. She is intent on you, focusing all of her energy on seeing and hearing. Right after birth this period can last up to an hour, longer if she stays with you.

The good news is that your baby will return to this state throughout infancy. This is a great time to engage your baby—talk quietly and look into her eyes. Lots of bonding goes on during this phase because of the easy nature of it all.

Active Alert

When you see your baby has his eyes open and is watching his environment intently, you know he is in the active alert phase. He might display a variety of facial expressions during this time, depending upon his mood. He moves, but not constantly, trying to interact with his environment.

Your baby can easily become over-stimulated in this phase. He might be irritable. You might notice generalized fussiness, or even something like hiccups or sneezes.

Before all of this over-stimulation puts baby over the edge, now's the time to try to help your baby calm down. You can use any fun, cuddly distraction techniques that baby seems to respond to well in practice. Not sure what to do yet? Start with picking him up to hold him close. This will give him a sense of security. If he is left unattended, this phase often leads to escalated crying. Though it's also quite possible that crying will follow even with tending, if you don't attempt to divert the meltdown, it will probably be a lot worse!

Crying

Crying is often thought to be a sign of hunger. But it is a very late sign of hunger, and generally speaking, you want to pick up on hunger signs before any crying occurs. (See page 30 for more on hunger cues.) Often, crying simply means that your baby has had enough of whatever you are doing. Or your baby has another need that is not being met.

Crying can be loud or soft. You might or might not see tears. Your baby might flail his arms and legs. Some babies will tightly close their eyes while crying and furrow their brow.

As your baby grows you will become more adept at figuring out which cry equals which need. Some parents get this fairly quickly, while some have a harder time getting a grasp. Every baby will be different, so just keep observing your little

During the quiet-alert stage, your baby is receptive to taking everything in. This is when you can get face-to-face and really try to interact. These moments can be special times to read or sing to your baby.

one. Time and experience will help you to put the clues together.

Your baby might have some techniques to help himself while crying, such as sucking a finger or thumb. Don't be discouraged if your baby isn't a self-soother right from the start. For many babies, it takes a while to learn to self-soothe, and they usually need some help to calm down, even before you can meet a need like feeding or changing a diaper.

To calm a crying baby, try various techniques, including:

- Swaddling
- Rocking
- Carrying
- Shushing
- Going into a dark room
- Using white noise
- Bouncing lightly in arms

You will soon learn which techniques work best for your baby. Don't hesitate to try multiple techniques until you figure out how to best calm and soothe your baby.

LEARN YOUR BABY'S HUNGER SIGNALS AND FEEDING CUES

Your baby has one big job. That job is to grow. In general, the majority of babies will double their birth weight by six months of age. Many babies will also triple their birth weight by the age of one.

To gain weight, your baby needs to eat frequently. The good news is that your baby is born with ways to show you she is ready to eat; these are called feeding cues. You will want to feed your baby according to her feeding cues rather than by watching a clock. This is particularly true at the beginning of her life.

Signs that your baby is ready to eat include:

- Turning her head from side to side
- Putting her hands near her mouth
- Sucking on her fingers, hand, or other objects near her mouth
- Rooting (trying to nurse on anyone when placed in a nursing position)
- Fussing, usually in conjunction with at least one of the other symptoms
- Crying frantically

These signs go in a progressive order. The sooner you see that your baby is exhibiting a feeding cue, the easier it will be to feed and soothe your baby. Once she is crying and/or frantic, you will need to try to calm her before attempting to feed her.

These feeding cues will be easier to see as you gain confidence in yourself and your baby, which comes with time. Remember: Watch your baby, not the clock.

BREASTFEEDING BASICS

Breastfeeding, while a natural process, is not something that happens automatically between mother and baby. It still has a learning curve. As you begin breastfeeding, you and your baby will learn best together. Hopefully, you have begun to learn about breastfeeding. Maybe you've read a book on it, or perhaps taken a class. But even if you don't have any background yet, some simple rules will have you breastfeeding like a champ in no time.

Baby's First Feeding

Your baby's first feeding should happen as soon after birth as possible. Typically, this is within minutes, but even after a difficult or surgical delivery you can be nursing usually within thirty to sixty minutes. The American Academy of Pediatrics has set up the guidelines to encourage an optimal first feeding.

When starting to breastfeed, the real key is to be calm, relaxed, and patient. Baby and mother should be skin to skin. Have baby wear his hat and his diaper and nothing else. If you are worried about him being cold, place a light blanket over both of you.

Use this time to love your baby. Hold your baby heart to heart. Don't worry about whether or not your baby will know what to do. He will actually

Carrying your baby close in a sling or pouch is a great way to get out of the house. Not only is your baby comforted by being close to your body, he's also protected from germs and other people who want to hold him. A great compromise for mom and baby!

take the lead in starting to breastfeed, and bob his head, looking for the breast. You might notice that he bounces, which is exactly what he is supposed to do when finding the breast. Give him a little neck support, which will be helpful. But let him find his way—you will be amazed.

Latching On

The method that you used to feed your baby the first time is a great latching technique. Once your baby gets the hang of nursing, offer him the breast when he begins rooting or shows signs of being hungry (see page 30). The heart-to-heart position is a great reference point, as it will keep your baby in good alignment while nursing. Don't forget to let baby lead the way, even when you are having difficulties. Your baby can help you if you will let him.

Always relax when you feed your baby. Sit in a comfortable position, keep your shoulders loose, and don't hunch over or tense your body. Tensing up will only make you sore, and it's harder for your body to let down milk when you are not relaxed.

Make sure your baby opens his mouth wide when he latches on to nurse. He should not be pursing his lips or clamping down on the tip of your nipple. Your baby's mouth should cover most of your areola when he latches on. If you don't think he has a broad enough latch, a good trick is to pull gently at his top and bottom lips to spread them out a bit more.

A good latch should not hurt. You might feel tugging as your baby learns to latch properly, but not pain. If you feel pain, slip your finger into the corner of his mouth to break the suction. Pop him off and try again. Don't worry if you need to do this often, even several times a feeding at first. It is important to teach your baby to have a good latch from the start. It can save you pain and problems in the long run, and your baby will be able to get a better feeding if he has the proper latch.

Your Milk Supply

The milk your body makes is called your milk supply. The best way to ensure that you have a good milk supply is to breastfeed your baby early and often. Newborn babies eat eight to twelve times a day at first—sometimes even more. If for some reason your baby is not able to nurse or does not nurse well at first, you should pump to help bring in a full milk supply and maintain it.

Don't panic if your milk does not come in right away. Breast milk can take a few days to come in. It is normal for this to take a bit longer if you have had a cesarean birth. Your baby will not starve. Newborn babies have tiny stomachs—they don't need huge amounts of milk as they are learning to nurse. Even before your breasts fill with milk, your baby will be receiving small amounts of valuable colostrum—the first, newborn milk, full of antibodies he needs. Colostrum also helps to rid your baby's body of meconium. If you are concerned that your milk supply is slow to come in, break out the breast pump to help you stimulate supply as needed, but do not be surprised or panic if you are unable to pump much milk. Remember, your baby is much more effective than a pump.

The best way to tell if your baby is getting enough milk is to watch the output in her diapers. (See more in baby's first week.) You can also watch your baby's behavior. Does she alternate periods of rest with periods of alertness and activity? Does her skin tone look good? Is she gaining weight? If so, those are all signs that breastfeeding is going well. If you have any doubts, seeing a lactation consultant or your pediatrician can be very beneficial. Despite what concerned or well-meaning friends or relatives might suggest, in most cases, unless otherwise advised by your pediatrician, you do not need to—and should not—supplement your milk with formula.

Supplementing with formula will only diminish your milk supply, as it will diminish the time your baby is sucking at the breast, which stimulates milk production. If you are eating and drinking enough, and you are allowing your baby to nurse at will when she is hungry, your body will produce enough milk to nourish your baby and help her grow. Trust your body—it is an amazing thing!

How to Best Feed Your Baby

You will hear many things about how to breastfeed your baby. Some of the advice you get might conflict. This is common, particularly in the hospital as you rotate through several nurses a day, who will handle your care and your baby's care. Taking a breastfeeding class before birth can give you the answers. You can also try to establish a relationship with a lactation professional before birth.

Some of the most common questions women have are met with greatly varying bits of advice.

Siblings will be interested as you breastfeed the new baby. They will most likely want to know if they were nursed and what they can do to help. Having something to do such as bringing you your drink, answering the phone, or reading a book together quietly, are all great ideas to make older siblings a part of the breastfeeding experience.

For example:

- How long should you let the baby nurse on each side?
- How often should the baby nurse?
- What schedule should you use?

If you are a new mother and want to make sure your baby nurses long enough, you might want to watch the clock. Don't. Clock watching is generally not your friend when it comes to breastfeeding. Allow your baby the time she needs to nurse effectively. She will release her latch when she's done. You can then burp her and offer her the other side. Some babies get very sleepy between breasts and need to be awakened.

Let your baby tell you when and how long a feeding should last. Remember, following your baby's lead will be one of your best tools in breastfeeding. Allowing your baby to nurse when and as she wishes is how your baby and your body will build the best milk supply. This is particularly true in the first few weeks. You are not spoiling your baby or setting her up for bad habits by feeding her according to her feeding cues. Although she should cue you to feed eight to twelve times a day, these feedings will not always be evenly spaced. Sometimes baby might sleep for a stretch of a few hours, and then cluster feed—feeding frequently in a shorter span of time.

Schedules are not best for babies, particularly at birth and during the first months of life. Babies need to eat frequently, because their stomachs are very small and require frequent filling. Your baby's goal is to double her birth weight by about six months of age. That is quite a feat. Your baby will figure out a schedule that works well with your family more quickly than you would believe if you just trust the process.

KNOW WHERE TO GO FOR HELP

Having a new baby is a lot of work. No matter how well prepared you are, it seems that life always throws you a curveball. So be prepared to figure out where and how to get help when you need it.

When to See a Lactation Counselor or Consultant

Breastfeeding is natural, but it also must be learned. As a new mom nursing a baby for the first time, it is incredibly helpful to have some guidance. Lactation consultants are professionals trained and experienced in breastfeeding techniques. You might find them through the hospital where you gave birth, your birth center, in a storefront setting, or from professional organizations like the International Lactation Consultants Association.

You should consider seeing a breastfeeding professional if:

- You are having pain or problems with breastfeeding, like sore, cracked nipples. Breastfeeding should not be painful! If it is hurting, then you probably need to help baby adjust her latch.
- Your baby is having difficulties with latching on.
- Your baby is having weight gain issues.
- You have twins.
- Your baby was premature.

- Your baby has physical problems that make nursing difficult, even if everything seems well.
- You have had previous breast surgery, including breast reduction.
- You have questions about using a breast pump.
- You are concerned.

Another category of support is not lactation consultants, but other mothers who have nursed. Connecting with other breastfeeding moms will be invaluable. You can find them in breastfeeding support groups, as peer counselors at Women, Infants and Children (WIC) Program, and through your childbirth or baby classes. La Leche League International offers breastfeeding moms' groups in many areas; there is probably one in or near your town. Refer to Resources, page 294, for more information on La Leche League. Talking to other women who have

Your partnership with your pediatrician is vital. You should feel comfortable calling your pediatrician for guidance with any questions or concerns. If you don't, you should find a new pediatrician.

been there is a great support, even when things are going well. These programs are designed to help you meet your personal breastfeeding goals, no matter what goals you have for you and baby.

WHEN TO CALL THE PEDIATRICIAN

When you interviewed pediatricians, you hopefully asked about their availability for phone calls. You probably imagined more daytime calls about appointments than anything. But in nearly every child's life there is a time you will need to call a pediatrician who is not in the office. Be sure to ask how to best reach him or her after hours. If you need to, call the daytime number first. Typically, the phone call will be redirected to an answering service that can help you locate your doctor.

You should call your pediatrician if your baby:

- Has a rectal temperature at or above 100.4°F (38°C)
- Projectile vomits
- Cries uncontrollably for several hours
- Shows signs of dehydration
- Has difficulty breathing or is wheezing

If you are worried for any other reason, follow your parental instincts and call!

Some emergencies warrant calling 911 or your emergency system right away. The best examples would be when your baby is not breathing, is having seizures, or is unresponsive. In such cases, the emergency medical professionals will alert your pediatrician for you at the hospital.

When you call your pediatrician, you will need to have some basic information handy:

- Baby's birth date
- Baby's age
- Your name
- Your phone number (where you can be reached)
- Baby's symptoms
- Duration of the symptoms
- Baby's temperature and how it was taken, if you think baby has a fever.
- Remember to have a pen and paper.

WHEN TO CALL YOUR OBSTETRICIAN OR MIDWIFE

There might be times when you are worried about your own physical health in these first few weeks. Remember to take care of yourself, because your own well-being will most definitely play into your parenting ability. You should call your doctor or midwife if you experience any of the following:

- Bleeding that soaks a pad every hour
- A foul odor to your discharge
- A temperature of 101°F (38.3°C) or higher

Postpartum Depression

While many women experience common "baby blues" because of hormonal shifts combined with the emotional and lifestyle changes that come with a baby, for some women, the problem is deeper. Postpartum depression (PPD) is a very real problem: It is estimated that up to 10 percent of women will experience depression in the postpartum period. Typically, at postpartum checkups, doctors or midwives should screen new moms for signs of PPD. Unfortunately, however, it is frequently missed.

Symptoms of PPD can include any combination of the following:

- Weight fluctuation
- Severe mood swings

- Lack of interest in the baby or difficulty in bonding
- Fatigue with or without insomnia
- Withdrawal from life, friends, and regular activities
- Thoughts of harming yourself or harming your baby

PPD can be caused by emotional, physical, or circumstantial influences, or a combination of all three.

If you want to learn more about PPD or you are concerned you might be experiencing it, go to *http://postpartum.net*. This site can be a helpful resource. It will give you more information on the signs and provide you with resources for getting help.

- Pain that pain medication doesn't alleviate
- Swelling, discharge, or redness from your cesarean section incision or perineum
- Signs of postpartum depression (see page 35)

Depending on the warning sign, you can decide whether to call immediately or wait until office hours. When in doubt, don't hesitate to call the office. If you feel it is life threatening, be sure to call 911.

Pain medications are a source of consternation for many new mothers. You want to be pain free, but you also want to be sure that your breast milk is not laden with unnecessary chemicals. The good news is that taking the oral pain medications prescribed by your midwife or doctor is generally not an issue, even for tiny newborns. In fact, a mother who has well-controlled pain is more likely to heal faster than if she were skipping doses. This is largely because getting up and moving helps your body heal by sending blood to the areas in motion.

Typically, beyond the first week after giving birth, you can either begin to wean yourself off pain medications altogether or move to over-the-counter medications. Even if you had a cesarean section, you should be able to move to round-the-clock medication like ibuprofen, using the narcotics by prescription for breakthrough pain.

GO OUT WITH YOUR NEW BABY

Now that you are getting into the swing of things, you're probably all the more eager to get up and go places with your baby. Some pediatricians recommend not taking sick or premature babies out for the first six weeks. For most healthy, full-term babies, however, going out is fine, as long as the people you will be around aren't passing your baby around too much.

Babies have weak immune systems and are prone to get sick quickly. They also tend to get very lengthy and invasive workups by doctors for even the simplest fevers. The good news is that breastfeeding helps to boost your baby's immune system.

When getting out of the house with your new baby, remember that you need to dress him in one more layer than you are wearing. Too many layers are just as harmful as too few.

Even if you are sick, your body has already begun building antibodies to fight infection in your baby. After birth you were passing along antibodies from everything you've ever come into contact with and already immune to. A perfect combination!

Still, to avoid situations that might cause your newborn to catch unwanted germs, consider limiting who your baby sees. You can do this and still have a social life. When you go out, protect the baby from being manhandled by using a baby carrier such as a Moby Wrap, Maya sling, or a Baby Björn. This allows you to go out and keeps baby right next to your body. Not only is it easy for you and comforting for your baby, but it also limits who reaches out for baby and allows you a chance to tell people that baby is not playing today.

For those who absolutely must hold the baby, like a sibling or grandparent, there are smart ways to limit contact for baby. First of all, anyone who is ill will simply have to wait until they are healthy. You should make even healthy people wash their hands or use hand sanitizer before holding the baby. Ask that people not touch your baby's hands or face. Since babies tend to put their hands in their mouths, this is an easy way for them to get germs, in spite of the kindest intentions.

Mama Moment

As a new mom, you are most likely riding a wave of joy and excitement, followed by extreme exhaustion. Remember that a good mother also takes care of herself. While you are taking care of baby, let people help you around the house and with meals. You might even be able to catch a much-needed nap. No need to be a superwoman here.

You might need pain medications during the first days or weeks if you've had a medically complicated birth. Don't worry about medication interfering with breastfeeding. Your doctor or midwife will be able to advise you about which medications are safe to take while breastfeeding. While some medication will get through the breast milk to your baby, it is not enough to cause harm. Usually after the first few days you can switch from narcotic pain medications to over-the-counter pain medications. The trick is to stay ahead of the pain.

WEEK 1

Eat

A newborn baby will generally eat eight to twelve times a day. Because your baby can't yet read the clock, she might not do it in any reasonably spaced manner. You might find that your baby cluster feeds, or eats every hour for a few hours at one part of the day. Remember, baby's belly is small and holds only a small amount of food. So while you might feel like you're starting another feeding after one has just ended, realize this is not how it will always be all day long, every day. The flip side of cluster feeding is that baby will usually have at least one or two longer stretches of time where she doesn't eat.

The key to feeding baby in the first few weeks is to make sure that baby is getting enough to eat. You can easily do this even when you can't see how much she is taking in. A happy baby is a well-fed baby. You will notice that your baby is active and alert during some parts of the day when well fed. She will lose less than 10 percent of her weight in the first five days and then begin to regain that weight. You should be able to hear your baby swallow while she is eating.

A hungry baby might actually sleep too much. So if you find that your baby sleeps a lot and you utter the phrase "good baby" to many people, stop to ask yourself if she is ever awake and in an active alert stage. If your baby is having weight gain issues or not-frequent-enough wet or dirty diapers, please see your lactation consultant and/or pediatrician.

Play

Playing is most likely not what you would imagine it to be at this stage. While your baby isn't going to throw a ball or engage in lengthy games, she can and will play. Each week your baby will be able to do more and more. Right now games are short and sweet.

A great game for these early weeks is one of facial expressions. Be sure to hold your baby close enough that he can see your face, about twelve to fifteen inches (30.5 to 38.1 cm). Then make slow and silly faces, something like sticking out your tongue. You might be pleasantly surprised when your baby imitates simple facial gestures. This is also a perfect game for small children and siblings. It is interacting with the baby but does not involve touching. These facial-gesture games are also great for helping a baby to learn how to open her mouth wide when it comes time for breastfeeding.

Holding baby near your face gives him a clear view. Those silly faces you make are entertaining, and they also give her a chance to study and replicate your facial moves.

Sleep

The good news is that a newborn baby likes to sleep. Unfortunately, they often don't sleep for long stretches or at times that you might find convenient. A typical newborn might sleep between thirteen and twenty-three hours a day at first. Some days this might seem like a series of naps that are five minutes long.

While it's not true that babies are nocturnal creatures, it might seem that way. Your baby was lulled to sleep by activity while in utero, so when you were walking and wakeful, baby spent a lot of time sleeping. This meant as soon as you got into bed, baby was awake. This pattern may or may not continue once baby is born. Read ahead to see what gentle techniques you can use to mold baby's sleeping to a happier medium.

HELPFUL HINTS: STEPPING REFLEX

Your baby was born with a stepping reflex. Check it out before it disappears. To activate the reflex, hold your baby up under her arms. Allow her feet to touch a surface, including your lap, and you can watch her step. As long as you support the vast majority of her weight, this is not harmful to her. It is also a great thing to record for her baby book.

WEEK 2

You are busy settling in at home with your new baby. As you get to know him, you will feel more confident in caring for him. As your body mends and heals, you will also have more energy, though sleep deprivation can be tough. Be careful and avoid doing too much. Let your body be your guide.

You might have a pediatrician's visit for your baby this week. This is considered a well checkup, meaning it is scheduled to ensure your baby's well-being and not because she has an active illness. She will be weighed and measured. You will have a chance to ask any questions that you have. Your pediatrician might also go over some safety tips for babies of this age and give you advice on the range of normal activities at two weeks.

Eat

Your baby is still not taking very long stretches between feeds, particularly during the day. This is likely to be the case for a few more weeks, though it will progressively get better. One day you realize that your baby has had several longer stretches without feedings during the day.

If your baby is sleeping more than four or five hours at a stretch, you should wake her to feed her. This is particularly true if she is having issues with weight gain. The majority of babies will have begun to regain weight lost after birth. Many might already be back up to birth weight or over their birth weight. You can stop waking your baby for feedings once a weight gain pattern is well established.

Play

The best way to play at this age is simply to hold your baby and talk or sing to him. Remember, his vision is best when he is eight to twelve inches (20.3 to 30.5 cm) from your face. When he is in his quiet alert phase, it is easier to keep his attention.

Choose a favorite book and read it to him daily. Babies learn by repetition. So while you might have the book memorized within the first two days, he still gets a thrill out of hearing your voice.

Sleep

If your baby was a great sleeper in week 1, this week might be a bit more of a shock for you. Some babies are a bit shell-shocked after birth and sleep more. Some, because of medications or procedures, simply sleep more. As your baby heals or processes those medications from her system, she might be awake more often and for longer periods.

Singing with baby is fun. It's a great way to express yourself without having to think of something to say. Share your favorite songs with your baby, and don't worry about how you sound. Your baby will love it!

If your baby slept a lot in the beginning, you might notice she is awake more this week. This can be a real treat during the day. It gives you a chance to play with your baby and enjoy her.

Nighttime waking will continue to be an important part of your baby's life. She will still need to eat around the clock, meaning that she will wake up to do so. If your baby is having trouble sleeping at night or for periods of longer than about two hours, try to see what you can do to assist her.

The American Academy of Pediatrics recommends that your baby sleep in the same room as you during the first few months of life, because it helps promote better sleep for moms and babies. If you are able to respond to her nighttime needs more quickly, perhaps she will be less awake and therefore easier to get back to sleep. Sleeping close together also helps moms' and babies' sleep cycles to sync up, making nighttime more restful.

WEEK 3

At this point you might be interested in leaving your house alone with the baby. Be sure to take a well-stocked diaper bag for the amount of time you will be gone. The best advice is to start with simple, short trips. You can always build up to longer trips with baby. Some common first visits include the grocery store and a friend's house. Even going out to lunch can be a treat! Whatever you do, getting out of the house is bound to be a huge morale boost.

Eat

Two big things happen this week in relation to feeding. First, at the beginning of this week babies usually have a growth spurt. Second, you might notice that your baby has one longer stretch between feedings, hopefully at night.

You can recognize the growth spurt when your baby seems to want to eat more frequently for forty-eight to seventy-two hours. This is temporary. This extra nursing is a way for your baby to tell your body to make more milk. After your body gets the signal and responds, in a couple of days, the frequency of nursing returns to normal.

The stretched-out feeding is a bit more difficult to pinpoint. You might not even notice that your baby is going four hours without eating instead of three, especially if this stretch comes during the day. Since your baby is still eating between eight and twelve times a day, it might be hard to see this longer spurt unless you are tracking the feedings. This is potentially helpful for babies who are having difficulties with feeding or gaining weight, but in general only serves to drive the schedule keepers (mom and dad) a bit crazy. Your pediatrician and lactation consultant can help guide you through it.

Play

Tummy time is great for playtime. Because your baby should sleep on his back, you will want to ensure that he has plenty of tummy time, meaning that he lies on his stomach while awake. On his stomach he can learn to hold his head up, developing those muscles as well as others.

At this point your baby may or may not be able to hold his head up. If he can, it is usually only for brief periods of time. While he is on his belly, offer him a toy. A mirror works very well because he can see his face. Resist the urge to pull out every toy you have been given. This might overwhelm him, cutting short his playtime.

Sleep

Night waking is still common, though sleep deprivation might be getting to you. This is not the time to start solid foods or sleep training, despite pressure from well-meaning friends and relatives and despite the temptation. It is important to remember that night waking protects your baby. It can help you respond to her needs and let you know she needs help, because she is spending more time in the active sleep phase.

Tummy time is important for developing your baby's head and neck muscles. It's also something that some babies like more than others. If your baby doesn't like to lie on the floor, tummy time while lying on your belly counts, too!

HELPFUL HINTS: BABY SENSES

Your baby's senses are intact from birth with some small varients.

Her sense of sight is not what you or I would see. Babies are extremely nearsighted. She will see best at a distance of eight to twelve inches (20.3 to 30.5 cm), perfect for when you are feeding her. As baby gazes up at you during nursing sessions, the two of you will experience some of your earliest—and sweetest—bonding moments. While she can tell the difference between light and dark, she cannot see all colors. She is able to see your face, but not in great detail. It is also normal for her eyes to have a slightly crossed look. That is caused by weakness in the muscles that will develop over time.

Your baby's hearing is also slightly immature. His inner ear is fluid-filled from his pre-birth days in amniotic fluid. This can slightly garble what he hears, so he will respond best to exaggerated sounds as well as high-pitched voices. If your baby does not seem to startle to loud noises, then you might be concerned about hearing loss.

Did you know that your baby can smell very well from birth? In fact, your baby can find your breast by smell alone. Your baby's sense of smell and taste are closely related. Your baby has a preference for sweet and can tell her mother's milk from another mother's milk.

Touch is very different for your baby. Having spent his life in the uterus surrounded by warm fluid, he is unaccustomed to most forms of touch. Some of the things that he touches might feel hard and irritating to him. Think of something as simple as the seam or button in an article of clothing. Something this small can irritate a newborn.

Be sure to provide your baby with lots of touch. Skin to skin contact is a great way to provide him with loving touch as well as natural warmth. Just put a diapered baby on your bare chest and cover both of you up. This works really well with nightgowns or shirts that button up the front. Simply button the shirt over the baby!

Waking at night is easier to bear if baby will eat and then go back to sleep quickly. Be prepared to minimize the length of time your baby stays awake by keeping the lights low and staying quiet, to convey that night is for sleeping, not playing. Have a diaper and wipes ready and very close to your bed to minimize the time it takes to change her diaper. You might also want to have an extra set of clothes available, just in case. Set up a small changing station on top of a dresser or even use your bed.

Hopefully, feeding time is faster now that you are getting the hang of it. If you feel comfortable, consider using an alternative breastfeeding position, such as lying on your side. This can be a real lifesaver for middle-of-the-night feedings. If you are afraid that you will fall asleep while feeding, try a book light and book. Some mothers also do social networking in the middle of the night with a laptop or handheld electronic device, like a cell phone, while feeding. If this does not interfere with your ability to get back to sleep, then go for it!

WEEK 4

Eat

Your baby is eating better and might even go longer between feedings. You should still be feeding her at least eight times a day, and many babies want to eat more frequently. You should still be doing at least one night feeding at week 4. Remember, your baby's stomach is still very small, and it can't hold much milk at one time! This is a developmental issue that will change. It is possible to force larger quantities into your baby, but this usually causes vomiting or spitting up of "excess" food. More food does not mean that your baby will sleep through the night.

Spitting up can also be caused by other issues. Reflux and overactive milk production, or even a strong milk ejection reflex, can cause a baby to spit up. Some babies spit up because they need more burping. If burping and other comfort techniques do not seem to help, mention your baby's spitting up at your next pediatrician's appointment. Your pediatrician can discuss several treatment options with you if you are concerned about acid reflux. Your pediatrician or lactation consultant can also share many helpful breastfeeding techniques if you have abundant, fast-flowing milk supply.

Your baby should have six to eight wet diapers in a twenty-four-hour period. Two or three bowel movements a day are also normal. Fewer might be okay in some instances, particularly in a breastfed infant.

If your baby is formula feeding, you will use about three or four ounces at a feeding throughout this month. The American Academy of Pediatrics says that this will satisfy most babies. If you have concerns about this amount, talk to your pediatrician.

Play

In the upcoming months your baby will develop new skills, including rolling over; to encourage baby to learn to roll over, make it a game. Place a blanket on the floor and sit with her. Place her on her back.

Place one hand on her belly and the other under her back. Gently help her roll from her back to her belly and belly to back. While doing so, in a singsong voice, say something like, "Rolling, rolling, rolling, rolling! Keep those babies rolling . . . ." Try to include your baby's name when you can. She will learn to love that!

Sleep

At the end of this week your baby is old enough to take a pacifier without greatly harming breastfeeding for most infants. The American Academy of Pediatrics recommends that you wait this long to start. Introducing a pacifier earlier can cause nipple confusion for baby and can diminish milk supply as it reduces sucking at the breast. Hence, pacifier use is discouraged until breastfeeding is firmly established and your body is producing full, adequate milk.

According to the American Academy of Pediatrics, several studies have shown that infants who sleep with a pacifier have a lower rate of sudden infant death syndrome (SIDS). This point is not proven yet. If your baby protests, you should not force the pacifier. Also, recognize your baby's nonverbal cues: If he sleeps with a pacifier, you should not force it back into his mouth if he spits it out. It's also important to remember that breastfeeding can cut the risk of SIDS in half for your baby. It is believed that breastfeeding babies awaken more easily and are not able to slip so deeply into sleep that they cannot arouse themselves.

Affirmation for Month One

I am filling my baby's basic needs of being fed, held, and loved.

What to Watch For Explained

Feeding difficulties occur most often because of pain in mom or due to **weight loss or lack of weight gain** in your baby. It is normal for babies to loose a bit of weight right after birth. Your body needs time to initiate the milk supply, though the colostrum helps your baby thrive and is all your baby needs, you will not see large weight gains in the first days. A loss of more than 10 percent of your baby's body weight or failing to gain after a week is when problems might need to be addressed. Nursing early and often will help you decrease the likelihood that you will have problems with breastfeeding, and your milk will come in sooner. Refer to pages 30–34 for advice about nursing.

A temperature of over 100.1°F (37.8°C) in a baby under two months of age is particularly worrisome because of their immature immune systems. Your baby's care provider will want to know this immediately to act quickly and find the cause. This can mean hospitalization and many tests. Sometimes this can include a spinal tap to check for intense infections that can have potentially devastating effects. Some practitioners will use antibiotics immediately to try to catch something, though it is important to remember that not every cause of fever is caused by something that can be helped with antibiotics. Be sure to talk to your practitioner about this before beginning medications.

A bluish tinge to the lips indicates that your baby is having trouble breathing. While it rarely happens, if you see your baby struggling to breathe or turning blue call for the medical staff at the hospital or birth center immediately. If you are at home, call 911.

Many parents are concerned about **labored breathing** issues. Sometimes this is because of the noises newborn babies make when breathing or how your baby breathes. Be sure to ask for reassurance from your baby's practitioner as to what a normal breathing pattern sounds like, which is faster than in an adult.

Your baby may also sigh and make other funny noises, particularly when sleeping. This is normal and not of concern. You might also notice that your baby sneezes a lot. Remember, up until birth he has been living in a watery, contained environment with nothing such as dust. Even the cleanest of rooms will cause sneezes and small coughs.

MONTH TWO

Week 5–8

Find a Rhythm

✓ Checklist for Month Two

- ☐ Consider learning about baby massage.
- ☐ Gather a baby emergency kit.
- ☐ Practice leaving baby with others.
- ☐ Prepare to go back to work.
- ☐ Deal with the changes of being a mom at home.
- ☐ Learn about vaccinations and your state's laws.

What to Watch For in the Second Month

- ☐ Excessive crying
- ☐ Vomiting and/or diarrhea
- ☐ A baby who holds his body stiffly or in a floppy manner

Be Sure to:

- ☐ Continue to support baby's head
- ☐ Respond to baby's needs
- ☐ Note if baby avoids physical contact like cuddling

Baby Skills:

In the second month, your baby:

- ☐ Smiles when seeing or hearing family
- ☐ Can see objects eight to twelve inches (20.3 to 30.5 cm) away
- ☐ Can follow objects in her line of sight
- ☐ Does not yet reach for objects seen
- ☐ Will notice her hands
- ☐ Turns toward light and sounds
- ☐ Can hold his head up to a 45° angle
- ☐ Holds his head up at a 90° angle
- ☐ Will begin to make more sounds
- ☐ Can hold head steady for brief periods when in a sitting position
- ☐ Can lift head when on belly— sometimes steady, sometimes not
- ☐ Will possibly bear weight on her legs
- ☐ Might be able to coo or laugh
- ☐ Will hold small objects, like a rattle

BABY DATA

Your baby is no longer a newborn! She has moved on to the infancy stage of development. While this is probably news to you, the first twenty-eight days, or roughly the first month, are considered completely separate in caring medically for your baby.

Survival was the basic theme for the first month; this second month of your baby's life is when you will really start to get the hang of things. You and your baby will find a rhythm that works well for your family. You will know more about your baby and feel more confident in your parenting skills.

Your baby is still eating every one to three hours, no matter how you are feeding her. The stomach at this point is still small and can only hold so much food. Breastfed babies may have cluster feeds, where they nurse very frequently but then have a longer time away from the breast. You will be giving your formula-fed baby about two-and-a-half ounces per pound (70.8 g per 453 g) of her body weight as a general guideline. Feeding her more will not make her sleep more and can make her stomach hurt. If she is still trying to "eat," it might be more from a need to suck than a need to eat. A pacifier might help this. Just watch that her weight gain remains appropriate. On the other hand, breastfed babies can do some extra comfort sucking at the breast, as they can control the flow of milk once they are done eating.

Sleep is still an issue; most families are not getting enough sleep. You might have one longer stretch of sleep during a twenty-four-hour period. This can be three or four hours long, or even five. Do not despair—sleep is coming for both of you.

The best news is that your baby is really start-ing to notice you. Your baby will smile at you, and you can see her whole face light up when you talk to her. Remember, she still can't see very far away, so you have to get in close. You can watch her practice some of her new physical skills and grow. It's amazing!

Your baby is growing and changing quickly. After the first month, the changes do slow a bit, but they are still remarkable. Don't forget to record your baby's changes with photos and a journal, even if you jot down just a sentence or two from time to time.

Mama Moment

As your body begins to heal and you start thinking ahead about being a parent, this month will seem much less overwhelming in some ways than your first month with a new baby. There will still be times where you feel like your life is a bunch of reactionary responses to everything, but a sense of control will slowly begin to take hold toward the end of this month.

Remember to take time for your-self. This truly does make you a better parent. "Me" time can look different for everyone. Some mothers want or need several hours several times a week. Other mothers need less time or distance. You should define how this time looks for you, be it going to the store alone, running out for a cup of tea or coffee, indulging in a massage or haircut, or even spend-ing a few quiet hours alone. A bare minimum is probably ten or fifteen minutes a day. This is your time, not time holding the baby or cooking or tending to someone else. Ideally your shower time shouldn't count either.

MONTH
2

MONTH TWO:
Bringing Up Baby

Your three goals this month are simple:

- Get out with your baby.
- Play with your baby.
- Know what happens at well-baby checkups.

CONSIDER LEARNING ABOUT BABY MASSAGE

Once your baby is about six weeks old, you can start learning about and practicing baby massage, starting with a baby-specific massage class. This is always a great option, as it gets you out of the house with your baby and around other new parents. If you do not have baby massage classes available near you, consider learning from a DVD or a book.

Massage is a great way to connect with your baby, and it gives you a way to help her calm down. It can also help alleviate some types of pain and problems such as gas.

Many parents incorporate baby massage into a bedtime or bath-time routine. Parents who work during the day enjoy being able to touch their baby. It is definitely a bonding time for mom, dad, or any other caregiver.

In class you will learn various massage strokes and sequences to help calm your baby. Some class-es also teach alleviation of gas and colic through

massage. Some classes will meet one time, while others meet for a few sessions. Be sure to ask if more than one person can come with you and your baby. This is a must if you have twins.

If a class is not available, some DVDs and books teach infant massage. These can be a nice substitute or even a refresher course after your class. Ask a massage instructor for advice on picking a DVD or book.

Beyond specific massage techniques, you might learn other interesting things from a class, including how to pick massage oil for a baby (particularly one without chemicals). You might even learn how to ask baby for permission to touch him—respect for baby begins very early.

Baby massage is a great way to incorporate touch into your baby's life. This can lead to a baby who is easier to soothe, but it is also calming for parents. Try to add a bit of massage into every diaper change, bath, or bedtime routine.

To find a class, start by asking other families who can provide you with the best recommendations. However, if you are the first in your group of friends to seek out infant massage classes, you can look in the newspaper, search online for availability, or ask your own massage therapist for advice.

When deciding which class to take, you will want to know:

- The instructor's philosophy on infant massage
- Where the class is held (location and room)
- The cost
- How many people will participate
- The age range of infants
- How often the instructor teaches classes
- What type of book or handouts you'll receive

Before signing up, speak to other parents who have taken the course, to get some feedback. Also ask any other questions you might have.

Once you have taken your class, you can incorporate what worked for you into your life. Use some of the tummy strokes to help alleviate gas, or try out the arm and leg strokes during a bath-time routine to connect with your baby. This will make touching your baby a nice time for both of you.

GATHER A BABY EMERGENCY KIT

As you and your baby become more mobile, it is wise to collect a set of items that you might need when your baby is not feeling well. While you might think of it as a first-aid kit, most baby emergencies requiring first aid would probably also require medical attention. Think of the kit as items you would have to run out to buy at 3:00 a.m. if you needed them in a pinch.

Here are some items you might include:

- Gas drops
- Bulb syringe
- Medicine dropper
- Thermometer
- Infant acetaminophen
- Infant ibuprofen
- Antihistamine

Keep these items in a basket or box that is easy to locate at all times. The basket will come in handy over the course of your baby's first year. Fever in the

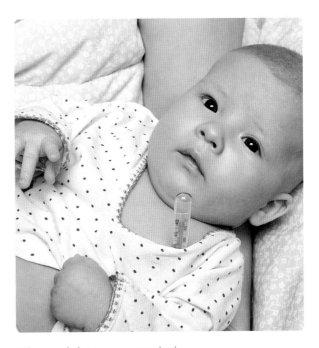

Taking your baby's temperature under the arm will usually suffice for most illnesses. Your pediatrician will let you know if you need to try a different route.

middle of the night? No need to worry; even in the dark, you know right where the thermometer is. It's often hard to remember the proper dosage of each medication, so it's smart to keep a dosage chart taped to the top of the basket. Most pediatricians give out these charts in their offices.

Go through your night emergency kit every year. Check for expired medications. You should also check that the medications are age appropriate, and update to the toddler versions of your infant medications when appropriate.

PRACTICE LEAVING BABY WITH OTHERS

There's no one magic moment when it's right to leave your baby with a sitter, and particulars of child care can be vastly different. Some families might simply be interested in going out for just a few hours without baby. Other families might need to prepare their baby for a day care or other child care situation. No matter how you will be using additional care for your baby, now is the time to consider trying it out.

This is more important if you will soon be placing your baby in day care, even if it is small, or a home setting. The idea behind practicing is to get both you and your baby ready for the separation. Getting ready involves the physical and emotional needs of both parties.

For example, both you and your baby might be upset about being apart. This separation can come as a shock to you. Many parents report that

they were eager to be alone and then incredibly sad when it actually happened. This initial separation anxiety won't last long, and it serves a purpose—to help you protect your baby. At this age, your baby is less likely to be aware that you are gone. Later, she may suffer from separation anxiety, but not usually at this age. This can actually make leaving her for a small portion of time much easier.

The more practical side of practicing for longer separations is that you can see what you will need, and you can practice your routine. You know you need to pack diapers, wipes, and food. But did you remember that your baby also needs her diaper cream? Perhaps a change of clothes, too? These small things can really make a big difference in

Baby's first hour away from you is a long one for both of you. Make it a smooth transition by preparing both of you for that time and rejoicing when you're together.

how your baby's day goes while you are gone. Some mothers find that if they send a blanket they have slept with, their baby sleeps better because she can smell her mother's scent. Play around and see what works for you and your baby.

For your first venture out, choose a time of day where your baby is mostly happy. If you know that she is going to be in tears and inconsolable around early evening, this is not the time to practice. Some parents choose a lengthy nap time; others do not. You will know what time is best for you and your baby.

Figure out where you will have this practice run. Will you have someone come to your home for an hour or two? Will you practice with your day care provider for a shorter amount of time? Only you can answer what will be most beneficial for your family.

Plan for what your baby will need while you are gone. It is always best to send too much rather than too little. Just don't get carried away. For example, one change of clothes is sufficient for most babies. Unless your baby is a major mess maker and you routinely go through multiple outfits, don't be tempted to send three changes of clothes.

Things your baby might need include:

- Baby bottles, ready to go
- A change of clothes
- Diapers (three or four)
- Diaper cream
- Wipes
- Blanket
- Comfort item

- Emergency numbers/information list
- Medications, if any

A diaper bag or small backpack can contain all of this nicely. If you are using cloth diapers or expect dirty clothes, a wet bag is also handy. If you do not use a wet bag, consider packing a small plastic sandwich bag for those messy emergencies.

Once your baby is ready to go, consider what you will need to bring for yourself. Keep your cell phone or pager nearby, if you have one. Make sure you program in the number where your baby is and also keep it elsewhere, in case your phone fails. You should also know the address where your baby is staying. You might want to consider using breast pads, in case your breasts become full and leak a bit while you're out. If you are going to be gone for a long time, you might also consider bringing a breast pump and baby bottles to collect the breast milk.

Hot Mama for Month Two

Wearing your pregnancy clothes can be depressing now that you have had the baby. Consider investing in a pair of jeans that fit your body now, and you can pack them away later.

More importantly, know where you are going out and why. If you have chosen something fun, go and fully enjoy yourself. Know that you will think about your baby while you are away. That is normal and to be expected. But also enjoy the time you have to yourself. Even if your outing is for your job or other business or educational venture, enjoy it! It can be a lot easier to concentrate when you are not holding a baby.

When your time is up, you will be ready to greet your baby. Your breasts might be really ready to feed her if you did not pump while you were gone. Most day care centers will have a place for you to nurse, and friends and family certainly will. Take what you learned about things you forgot to bring or plan for and help make the next time a success!

Remember, by starting early and going out for small amounts of time, you can ease into using child care. This practice will make it easier for you and your baby to be apart. There is no one right time or place to do it. Some mothers are more bothered than others about being away from their baby. If you are not overly concerned, then that is perfectly fine and normal. It is also normal to be concerned. There is no one right way to feel.

Baby carriers are a great invention. You can carry your baby safely, nurse discreetly, and still snuggle up hands free. There are a wide variety of carriers to choose from, but don't feel you have to limit yourself to one type of carrier.

LEARN TO CARRY YOUR BABY IN A CARRIER

A baby carrier is invaluable for getting through daily activity with your little one. They come in several varieties, including baby slings, wraps, front packs, and even backpacks. While they are all slightly different, the many types serve basically the same purpose: to give you a way to carry your baby with support.

The benefits of a baby carrier are many. First, they can keep you closer to your baby. Particularly for babies who like to be held all the time, a baby carrier can be a huge relief. Being carried

around closely on mom or dad might help to calm and soothe your baby, particularly if he has fussy periods. And, of course, a baby carrier will free up your hands, making you a great multitasker! Using a carrier for your baby can be key when shopping, walking, or simply going out and about.

Baby slings are usually made from a long piece of fabric. They can be tightened with rings, as with a Maya sling, or tied strategically to secure your baby, as with a Moby Wrap. The ring slings can have padded or nonpadded sides and/or shoulders. The choice is one of personal comfort for most parents. Try a few out until you figure out which works best for you. It is nice to have a sling around, because they usually allow you to carry your baby in a number of different ways: for example, front facing or inward facing, hip carry or front carry. These types of baby carriers can generally be used from newborn to toddler stages.

Front packs are best for a slightly older child. They might offer fewer ways to carry your baby, but they are more readily available at the baby stores. You might find options that allow you to carry your baby facing inward or outward. Be sure to check the weight and skill requirements. For example, your baby might need good head control before he can sit in a particular carrier.

Backpack carriers are for babies who are six months and older. These are harder to use and less comfortable for long periods of time. They are not used as often in daily life; they are more for hiking and other outdoor activities. Choosing which style is right for you is not hard. Try a few out. Talk to some friends about their baby-carrier preferences. See what is available locally and ask about return policies. Look online for other options, particularly if your local options are slim.

If you plan to share your baby carrier with dad or someone else, make sure that it is adjustable. Moby Wrap–type slings are best for this. However, other wraps are becoming more adjustable, rather than coming in multiple sizes.

Many baby wraps and slings come in several varieties. When choosing a pattern and fabric type, keep in mind:

- Who will be wearing it?
- Could it work for a girl or boy? (Reusable!)
- Will it hide or mask baby stains?
- Is it something that you like?
- Is it easily washable?
- Is it overly bulky or lightweight?
- Does it stretch too much for you, or does it keep its shape?

Before you choose a particular carrier, make sure you have tried it out for an extended period of time, so you are sure it is comfortable. Remember, baby will only get heavier over time!

In the end, choose the best fit for your lifestyle. Start by using your carrier early and often to get yourself and your baby used to it. You may be really amazed how easy this can make your life!

MONTH
2

PREPARE TO GO BACK TO WORK

You have probably spent a lot of time deciding what is best for your family when it comes to your working or not. Sometimes the best choice for your family is for you to go back to work. This can be hard emotionally, but you can do some things to ease any uncomfortable feelings.

Plan for your first day back at work before you get there. Consider a visit to the office with the baby shortly before you are scheduled to go back. This gives you a chance to show off the baby and get the lay of the land before your first day back. Remember, when you go to your workplace, try to make it when there is some downtime, like lunch or another break. While there, be respectful of your coworkers' time.

Pick your start date wisely. Some mothers choose to go back midweek. This gives them a short week work out any difficulties they have. It can also be easier on you and your baby separation-wise if

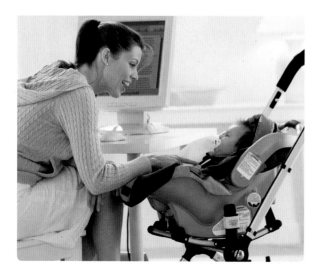

after only a few days you have a weekend to spend time together. If a short week isn't feasible, see if you can start back with half days for similar reasons. Easing into your workweek is not a bad idea when you have been off, even for just a few short weeks.

Be realistic about being back at work. You will most likely not hit the ground running. There will be an adjustment period for you job-wise. This is to be expected; don't let unrealistic expectations add to your frustrations. Be patient—your work routine will all come back to you quickly enough.

If you find that you are missing your baby, take a few minutes to think about her. Clear your mind of work and let yourself have a moment. Bring a photo of you and your baby together for your desk, even if you have to place it inside your desk. Separating can be difficult on you, particularly if going back to work was not your first choice. Do not panic; every day will not be as hard as the first few days.

You might also find that once you get to work, you get busy. Then, before you know it, it's time to go home. Maybe you didn't think of your baby frequently. This is can also happen, and it doesn't make you a bad mother—just a busy one!

Some mothers can't wait to get back to work. This is not a bad thing at all, and yet if you feel this way, you might feel guilty for being ready to leave your baby. It is simply a personal preference and

If you can, try alternative work arrangements. Job sharing, flexible hours, and possibly working out of your home may be options to help you as you re-enter the work force.

not a reason to feel good or bad. If you fall into this category, go back to work and know that you have made the right decision for you and your family. Your baby can be engaged in plenty of ways when you are home; it just takes some thought and planning on your part.

The following are some suggestions that will make going back to work easier on you and your baby:

- Planning ahead for a slow start
- Easing into work and child care
- Being realistic with expectations of what you can actually do
- Feeling good about the care your baby gets while away from you
- Taking time to realize what you're doing for your family

Using a Breast Pump at Work

If you are using a breast pump at work, you will need to think about a few things. The first thing you will need to do is decide what type of breast pump you will need to help you nurture your baby. Once you have chosen a pump, you will need to consider where you will use it at work.

Some offices offer a special room for mothers to use their breast pumps. At the moment these are few and far between, but we are getting more every day! Don't hesitate to ask your company to take the initiative to carve out an appropriate space at your workplace.

If you have your own office with a door, this might be the perfect space. You can simply make a sign for your door to indicate that people should come back later. It need not tell everyone what you are doing unless that is important to you. Sometimes a closed door is enough.

If this is not an option, consider asking someone who does have an office for a loan when you need to pump. This can be hard to do, but you might find that the other person is very supportive. Other options include a conference room, a break room, a storage room, or someplace similar. The most important things you'll need in your pumping space are a place to sit comfortably and an electrical outlet. Some mothers use their car as a place to pump.

Once you have found a suitable place, you will need to think about storing the breast milk. If you have an office fridge, you can easily use that for keeping the breast milk. If not, many breast pumps come with insulated containers and ice packs to keep your milk cold until you can get home.

ADJUST TO BEING A MOM AT HOME

Some mothers will not go back to work outside of the home. This might or might not be your choice, but there is plenty to be done at home, and it is a very hard job. Taking care of your family, your home, and perhaps even going to school or working from your house can be a lot to manage.

What Do You Do All Day?

One of the most dreaded questions that stay-at-home moms get asked is "What do you do all day?" Many of the images of stay-at-homes, while changing, still involve peaceful, sleeping babies and a clean house, with mom on the couch watching television. Nothing could be further from the truth.

What no one ever tells a stay-at-home mom is that baby and child care can take up a big part—if not the majority—of your day. You have to feed the baby and yourself. You have to change diapers. You have to play with the baby, give her appropriate stimulation, and keep her safe. Baby and child care is your main job, in fact. The rest—the house, the bills, the grocery shopping, and errands—are your second job: the things you need to squeeze in on top of that first and most important job of caring for your child. And child care, for a stay-at-home mom, is a 24/7 proposition.

As you get adjusted, you will probably find time to do some laundry here and there, since your baby can produce a lot every week. Perhaps you'll even sneak in some house cleaning during the day. Maybe you even do some errands like grocery shopping, dry cleaning, and the like. You also have pediatrician appointments for your baby and perhaps some other appointments to keep.

All in all, a stay-at-home mom's life is usually so jam-packed that at times, you'll spend the day in ways you can't even remember. Most stay-at-home moms rarely feel like they have any quiet time, nap time, or television time. The life of the stay-at-home mom is busy and hectic.

Social Circles

Particularly if you have been out in the working world for several years before having children, making the choice to stay at home, although rewarding, can amount to nothing short of culture shock. Socially, some stay-at-home moms feel like they do not get the adult time they were used to and need once they are at home. This can be very isolating. When possible, you should seek out ways to stay involved with other adults, even if it is with your baby. Playgroups, music, and gym classes are all great ways to increase your time with other adults.

A lunch date at least once a week is also a great sanity saver. This can be with your girlfriends, your husband, or even new friends who also have babies. These outings will provide you with other social outlets. If money is an issue, these lunch dates can even be done at homes, rotating every week. Packing a picnic is also an option for nicer weather days. If your husband has a place to eat at work, you can even show up with lunch already made.

New motherhood, particularly if you stay at home, can often feel like you're throwing yourself into your baby nonstop. Do not neglect the social aspects of life. If you do, you will find yourself becoming depressed. If you don't know people where you live, get out and find some. Nothing sparks conversation as easily as kids—and new mothers can usually relate to each other easily based on shared experience! If you just get out with your baby and look to meet other new moms, you'll be surprised at how quickly you will connect with new friends.

Working from Home

Some mothers try to juggle work or school while being a stay-at-home mom. This can really be a great compromise for many families. The problem is that it can be a very tough balancing act.

Depending on the work you do, you might need to have quiet time for phone calls or tasks requiring deep thought. These will need to wait for baby's nap time. While your baby might not always cooperate, this goal is a start.

You might want to consider setting office hours. Decide how much time you need to work every day. Block off those hours. Perhaps you can do them later in the day when your partner is home to help you with baby care. Some work might be possible to do with your baby snuggled on your lap nursing. Or you might at some point need to consider a babysitter for a few hours a few times a week. This will largely depend on what type of work you do and what the requirements are for your job.

Working from home sounds ideal, but it does take some work to figure it all out. Don't panic if things don't flow perfectly at first. You will get the hang of it as you navigate the twists and turns.

Balancing It All

Balancing the many tasks of a stay-at-home mother is not easy. You are juggling your baby, your home, yourself, your relationships, and your work, be that your housework or your business or school.

Be sure to be honest with yourself about what you can and can't do. Take care of yourself. It is okay to say that you need something. That something might be more help, more time, or more space.

Talk to other moms who are also in the middle of their own juggling acts. What works for them? What didn't work? Perhaps you can find some answers that are helpful for your own life.

LEARN ABOUT VACCINATIONS AND YOUR STATE'S LAWS

At the end of the second month of life your baby will have a well visit with your pediatrician or nurse practitioner. During this visit, vaccinations or immunizations will be discussed. There are multiple types of vaccination schedules, but the most common is the one recommended by the American Academy of Pediatrics.

Other physicians and organizations have suggested alternative schedules. Some of these are based on many parents' reluctance to vaccinate their children, or to give so many vaccines at one time. Many pediatricians will debate parents over alternative vaccination schedules. If this is important to you, you will want to ensure that you find a pediatrician who supports an alternative schedule.

Infant immunizations are a difficult issue. Fear and misinformation abound on both sides. Drug companies and those who manufacture these immunizations have been less than forthright and have put potentially harmful chemicals in the vaccines. Now there is a rift between parents and their baby's care providers. This is the real problem, as both are holding firm and neither wants to budge.

Parents need to understand that pediatricians are only advocating for what they believe is healthiest for babies. Pediatricians need to understand that parents are doing no less, just that what they feel is best might be different. The two groups need to be cognizant that they are both fighting for what is the best for babies, and that it won't be accomplished by refusing to listen and digging their feet into the ground.

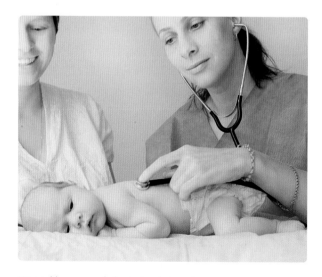

You could nurse your baby during shots and other painful procedures at the pediatrician's office. It is a great way to reduce pain and crying. If your practice isn't accustomed to it, ask them about trying it. It's pretty amazing!

Most parents and pediatricians who are open to learning from and listening to each other are much more likely to be pleased with the decisions made. It is in this spirit of partnership that questions can be answered and fears allayed. Then both sides are heard, and what is truly right for your baby will be done.

Immunization protocol can be governed by state law. But the vast majority of states also have exemptions available for vaccination schedule changes, delays, or vaccine refusal. You will need to check with your state health department to find out what needs to be done should you require an exemption.

If you decide to begin immunizations, you can do much to do lessen the pain of the injections. The American Academy of Pediatrics and others suggest that you nurse your baby while she receives her immunizations. This is really quite simple to do, but some pediatric offices might not be familiar with the procedure. Feel free to lead the way!

Simply nurse your baby in a position that is comfortable to you. Ask the person giving the injection to show you where they need to inject. You can move your body around so that they have a better view of the area they are looking to inject. The vast majority of babies will stop nursing briefly to look either at you or in the direction of the injection. You might want to hold your baby a bit tighter, should she move when getting injected. This is no different from how she would be held for an injection without nursing. You also have the option of leaving your baby alone during injections if you are upset. However, this is not generally advised, as baby will do better if you are present.

If you prefer, you can also simply hold her without nursing, and then nurse as soon as the injections are done. If she takes a pacifier, you can try to give it to her while the injection is happening. Some babies are better at dealing with this than others. The nurse practitioner or pediatrician might suggest alternate comfort measures as well. This may or may not include giving your baby medications like infant acetaminophen.

Before you leave the pediatrician's office, be sure that you know about what the possible complications or reactions to a particular immunization might be, and what you should do if they occur. Some side effects are common and can be easily dealt with at home. Other reactions require immediate attention from your pediatrician or emergency room. Be sure to have a list handy, because relying on your memory is not the best approach. You can also leave this information sheet with your baby at day care, grandma's house, or wherever she might be in the first days after her immunizations.

Common reactions to vaccinations include:

- Fever
- Crying
- Pain at the injection site
- Redness at the injection site

Uncommon reactions can be seizures; lethargy; prolonged, shrill crying; and others. Your pediatrician will let you know the exact signs of complications based on which immunization your baby had.

Be sure to ask for a copy of the vaccination schedule you have agreed upon. If you do get vaccinations, you will also want a copy of the vaccination record. Typically, you'll need to present this at day cares and schools. It is your proof that your child has been immunized. If it is lost, your child might have to receive the vaccines again.

FIND A PLAYGROUP OR MOTHER'S GROUP

Connecting with a group of other mothers and babies can be a lifesaver. You can find them in your social or religious settings, or even through specialty groups such as breastfeeding support (look up the local chapter of La Leche League in

Being with other mothers is a great way to start getting back into the real world. Connecting with other mothers will give you an outlet for sharing your feelings and challenges.

your area) or early preschool groups (as an extension of the school—think of it like a sibling playgroup). These groups serve many purposes, from social outlet to a chance to get out of the house and learn about baby, parenting, and other topics.

Sometimes you will have choices among groups available to you. Some are more casual, and others have a clearly defined structure. Some have an educational component, while others are more social in nature. If you have choices, go to a couple of meetings for each before deciding which groups work best for you, your baby, and your schedule. If you like one more than the others right away, you might be able to make your decision easily. It can be harder if you like them all. Then your choice might depend on you and your baby's lifestyle.

You might also join a group and then later decide it is no longer right for you. Then you can start the process over to find the best group. If you were involved in only one group, consider starting a small mother's/playgroup of your own. That will give you more control over issues that are important to you as a parent.

If you are looking to start your own playgroup, first contact families you know who have infants about the same age as your baby. It can be especially beneficial if you already know and like the parents. If you do not feel like you know a lot of people, you can try to find others by contacting those families you met in childbirth class and in your other baby support groups, such as La Leche League meetings or your local birth network.

You will need to discuss important details for your group's setup. For example, when and where will you meet? Daytime meetings might be great if the members of your group have flexible work hours or do not work outside the home. But if your work schedules vary, you might find you need an alternate time. Location works very similarly and depends on where your member families live. Often, rotating among members' houses, or meeting at various other locations such as playgrounds, can work well.

Setting rules might be important to your group, or you might prefer to keep things more informal. Before you make a decision as a whole, it might help to talk to other groups about the pros and cons of formality. This could be an eye-opening experience.

WEEK 5

Eat

Chances are you have feeding your baby down pat by now. If you had a rough start with breastfeeding, you might still have a few lingering issues to work out. Hopefully, by the midpoint of this month most issues will have resolved themselves. Continue going to support groups, even if you don't think you have breastfeeding issues anymore. You never know when new questions will crop up, and these groups are valuable social times that will help you connect with other mothers. Groups will also help you address other upcoming issues, including dealing with food challenges, starting solids at the appropriate time, teething, weaning, and more.

If you are feeding your baby infant formula, you might already have found the formula that works for your baby. Many families at this point are still experimenting to see which works best for their baby. Your baby might have an allergy or sensitivity. Such complications can cause him pain and distress.

Your pediatrician can help you find the right match for your baby, though it might take some switching around. Some babies require specialty infant formulas that are more expensive or even prescription based. The following are some possible signs of a problem with your baby's formula selection:

- Fussiness or crying soon after a feeding
- Runny nose, usually constant
- Red, rough rash on baby's face or bottom, particularly his anus
- Distended/swollen belly after eating
- Hard stools (constipation)
- Gas
- Spitting up or projectile vomiting

If your baby has one or more of these symptoms, you should make an appointment to see your pediatrician. Together you can try to figure out what, exactly, is bothering your baby. This can help you choose a replacement formula. When your pediatrician recommends an infant formula, be sure to ask why this particular brand is better than other brands. Does it make a difference medically, or is it simply a brand they recommend for other reasons? Some mothers might also be able to relactate, if

they wish, with a lot of help and support from their lactation professionals and their pediatrician. Banked breast milk is also available for infants who simply will not tolerate infant formulas.

Babies who are partially breast and partially formula fed might have some of the same issues, even though they are getting at least some breast milk. How great the symptoms are is typically proportionate to the amount of breast milk being given. Try to adjust this amount until you see the signs of distress decrease to a tolerable level.

It is also true that some breastfed babies react to food their moms eat, although this is not always the case. If you suspect a problem with your diet and your baby's tolerance levels, you should keep a food log for yourself. It should include not only what you eat but how your baby responds. The vast majority of issues are centered on dairy products. You can try eliminating them from your diet, though it might take a few days to see improvement. You might also note that some foods like ice cream cause a problem, but cheese in a casserole does not. This is where your logs come in handy! Other types of foods might cause gas, but not the allergic reactions that can come with the cow's milk proteins in most formulas or in mothers' diets. Some top gas offenders include cruciferous vegetables and beans. Ask your pediatrician or lactation consultant about taking a product that treats gas to see if it will ease the issue.

Play

At this point your baby will want to interact with you, and this is the best form of play at this stage of development. Keeping in mind her abilities and what she is not capable of, you can actually do more than you think. Simply use her senses to help her become aware of her surroundings.

Consider using a crib mobile or picture cards positioned about eight to twelve inches (20.3 to 30.5 cm) from her face, where she can see best. You can keep them stationary or you can move them very slowly. Your baby will follow with her eyes, but it's out of sight, out of mind at this age. Also, moving things very quickly will not create a lot of fun for baby.

Colors that are easily discernible from one another and high-contrast images are best. Babies also love faces, so there are plenty of ways

Most parents know that using a car seat is the safest thing they can do when transporting their baby. Many people do not realize that more than 90 percent of parents make potentially deadly mistakes with car seats. Consider taking a car-seat class or visiting a professional car-seat installer or safety technician.

You can find car-seat safety technicians at many local fire stations or at some vehicle dealerships. These people have been specially trained in safe car-seat use and installation.

Did you know that the vast majority of car-seat add-ons and attachments are not tested for use in car seats? This means that they might actually make your baby's ride in a car seat dangerous. Consider other options before buying additions such as toys, neck braces, and so on. For more help, you can talk to your car-seat installation technician.

Your choice of car seat is important. You should choose something that will continue to grow with your baby.

to use photos from your family album or even pre-purchased toys. This would make an excellent project for older siblings or relatives. Simply have them select photos to use in pre-made books with plastic sleeves (designed for babies).

Holding your baby and letting him look at your features will also be fun for you and baby. In the midst of your sleep deprivation you probably will not realize how quickly your baby is changing. Try to take a few minutes to simply look at your baby and play every day.

Sleep

Try to minimize nighttime waking or the length of time your baby is awake during these early weeks. Now that you mostly have the hang of feedings, try to keep everything calm. You can try many things to prevent your baby from waking up completely or having trouble falling back asleep.

Some tips for keeping night feedings low-key include:

- Respond as quickly as you can to your baby so he won't become wide awake or hard to calm. The longer you wait, the more likely he is to be fully awake, and therefore harder to encourage back to sleep.
- Keep the lights low. Use a night-light if needed.
- Remember that this is not playtime. Use only as much activity as needed to perform your tasks.
- Speak softly and quietly to baby, as needed.
- Be prepared for night feedings and diaper changes to minimize what you need to do. Have your supplies ready and nearby.

As you gather the skills for nighttime parenting, this becomes easier. Figure out which techniques you can use now and add the rest to your bag of tricks for the future. Most parents find that the key to minimizing lengthy, middle-of-the-night stretches of wakefulness is immediate response to baby.

WEEK 6

Eat

Breastfed babies might experience another growth spurt this week. Yet again, your normal feeding schedule will be turned upside down. Perhaps you had settled into an every-three-or-four-hours routine, and for a day or so you find your baby wants to nurse more frequently. Just as in the second-to-third week, this is simply a way to tell your body to produce more milk.

You might also notice a change in your breast-fed baby's bowel habits. While perhaps he used to have a bowel movement with every meal, he might now drop down to once or twice a day. Good news—those nighttime diaper changes might soon be a thing of the past! Some breastfed babies, after the first month of life, have bowel movements every other day or even just once a week. This is generally not a cause for alarm or concern as long as the bowel movement is not hard or pebble-like in quality.

If you are supplementing or using formula, you might be giving your baby four to five ounces (113 to 141 g) at each feeding. This amount will increase slightly every month until you have made it to about

TIP

Breast Before Bottle

Do not mix breast milk and infant formula in one bottle. If you need to supplement a feeding with infant formula, first feed the baby breast milk and then feed him

es

ə

eight ounces (226 g) per feeding. Your pediatrician can help guide you to see if you need more or less.

Play

Smiles! Your baby might begin smiling at you around now, if she hasn't already. These first "real" smiles are a lot of fun to receive. They can also make the hard work of parenting seem very worth it in just a few seconds.

Consider smiling games with your baby. Do you want to see her smile? Then show her your best smile. She is likely to reciprocate. Try out different smiles with her as you talk to her.

Simply having positive interactions is a good thing; the smiles are the bonus. Big, exaggerated smiles are good for babies to see. Remember, keep baby close, between eight and twelve inches (20.3 to 30.5 cm), to get the best response. Try placing the baby on your lap while making the faces and smiles. Remember to give her a minute to respond. It still takes her a while to get the hang of moving her body—even small movements.

Don't forget to snap lots of pictures during this time. Have someone take pictures of you playing smiling games with your baby. Then switch so you can be the photographer. These smiles are the real deal now—don't let anyone tell you they're just gas!

Sleep

The middle of the night looms large when you are sleep deprived. The days might feel short, but the nights are long. Those feelings are typical for new parents. Don't panic. Sleep-filled nights are coming. Hopefully, you are occasionally getting a lengthier stretch of time at night to sleep. If not, then with any luck you are at least figuring out some coping strategies. Remember, nurse lying down if you can! And try to get to your baby as quickly as possible when she stirs, so that you can feed her before she fully wakes up. That way, she will go back to sleep more quickly and easily.

Helping your baby ease into sleep as an infant is an important part of building sleep habits for life. Just as you might have trouble transitioning from one area of your life to another, and need to take a moment as you walk in the door from work, babies also have transition issues. Even as adults, we are sometimes so over-stimulated or preoccupied that we can't settle down to sleep. Imagine what it's like for an infant, who is constantly seeing, learning, and trying new things every day! No surprise that settling a baby down into peaceful sleep can be challenging.

Even when your child is an infant, you can establish a good bedtime routine to help him settle. A predictable, enjoyable bedtime routine also signals that sleep time is approaching. In many families dad does the bedtime rituals so that mom can relax or do something else.

Your bedtime routine might include:

- A bath
- Baby massage
- Diaper change
- Change of clothes
- Short picture book
- Feeding
- Lullabies
- Anything that feels right for your family

The goal here is low stimulation for your baby. Keeping him calm helps to prepare him for restful sleep. As he eases off to sleep, you should consider your bedtime rituals as well. Sleeping when the baby sleeps is hard for some but allow the gentleness of the bedtime routine to help you as well.

Reading to your baby every night is a great ritual. Don't think you need to get a new book for every day. You can rotate among a few of your favorites, or even read the same book over and over. Babies respond well to this sort of repetition, and the books will become a welcome familiarity.

HELPFUL HINTS: POSTPARTUM PLAN

This week you will have your six-week post-partum checkup. The purpose of this visit is to check how you are doing physically and mentally. Many mothers do not know that once the umbilical cord is cut, their midwife or obstetrician is no longer in charge of the baby. The baby does not need to be at the visit, but it is nice to show off the baby to the nurses and medical aides you have seen throughout your pregnancy. Plan to bring your stroller or someone with you. It might be difficult to manage your baby during this visit.

You should come with a list of questions that should include:

- Questions about your birth experience
- Lingering health issues
- Information on birth control methods

Birth control is the big question at this visit, and one that directly affects your baby. Nursing mothers have many birth control options. Combined-hormone birth control pills (estrogen and progesterone) are not recommended. However, progesterone-only birth control pills, the mini-pill, are safe for breast-feeding but may not be as effective. You can also use the intrauterine device (IUD), foams, a diaphragm, and condoms. Be sure to talk about ways to know if a medication can cause issues with your milk supply.

This visit can be very emotional—you might feel sad that you are leaving the regular visiting schedule and miss the sense of well-being that came with regular appointments.

It also might be upsetting if you have questions about your birth experience. Now is the time to ask those questions. You might want to request a copy of your doctor's medical records from the hospital or birth center where you gave birth. If you have specific questions about your records, you should order them a week or two before your postpartum checkup. If all of your questions aren't answered, make another appointment to finish your conversation.

Before you leave, you will need to know when you should be seen again. You should have a list of your medications and their instructions. You might also want to get an itemized copy of your bill for future reference.

WEEK 7

Eat

If you are heading back to work next week, you might consider trying out a baby bottle or specialized cup with your baby. She will probably have no problems switching back and forth at this point in your breastfeeding relationship, though some babies do. However, if you try to give her a bottle or cup, she is likely to resist it. After all, you are right there for her, and she's probably going to want to breastfeed. Many moms will find their partner is a good alternative when it comes to trying out bottles. Your baby has a relationship with this person but she does not associate food with him, so taking a bottle from him won't be an affront to her senses.

You might have to try a couple of types of baby bottles before you find the one that works for her and causes less gas. Also, certain baby bottles are harder to clean, carry, or feed with than others. Some babies also display a temperature preference. For example, they might prefer to have bottle- or cup-fed milk at room temperature.

If your baby seems to have issues with nipple confusion, go back to the breast completely for now. Since you still have a few days before you need to figure something out, this will be best. As you are doing that, regroup. Be calm. What is your baby resisting? Is it being away from you? Is it the feeding? Some babies will only take feeding from strangers, while others want the temperature of the liquids changed. You can also consider different baby bottles or different products like specialty cups, finger feeders, or specialized spoons. This ensures that baby gets fed without hassle. You can also talk to your local lactation professional for support and help to see if something obvious can be done to help your baby with nipple confusion.

The only sterile formula is ready-to-feed and premixed. All other powder formulas are potentially contaminated. The government has standards for the manufacturing of infant formulas. Each company has to meet these requirements and various testing agencies like the Food and Drug Administration and the Centers for Disease Control and Prevention test infant formulas, often with surprising results. Be sure to check regularly for infant formula recalls.

Play

Your baby loves to move, but cannot quite figure out how to move all his parts at this point. Help to stretch him as you play by moving his arms and legs. Gently place your baby on your lap or on a blanket on the floor to begin.

Grasp his arms and lift them gently above his head. Consider saying silly things like, "How big is baby?" As you lift his arms say, "So big!" Big smiles and sing-songy voices are still little baby favorites.

You can also cross his arms over his chest. First place his right arm on top. Then switch and have his left arm on top. This should not be a fast, jerky movement. You do not want to hurt him, just move with him. Consider adding more silly phrases like "Give yourself a hug!"

You can do similar movements with his legs. Bicycle pedaling is an easy one. Just remember to be slow and deliberate in your movements. No need to run the race now! There is plenty of time later.

Sleep

As your baby gets older, she will need to figure out how to fall asleep on her own. It's easiest on the whole family, including your baby, to start this process gently, in small increments, beginning with a general awareness of sleeping habits and patterns.

Start to make note of how many naps your baby has per day. Does there seem to be a pattern? Can you notice signs of a sleepy baby just prior to a nap? If you have not noticed yet, now is the time to take note. You can jot this down in a simple notebook or purchase a specialty book made for this type of chart. Many families find it easier to use a charting program online, like those listed in the Resources section.

Baby is completely engaged with you as you play. Helping your baby to incorporate movement and song is a splendid way to spend a few minutes.

HELPFUL HINTS: BIG CHANGES

As your baby gets older, you will need to pay more attention to the world around her. Your changing table is one of those things that quickly can become dangerous for your baby as she develops. Be sure to always have a safe changing area.

Make sure your changing table is sturdy enough not to topple over when you place the baby anywhere on it. This means the edge or the center. Sometimes changing tables adapted from other pieces of furniture are less able to withstand baby's weight near the edge, resulting in a hazardous spot.

Be sure to have a safety belt on your changing table. Insist that anyone who changes your baby's diaper use the belt at every diaper change. This can help prevent nasty falls from high places.

A good changing area will also have storage for everything you need. It is critical that you do not take your eyes off your baby as you are looking for a diaper, wipe, or anything else. As she learns to roll over, your baby has a bigger risk of falling. Always remember to keep one hand on baby, even with the safety belt.

Acting immediately to get your baby to bed when she begins to get sleepy is the easiest way to encourage self-soothing and sleep behaviors. When you see the signals, it's best to respond by placing your baby where she will sleep. Laying her down drowsy and nearly asleep will allow her to relax into her nap or bedtime.

This is not to say that every baby is ready for this at this age. It is merely something to begin trying. If your baby cries or resists, he is not ready to go to sleep alone. Listen to your baby and your parenting instincts. These will serve you well, where peer pressure from other people or other parents is not particularly helpful. You know your baby best.

Hopefully, once your baby is asleep she is a sound sleeper—most babies are. Remember, the womb wasn't quiet, so everyday sounds should be fine.

WEEK 8

Eat

Many parents have questions about starting solids, particularly cereal, at the end of the second month of life. In general, the American Academy of Pediatrics does not recommend starting solids until at least six months. This is true for breastfed and formula-fed babies.

When babies are ready to eat solids, they display definite signs, such as having enough body control to sit upright and being able to pick things up between their thumb and pointer finger. Their tongue thrust reflex diminishes as well. Many babies will actively begin to show interest in food and even try to grab it and put it in their mouths. This usually occurs sometime around the middle of the first year. (For more on readiness signs for eating solid food, see page 143.)

Starting solids too early can cause allergies and other gastrointestinal complications. Many parents believe that starting solids at this point will help their baby sleep through the night. While some parents do see an increase in late-night sleeping, remember that waking up at night can be a protective benefit for your baby so you can respond to her needs, in addition to reducing the risks of allergies.

If you think you need to start your baby on cereal, be sure to discuss it with your pediatrician. She can explain ways to determine if your baby is a good candidate for starting solids early and can even assist you in beginning solids, given that your baby is probably not physically ready to eat them.

(This would relate to issues with tongue thrust, inability to sit well unsupported, and lack of head control.) There might be ways to avoid beginning solid foods and still correct any issues that you are having with your baby's health.

Sleep

At this stage of the game your baby is still eating in the middle of the night, maybe more than once depending on his weight and other factors in your life. This means that you are still up at night. It is still possible for your baby to sleep for a much larger chunk of time in one stretch, but don't be discouraged if it isn't happening reliably yet. One of the keys to getting this lengthier stretch is the amount of time your baby is napping during the day.

The vast majority of babies actually take multiple naps during the day, especially at this early age. Your baby will get between six and eight hours of sleep during the day at this stage. He will probably have two or three solid naps and several smaller catnaps in between.

If your baby is sleeping for longer, solid stretches throughout the day, be mindful that this can cause more wakefulness at night. To stop lengthy naps during the day you can work on keeping him up longer before his nap or wake him a bit earlier from the nap. Doing this in ten- or fifteen-minute increments can help to ease your baby into the changes without disrupting his life too much. Since all babies are different, there is no one definite way to know if your baby is ready for nap changes—you might simply have to try it a few times, and then proceed according to your baby's cues.

MONTH
2

HELPFUL HINTS: TUMMY TIME

Now that your baby is starting to hold his head up, it's time to think about starting tummy time! The American Academy of Pediatrics now recommends that babies sleep on their backs but pediatricians are finding an increase in *positional plagiocephaly*. This is a temporary flattening on one side of a baby's head due to lack of alteration in position. The best answer to prevention is tummy time, which is simply allowing your baby to play on her stomach.

Your baby will grow to enjoy this exercise more as she gets older and can move and control her body better. Your goal should be two sessions of at least ten to fifteen minutes per day. Your baby might not be able to handle that amount of time at first, so start slowly with just two or three minutes whenever you can, and build up from there.

Play

As your baby grows, he is ready for new challenges. His grasp is developing, and he will hold on to toys placed into his hands. A small rattle with a slender handle is a really good plaything at this age.

Take the rattle and place it in baby's hand. He will grasp it without thinking about it most of the time. He might spontaneously move his hand and unwittingly shake the rattle. If he doesn't, then you can gently shake his hand so that he can hear the noise. He may or may not have found his own hands yet, so this will surely delight him.

Be sure that you switch the rattle from hand to hand. This helps your baby to develop both sides of his brain and to use both hands while playing. Just be careful—in a blink, he might bonk himself accidentally on the head with the rattle.

Affirmation for Month Two

I am learning how to read my baby's cues.

What to Watch For Explained

Excessive crying is something that can be very bothersome to you and your baby. While all babies cry, typically up to three or four hours a day though not in one stretch, excessive crying can mean that something is wrong. Your baby cries for nearly all their needs. This can make distinguishing the cries hard to do. Going through the basics of feeding, calming, diapering, loving, and swaddling can help. Though occasionally you will have a baby who still cries for lengthy periods or for a longer than normal total period during the day.

If your baby is one who cries more than three to four hours or has long periods of crying with little or no break, you may suspect that something is wrong. Colic, which is typically thought to begin after the first month, is an elusive and mysterious diagnosis. A good review of your baby's health is in order. Is your baby gaining weight? Is your baby ill? Does your baby have needs that aren't being met? Your pediatrician can help you go through a list of possible causes and potential solutions. Your pediatrician may find a physical cause and that may help immensely. It might be something as simple as burping better to help relieve swallowed air. You may also find that a simple change in your diet can be helpful if baby has a reaction to something you are eating—the most common would be dairy. Your lactation consultant or LLLI group would be helpful in learning about elimination diets to see if this is true. If you have added formula or changed formulas, that may also be a cause of excessive crying due to changes in baby's diet and bowel habits. Seek advice from your pediatrician.

Vomiting and diarrhea are potential signs that your baby is sick. Vomiting can be difficult to tell from spitting up. If your baby does not spit up after eating, and you have made no changes to your baby's diet, then vomiting should be suspected. If you have made changes or if you have a baby who spits up frequently, look for a different or foul smell to what is coming up.

Loose stools are common with a breastfed baby. You will see many bowel changes over the first weeks and months in the bowel movements of your baby. Making changes to baby's diet can cause a variety of problems with bowels. Foul smells and severe color changes may make you suspect diarrhea, but true diarrhea can occur in babies who are and are not breastfed.

The biggest issue with both of these issues is dehydration in your baby. Breast milk is the best thing for your baby, even if he is vomiting.

While you may be thinking that you wouldn't drink milk if you were vomiting, breast milk is not a dairy product and will keep your baby hydrated, even in the small amounts that your baby is retaining. If your baby is not breastfed and you are concerned, ask your pediatrician for advice on a diet for your baby. Be mindful of the signs of dehydration which can include the following:

- Crying but no tears
- Lack of urine output
- Dry mouth
- Sunken fontanels

You should seek help immediately.

A baby who holds his body stiffly or in a floppy manner can be indicative of a problem. Your baby may be experiencing problems with muscle tone. This could be due to illness or developmental issues.

At first, if your baby is floppy, you may think that you simply have a baby who is unable to hold themselves up yet. As you notice that your baby is not developing or moving forward or you see other babies are able to do things that are age-appropriate, you will ask questions. Your baby's practitioner is the best person to talk to about your concerns.

MONTH THREE

Week 9–13

Take It All In

✓ Checklist for Month Three

- ☐ Consider professional portraits for your baby.
- ☐ Schedule a date night.
- ☐ Defend against diaper rash.
- ☐ Learn how to play with twins.
- ☐ Check in with older siblings.

What to Watch For in the Third Month

- ☐ Not making eye contact
- ☐ Smiling when seeing a parent's face or hearing their voice
- ☐ Reaching for objects
- ☐ Poor head control when sitting or being pulled up
- ☐ Calming to soothing sounds when he can't see you

Be Sure to:

- ☐ Support baby's head
- ☐ Watch for new skills

Baby Skills:

In the third month, your baby:

- ☐ Can lift his head up while on his belly
- ☐ Will turn toward sound
- ☐ Can hold her head up to a 90° angle
- ☐ Will bear weight on her legs when in a standing position
- ☐ Will begin to try to roll over; some babies will roll in one direction
- ☐ Will reach for objects within her grasp
- ☐ Can grasp small toys when placed in her hand
- ☐ Will open his hands more
- ☐ Makes eye contact
- ☐ Can hold her head up longer during tummy time
- ☐ Will vocalize more
- ☐ Can recognize family members
- ☐ Might develop a preference for male or female voices
- ☐ Will continue to learn to laugh or giggle

BABY DATA

Your baby is really starting to play now! In addition to the great smiles and coos he is giving, your baby is also getting more physically active. You can watch him lift his head really well now, though his head will begin to bob as his neck muscles tire.

Your baby is also opening his hands more and is even able to grasp toys. And he's probably still bonking himself on the head with that rattle in his hands. That will really surprise him, as he still has no idea how it happened. If you hold him in a standing position, he might even bear weight on his legs, though he won't be ready to walk for several months to come.

Your baby will still be eating frequently, but is probably moving closer to the every-three-hour mark for most feedings. However, some babies who are on the smaller side or who need to gain more weight might still be eating more frequently. The

Sleeping and feeding might still dominate your life, but hopefully those are sessions are shaping up into a workable pattern for you. This can be harder with more than one baby, but it's still doable.

number of wet and soiled diapers your baby has still remains the best way to tell that he is getting enough to eat.

Your baby might be down to one nighttime feeding, but might also still need to eat more frequently. (Particularly if you are breastfeeding and cosleeping, your baby might be feeding more often during the night, and you might not even realize it as much if you are not getting up. If your baby is simply nursing while lying down and going back to sleep, these wakings are probably easier to bear and do not disrupt nighttime sleep as much as they would if she were fully waking, fussing, and crying.)

Sleep is still on your mind, and you're probably thinking you would prefer to have more. The good news is that you probably have figured out a daily napping routine. Now if you would only remember to nap occasionally when the baby naps. Some babies are sleeping well at night by this point, but trying to figure out how to get your baby to take her longest sleep period at night is not always easy for every family.

CONSIDER PROFESSIONAL PORTRAITS FOR YOUR BABY

Your baby is growing! What better way to commemorate that than with some professional photos? Baby photos are often fairly inexpensive if you shop around. Photographers know that if they make you happy with a tiny baby, you will bring your growing family back time and time again.

Look for someone who has experience with babies, not just someone who takes good photos. Sometimes you might get good pictures at a good price, but it's not worth the frustration or aggravation if the photographer isn't comfortable with kids. You can ask around or look online at various photography Web sites. If you have friends with kids, be sure to ask their opinion of local photographers.

Don't forget to have a few really nice professional photos taken while he's still a tiny baby! You don't have to spend a lot, but do make it a priority. When you look back at them in years to come, you'll be glad you did.

MONTH 3

You can also try places in local malls or department stores. Some larger chain stores might not have photo centers built in, but they might have a travel center. Such options can be less expensive. Your local university or photo store might also be able to put you in touch with some beginners who are looking to build their portfolios. This might translate into less-expensive photos for you. Digital cameras are also easier for catching your baby's smiles and expressions quickly. Be sure whomever you choose brings a digital camera along.

Consider what you are looking for. Do you want a series of growing-up shots, say at three months, six months, nine months, and a year? Or do you prefer a one-off photo shoot? Some photography centers will give discounts for multiple purchases during baby's first year.

Although an actual photo session might be free at certain places, it's easy to lose your shirt and overspend once you see your baby's adorable photos. Be prepared ahead of time with a list of how many photos you need and in which sizes. Your list should be detailed enough so you know, for instance, that you want four 5 × 7 (12.7 x 17.8 cm) shots for grandparents and sixteen wallets for other family members. This will help you to be wise in your purchases.

Schedule a time of day that your baby is happy and awake. If your baby is always napping at two in the afternoon, this is not the appropriate time for a photo shoot. Your baby should be well fed, but not stuffed to the point of spitting up.

Be sure to bring a change of clothes, a favorite toy, and a blanket or two. Do not dress your baby in the clothes for the photo shoot until you are at the studio. This is a surefire way to get the clothes dirty before the photos are even taken. If you are planning a bare-bottom shot, use a very loose cloth diaper for a few hours before the photo shoot. This will help to avoid lines and creases from diapers on your baby's bottom.

MONTH THREE:
Bringing Up Baby

Your three goals this month are simple:

- Learn ways to make your baby smile.
- Watch for alterations in baby's rhythm.
- Know what's going on in your family.

SCHEDULE A DATE NIGHT

As you start to get the hang of the new-baby thing, you might wonder when or if you will ever get your life back. The good news is that you will get your life back—or you'll at least get a life back, even if it's a bit different from the one you had before baby. The bad news is, it could happen more slowly than you might like. You, however, have a lot of the control over this issue. One way to start is to consider instituting a date night.

Reconnecting with your partner, even for a short period of time, can help you both immensely. The first thing to remember is that this time might be shorter than it used to be, and it might not occur as frequently. But that does not mean you must give it up.

When planning a date remember that you need to be open to many options. If a date night used to mean going out dancing until the wee hours of the morning, perhaps you need to rearrange your thinking and head out earlier so you can be home earlier. Or maybe you need to alter your plans altogether and scale back a bit in the beginning. Remember, just getting out of the house alone with your partner is what matters!

If you're used to going out together at night but that is now a challenge with baby's bedtime, consider a different time of day for your outing. Perhaps you have free babysitting one weekend morning. Grab your partner and head out for breakfast instead of dinner. You might also consider walks, movies, grocery shopping alone (don't laugh!), and even coffee and the morning paper.

Sometimes date night might include the baby. This might be particularly true if you have older children. It can be easier to find child care, or it might be your preference, to find someone to watch your older kids. If that's the case, plan for baby-friendly places. Go when you can get child care and when your baby is in the best mood possible. This can mean trying to go during a nap time or avoiding times when you know your baby is likely to melt down.

If your first date night was a success, move forward with planning future events. As your baby gets older, you will have more options for places to go with baby. With a slightly older child you are also likely to get more offers from babysitters.

Reconnecting with your partner is important. Don't have unrealistic expectations for your first dinner alone. Think about a quiet evening after baby is in bed and a nice dinner at the table.

Hot Mama for Month Three

Get out of the stretch pants. They aren't helping you and can give you room to expand without realizing it. It's time for real clothes, even if you have to buy some new ones.

MONTH
3

GOING OUT IN PUBLIC AS BABY GROWS

While you might feel it is a bit easier now to go out in public with your baby, there are still concerns. Previously you had to worry about getting out of the house with the baby and everything that went with him, including the diaper bag, stroller, and so on. You might also have been avoiding public places for fear of germs. Germs are of particularly concern to families of babies born prematurely or chronically ill. You should also use caution and be wise in your choices for where you are going and how you are going to let your baby greet the world.

When going out, the first concern is obviously your baby's safety. She is still susceptible to germs, though her immune system is growing stronger. You will want to keep strangers from touching your baby, particularly her hands and face.

As a new mom, getting out and about is great for your mental health and a necessity. Taking baby with you is something that many families need to do but also enjoy. Using a sling or carrier can make it a breeze.

You can do your best to avoid strangers by using a stroller shield or simply by carrying her facing you in a sling or baby carrier. This keeps prying hands away easily without your having to say a thing. If this doesn't deter someone, be prepared to ask them not to touch your baby. You can say this in a friendly manner or your can simply ask them to back away from the baby. If you want to allow someone to touch your baby, simply use your judgment and some hand sanitizer.

Avoid loud noises like concerts, which can upset small babies who don't understand yet what is going on. Do not use your baby carrier if you are participating in sports such as horseback riding, bicycling, or anything that can cause harm—common sense should prevail here. Just enjoy yourself in general when you go on outings at this stage. Babies at this age are still very portable without being a handful. Just wait until you are chasing your little one around in just a few short months!

DEFEND AGAINST DIAPER RASH

Most parents dread diaper rash. It certainly is not any fun for your baby either. The best thing to do is understand how diaper rash happens and to know how to prevent it. Here are some of the basics:

- Change your baby promptly. Urine and feces will cause his skin to break down and leave open sores that are painful and unsightly.
- Do not use talcum powder. It can get caked into the crevices and actually cause diaper rash.

- Be careful what you place on your baby's bottom. Do not use soap, as it can dehydrate the skin, making it more prone to diaper rash.

- Be sure you have cleaned the entire diaper area very well. This can mean moving testicles to get underneath them, or opening the labia slightly to help remove feces. Wipe front to back and change wipes frequently.

- Remember to dry your baby all over before putting her diaper on. Diaper rash in the leg creases is not caused by diaper-area hygiene but usually poor drying after a bath.

Diaper rash is more common in formula-fed babies because of the chemical changes in their stools. Antibiotics and other medications can also cause your baby's skin to break down.

Switching to cloth diapers might be a good option if your baby experiences frequent diaper rashes in disposable diapers. If your baby is in day care that does not allow cloth diapers, just use disposables during the day and then switch to cloth at night when your child is home. You might also be able to get your pediatrician to write a note allowing you to use cloth even at day care for medical

MONTH
3

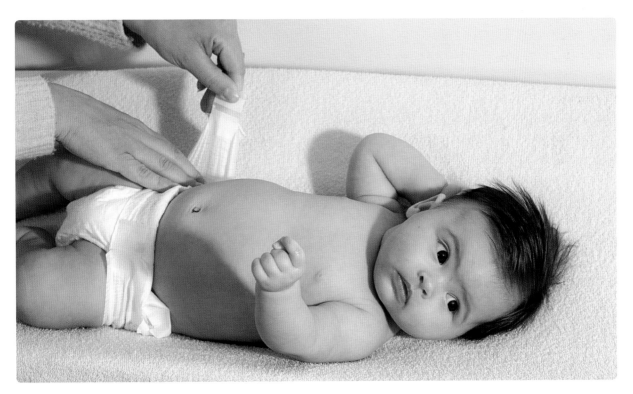

The key to a quick and easy diaper change is in being prepared. Sometimes that means meeting the task with at least two diapers, in case accidents happen mid-change!

reasons. Just be sure to wash and rinse your cloth diapers and wipes really well. If they don't get clean enough, they can hurt your baby's skin.

If you have a heavy wetter, try adding a cloth doubler to a cloth diaper to improve the absorbency and to wick the moisture away from baby. You might also want to consider a disposable at night if the doubler does not help.

Give your baby plenty of air time. Simply let the baby lie on a diaper with her bottom exposed to air. This allows healing and drying time. Most babies at this age enjoy a bit of nakedness.

Go lightly on diaper creams. They are best used as barriers for overnight when your baby sleeps for longer periods. Once a rash has occurred, they might actually hinder healing by not allowing the sores to get enough air.

Call your doctor if you don't see improvement relatively quickly or if the rash continues to get worse, bleeds, or develops small blisters. This rash might be related to thrush, a yeast infection, or other problem that requires medical treatment.

Even the most prudent mother will find that her baby gets a diaper rash at least once in the first year. It does not mean you are not doing your job. Sometimes it simply happens. Prevention is your best bet, but quick attention on your part and attention from the professionals when needed will help your baby's bottom stay healthy and diaper-rash free.

LEARN HOW TO PLAY WITH TWINS

Having twins can be a blast! But twice the baby is sometimes more than twice the work. Then again, sometimes twice the baby is more than twice the fun, too. Playing is definitely one of those times.

At this point in your parenting of twins, you are coming to the surface and able to think about something other than getting through the next feeding, sleeping, and changing diapers. That means you are most likely ready to start playing more with your babies, to add some fun to the mix.

Playing with twins is different from interacting with a single baby—you are trying to entertain two babies and teach them—all at once. This can seem to be an overwhelming task.

If you have twins, consider spending some one-on-one time with each of your babies. Each parent can take a baby individually for a while and play the same way you would with a singleton. If both parents are not available at times, you can ask a babysitter, friend, or other relative to jump in

Having twins may be twice the work, but it's also twice the love and enjoyment. It's fun to watch the bond between them grow closer as they entertain each other.

and play, too. This might be one of those rare times when the babies' schedule disparities can also work out well: If one baby wakes up earlier or goes to sleep sooner than another, you'll be able to catch some one-on-one time.

You can use other products to help you juggle one-on-one time with twins. This means that one baby is enjoying the bouncy seat or crib mobile while you play with his sibling. You can also use the swing to allow you some individual time. At this age, babies often love mechanical swings.

One-on-one time is important but not always possible. So get ready to play with two babies! At this age, you can lay both babies on the floor together (on a blanket or a play pad) without their rolling on or wrestling each other! Sit between both of them and place a hand on each one's belly or leg. Try singing songs and tickling your fingers up their legs to their necks—one hand per baby. Try finger play with songs like "The Itsy-Bitsy Spider," "Head, Shoulders, Knees, and Toes," or "This Little Piggy." You can play these games easily with both babies at the same time, and yet provide some individual touch.

When babies are on their bellies, a two- or three-sided tripod mirror can be helpful. Place the babies head to head with the mirror in between them. If you don't have a mirror, you can use this same position to allow your twins to look at each other, which is also beneficial. This provides them with belly time and the ability to see faces. As one starts to roll around, you might have to transport your little one back to the original belly position.

Mama Moment

This month is the light at the end of a busy tunnel! You've settled into having a baby and you've made it through the early newborn phase. Now that you are feeling better and your baby is becoming more social, life might feel a lot easier at times. Hopefully, you have figured out some routines that work for you and your family, and you are ready to tackle the world. (Some days, at least.)

Just don't get overly ambitious, and consider lying low for a while when necessary. Remember, this stage is all about finding the right balance for you and your family. Go out and have fun with your baby, but remember to come home to recharge your batteries as well. You will also start remembering that there are other people in your life beyond the ones you see every day! Enjoy rekindling all of those familiar friendships and relationships, and get ready to begin some new ones as you meet other moms.

Try playing fun bouncing games with both babies in your lap. While they are small, you can pick them up and do this yourself. As they grow and get older, you might need help. Try lap games while sitting on the floor. Wiggling babies and a full lap can mean a baby is more likely to fall off.

Also try using a sling or other baby carrier to help you play. You can use two carriers or one, depending on the type of carrier and the age and size of the babies. Strap both babies into the carrier and have a dance around the room or a walk around the block. This can be entertaining and fun for everyone—plus it's exercise for you. As you grow in confidence, you will be able to do that more often.

As your babies grow, your ability to play comfortably will continue to increase. Developing confidence is usually the biggest issue when it comes to managing two babies or more. Once you have that, you are able to get in lots of quality playtime.

As time goes on, siblings might feel more and more sensitive about the time and attention the new baby takes away from them. Incorporate siblings into time spent with the baby, but also remember to spend some alone time with your older children, even if it's simply reading a book together at night.

CHECK IN WITH OLDER SIBLINGS

Now that you have gotten the new-baby routine down, you should check in with your older children. Even if they seem to be doing fine, it is a good idea to ensure that you are able to give them individual attention and time. This will help to alleviate future problems and help you to see any minor issues that might be beginning.

In really young siblings, you might be over the daily tantrums of having a new baby at home, but not always. Be mindful of leaving younger children alone with the baby, even for a few minutes. They can quickly become bored or play too roughly.

When bottle feeding, allow your baby's hunger to guide you and not the amount of formula that is in the bottle. This teaches your baby to know to stop eating when full.

Older siblings might not act out in the same ways as younger counterparts, but they can still be quite upset. You might hear about problems from teachers at school or other adults. Although these problems might not seem related to having a new baby, most likely they are related. You might see:

- Lack of concentration at school
- Bedwetting
- Picky eating
- Aggressive behavior
- Whining

Each of these is a small cry for attention. Try to find several times during the day to devote just to your older children. Sit down to go over homework with them, read a story together, or just sit and talk, but not while you are holding the baby.

The vast majority of siblings take a few months to work out the kinks. If your older child seems to be taking the issue harder than other kids or behaving very much out of character, be sure to talk to your pediatrician. They can guide you regarding what's normal and what's not.

WEEK 9

Eat

Bottle feeding should be done lovingly and not merely as a task. Too often we look at bottle feeding as something to get through as quickly as possible. Remember to use this time to snuggle and love your baby.

When giving your baby a bottle, no matter what is in it, always listen to her. She will know when she is full, and she will stop sucking. Continually putting the bottle back into her mouth might cause her to suck and even to finish the bottle, but it can also make her uncomfortable and overly full, even to the point of vomiting.

Another thing to note is that during bottle feeding, you should switch sides when holding your baby. Often there's a tendency to use only one side, usually so that your dominant hand can feed the baby. But it is in baby's best interest to switch sides, as with breastfeeding. This helps to stimulate your baby's brain.

Sleep

So your baby sleeps really well. You keep reading this book, and talking to other parents, and hearing about babies who just do not sleep well. But you really don't understand. Is it possible for your baby to sleep too much?

The answer is yes. While people's need to sleep varies by individual, even infants have parameters. Typically around this age about fifteen hours of sleep per day is average. But if your baby is sleeping much more than that, you should talk to your pediatrician.

The concern is that your baby needs an inappropriate amount of sleep due to underlying medical issues. When your doctor hears you say you have a "good baby" who sleeps "all the time," his ears will probably perk up. Is the baby growing well? Is the baby eating well? Is the baby interacting socially with the people in her life? Sometimes

Safe Cosleeping Guidelines

Sleeping near their parents can help soothe some babies, and it can help particularly if you are nursing, as you can easily roll over and feed your baby while lying down. If you are cosleeping with your baby, you should be aware of and follow some safety guidelines. These rules are designed to help you and your baby sleep together safely:

- Do not sleep with your baby if you or anyone in your bed has been drinking or taking pain medication.

- Make sure your bed has a hard, firm mattress.

- Remove all of the fluffy bedding or pillows.

- Take the comforter off the bed and replace it with a heavy-duty but lightweight blanket.

- Do not cosleep with an obese person in your bed.

- Do not use products sold to keep your baby in a specific position in bed.

sleeping too much is not an issue—just a baby who likes to sleep. Sometimes this isn't the case, however, so let your doctor help you decide.

Play

Choosing the right time to play with your baby is as important as how you play with him. Your goal should be to find time when he is well rested and not hungry. If you can combine this with a time when he is most alert, you have found the perfect moment.

For some babies, this is morning time. Usually after they wake up from a longer period of sleep and have been fed, they are ready to play. Watch your baby for signs of being ready to play. This might

HELPFUL HINTS: AVOID BUCKET SYNDROME

Parents today have a wide variety of options to carry or contain their babies. You can choose the car seat, the baby carrier, the crib, or the stroller, and various other items are available as baby gets older. While these all have their time and place, be careful to avoid bucket syndrome.

Put simply, bucket syndrome means your baby basically spends his entire life in a bucket. You might find that you remove your baby from the crib and place him in the swing. From the swing, he goes to the car seat and then right on into the stroller. This can lead to positional plagiocephaly, as well as a baby who never gets held or has the opportunity to explore freely.

Now certainly these items have their purpose. No one would really argue that a car seat, when in the car, isn't a good thing. But what about the baby who sits there all the time? Not only is it bad for your baby to stay in one place and not be able to see different sights, but physically it can be detrimental because he can't move around much or in different ways.

The bigger issue is that babies need touch. Touch has been shown to physically and mentally help stimulate your baby's growth and development. It feels great for baby, and you'll enjoy it as well. If you must contain your baby occasionally, that is fine, but do monitor your use and consider other ways to carry baby that might be a bit more bucket free, such as slings and baby packs. You can also encourage those who help to care for your baby to adopt similar methods.

mean engaging eyes. He might smile at you in an attempt to get you to play. He might even "call" for you using his voice. These happy noises are signs that he wants to play with you.

If you are not available in the morning or if your baby is not a morning person, don't despair—there are plenty of other opportunities to play. You must watch your baby for signs of wanting playtime.

That said, be mindful that playing right before bedtime is not a great option. If you have been working and you come home thinking you should eat dinner, then play, and then go to bed, think again. You will want to play first so that your baby has a chance to calm himself down before bed. Being able to wind down before sleep is a big benefit for both of you. Remember, keep things calm and quiet before bed.

Playing with baby in bed is fun! If you've both just gotten up, you are typically in better moods. Early-morning playtime is a nice way to start the day slowly before rushing off to the real world.

WEEK 10

Eat

At this point, maybe you've tried breastfeeding in public and maybe not. If you are choosing not to breastfeed in public because you are concerned about modesty, consider trying it now. There's no need rush off to the bathroom in a restaurant or hide away in a back room at a family party. By now in your breastfeeding relationship, you are probably more comfortable with nursing. This means you are able to be a bit more modest, more easily.

For your first attempts consider being someplace where you know the people around you. This can even be at your house. Practicing will help you gain confidence.

Nursing clothes are probably the easiest way to stay modest while nursing. They are designed to help you cover up and nurse at the same time. But you don't need to go out and buy an entire wardrobe of nursing clothes. A few good nursing tank tops will go a long way when worn under other shirts and sweaters. In fact, as you get more resourceful with your nursing tactics, even regular T-shirts and tank tops can work if you layer, for example, a button-down shirt over them to help keep you covered.

With or without nursing clothes, you might decide to try a nursing cover or blanket. Some babies refuse to nurse covered up. Other babies don't care. This is also something to practice before you are ready for the big time.

If you are still nervous about nursing in public, try nursing your baby in front of a mirror first. It's a great reality check. You'll quickly realize that you can see more when you look down at yourself than anyone else can see when they look straight at you. And remember this: If someone is looking so closely at you to be able to see anything, then it's their problem, not yours. No one should be staring that closely at a breastfeeding woman, out of respect for both mother and baby's privacy! Once you have developed a level of comfort, take your newfound skill out and try it!

Play

Simple play is usually the best play. Learning that while your baby is young is a gift. Learn to make your baby smile these first few months. This can really help lighten your load as a parent and help you to connect or bond with your baby.

Combining your voice and touch is the best toy your baby can have at this junction. Remember to be close enough for your baby to see you well, about a foot (30.5 cm) away from her face. And touch her as you talk to her. In fact, make a game out of it.

MONTH
3

You've gotten the hang of nursing! Now that you've become more confident, remember to stop and enjoy it. Your body is nurturing your baby just as it did when he was in the womb. Isn't that amazing?

Sing her a song about tiny spiders and "walk" your fingers up her belly. Sing her a song about marching ants and "march" your fingers across her chest. If you are singing about being happy, smile really wide so that she can see what "happy" is. This type of play is a great way for your baby to learn all sorts of things about language, emotions, and what's going on around her. She is also going to love the sounds and motions, such as clapping, that can go along with singing, even if she is not able to repeat them herself at this point.

Find time every day to sing and play with your baby. You will find that you look forward to this time together. To make the most of it, be sure to choose a time of day when she is well rested and not hungry. This will enhance the experience for all of you.

Sleep

Your baby might fall asleep in inconvenient places such as the car seat or the baby swing. This can be fine for the occasional nap or brief period of sleep. But in general, you do not want your baby to sleep in these places for long periods of time.

Car seats are made to allow your baby to sleep while being transported. This means you can be out at the grocery store, and if the baby falls asleep on the way home, you can take the baby into the house—still asleep. But long periods of time in the car seat can be hazardous to your baby's developing spine. All the pressure over long periods can be too stressful.

Another problem can be that your baby learns to sleep in the car seat, stroller, baby swing, bouncy seat, or anywhere but where you would like her to sleep. You could be setting yourself and your baby up for sleep issues in the future. This doesn't mean that you should never allow your baby to sleep in these places, just that you need to ensure it's an occasional thing to prevent some physical and emotional issues later.

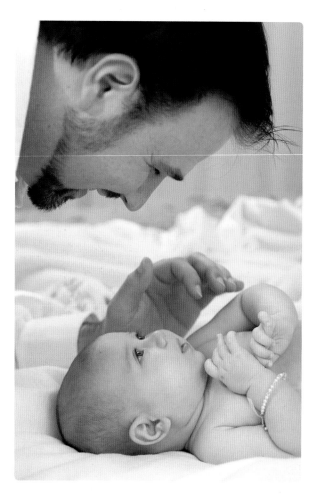

Finger play and songs are great for babies. They can learn so much about rhythm and movement through these simple games.

HELPFUL HINTS: BABY SKIN AND RASHES

Your baby has mostly likely outgrown the baby acne phase. You might notice that he still has some splotches or marks on his body. Many babies have what are called stork bites or angel kisses. These are non-raised red, splotchy areas on the back of the neck, at the hairline, and between the eyes. These are not problematic and usually fade over time, though they can become red if your baby screams.

Other skin issues that might arise are allergic reactions to chemicals, particularly in their clothing, such as laundry detergents or soaps. You might notice red areas near the seams of clothing or where clothes are tight on your baby's wrists or ankles. The first thing to do is rinse your clothing twice after you wash it, before you dry it. If this does not alleviate the problem, switch to a dye-free, perfume-free laundry detergent. You do not have to use laundry soap made for babies, but you can.

You will also want to check clothing for elastic banding. This can be irritating to your baby's skin. Choose clothes without this banding or flip the banding to the outside by rolling up the sleeves on outfits.

If your baby suffers from eczema, you might notice red, rough patches in various places on the body. Use a moisturizing lotion with no perfumes and minimal amounts of chemicals. Your doctor might be able to offer you some samples of a variety of creams. Avoid hot baths and excessive drying. Some doctors refer to eczema as the "itch that rashes." Don't panic, but do treat it by keeping you baby's skin moist with creams. If your baby has a bad case of eczema, your pediatrician might suggest a prescription treatment.

MONTH
3

Rashes can be worrisome, particularly on baby's face. Know that it is fairly common to find discolorations on baby's tender skin. If you are concerned, be sure to bring it to your pediatrician's attention.

WEEK 11

Eat

If you need to warm up breast milk or other baby bottles, do not use a microwave. A microwave can destroy some of the beneficial parts of the breast milk. It can also leave hot spots in any liquid, which can burn your baby badly.

An alternative is to run the bottle under warm tap water. This might be slower, but it is better for your baby. You can also use bottle warmers in your home or car. If you know that the baby will need a bottle soon, you can start the warming process by placing frozen breast milk on the counter. Never put warm breast milk or formula back into the refrigerator or freezer.

Play

Using sign language with your baby is a great way to communicate together. Babies are capable of thought but unable to express it effectively during this first year of life. Most babies will not begin to talk until the very end of the first year, and even then, they do not have the vocabulary to say what they really mean. Using baby sign language can help you give your baby a way to express himself a bit better.

It is very simple: Choose a single sign or two from American Sign Language (ASL). Pick a sign that means something in your baby's life: Typically, it will have to do with food or diapers. A good first sign is usually "nurse" or "milk."

When you see your baby is hungry or ready to eat, show him the sign as you speak. Ask, "Are you ready to nurse?" Use whatever word you would use for *nurse*. Do this while showing him the sign: your hand sideways, thumb side up, opening and closing. Use the sign every time you feed him.

After a few weeks, consider adding a second sign. "More" as a sign always works well. You might also consider manners, such as "please" and "thank you" as first signs.

You might feel a bit silly at first. But realize that your baby is paying attention. After a while, sometimes months, you will notice that your baby is trying to respond. It might not look exactly like the sign you are making, but it is a start. For instance, rather than opening and closing his hand in an organized fashion, he may try to do so wildly, which looks more like waving fingers, but if he does it every time you go to feed him, then it's the sign!

Continue to add signs as you and your baby like. There are also many books about using sign language with children. Some are meant for the adults and some for the babies. Be sure that you find a book using ASL as its basis. Sign language is also great when your baby is a toddler or older. You can use it to ask embarrassing questions or address discipline issues without being loud and screaming, "I have to go potty now!"

You might also want to look for baby sign language classes. This is a great place to find other parents with similar interests as well as similarly aged babies. If you can't find one, go for the quick ASL course for adults.

Baby Signs

Using sign language can help your baby communicate at an early age.

Daddy

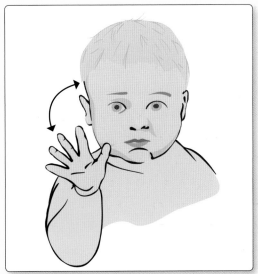

Mommy

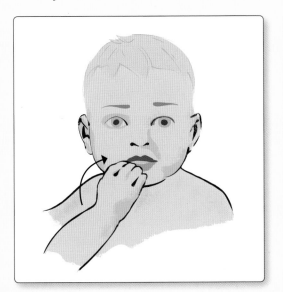

Eat

Thank You

MONTH
3

Sleep

Have you checked your baby's sleeping area for safety issues recently? Sometimes as you start falling into a routine, things creep up that you did not intend. Has a toddler thrown a stuffed animal into the crib? Are the crib sheets secure? Do you have the bumpers removed? If you are cosleeping, do you have the winter comforter on your bed now when the summer-weight one was lighter and safer?

Try to remember to do these safety checks every so often. It will help to keep your baby safe during slumber. It is so easy to fall into a pattern and not even "see" the danger in the crib.

In addition to safety checks, you will always want to place your baby in the crib safely. The safest way to place your baby in the crib is the feet-to-foot method, where you place his feet toward the foot of the crib. This prevents him from moving up and potentially wedging himself between the mattress and the crib.

Pacifiers might be fine for falling asleep, but once they fall out of baby's mouth, leave them; never force them back in. Also, never tie your baby's pacifier to him. This will minimize the risk of strangulation.

HELPFUL HINTS: PACIFIERS

Many parents have questions about pacifiers. When you were first working with your baby to nurse, it was more important that he learned to suck at the breast. Now as your baby grows, he may need to suck when he does not need to eat. Enter the artificial nipple: the pacifier.

If your baby is nursing well or taking bottles well, introducing a pacifier is not a problem. Lactation consultants generally recommend waiting until this point or until your baby is more than one month old. Recent studies linking pacifier use to a reduction in sudden infant death syndrome (SIDS) during sleep times has increased awareness about pacifier use.

Do not panic if your baby will not take a pacifier. Pacifier use is, by all means, not the only link to reducing the risk of SIDS. As mentioned earlier in this book, you will also want to leave the pacifier out of your baby's mouth once he has fallen asleep and has spit it out. You should not force the pacifier back into the baby's mouth.

WEEK 12

Eat

It's already growth spurt time again! You may notice that your baby seems ravenous no matter how often you are feeding her. She might consume more food or spend more time breastfeeding for forty-eight to seventy-two hours.

Her growth spurts are normal and are a signal that her body needs more energy. This will also mean that new physical and mental abilities are following. If she has not gone back to her normal schedule or something reasonably close, you might discuss it with your pediatrician or lactation consultant.

Play

One thing you've probably learned early on about your baby is that he loves playing with you. While you probably love playing with your baby, there will be times when you are not around to play with your child. Or there might be times when you would like him to play alone, even for a few minutes.

These days, it seems like every child's toy needs batteries! But some toys entertain baby without batteries. Some examples are the chairs that move based on your baby's movements, frequently called bouncy seats or bouncers. Many come with a built-in toy bar that goes across the front of the seat for added entertainment.

Your baby will eventually learn to move the seat or bat at the toys, but even in the beginning they can be lots of fun for baby. He might find the toys stimulating to look at or even find that his own random movements move his chair. These are great places to rest baby for a few minutes.

Another fun toy for baby might be a play gym for the floor. These are simply padded mats with toys strung above baby's head. You can also use a blanket and separate toys for the same trick. One must-have toy is a soft mirror designed for babies. They are frequently made in a tripod shape so that they will sit on the floor without toppling over on your baby's head. Babies sure love to look at other babies, even if they don't realize they are looking at themselves!

Sleep

Have you tried music to help your little one sleep? Playing calming music, such as lullabies or classical music, can calm your baby and lull her to sleep. You can also try white noise or the sounds of nature.

Mirrors are a baby's best friend. Your baby will probably spend lots of time "talking" to the new baby on the block without realizing at first that the new baby is really his own reflection.

HELPFUL HINTS: NO SMOKE

We all know that smoking around a baby is bad. Harm from secondhand smoke leads to more frequent and more severe illnesses for your baby, including asthma, upper respiratory infections, and ear infections. Now we are learning about thirdhand smoke which is carried around on your clothing from being near smoke or from smoking. New studies are showing us that thirdhand smoke is dangerous for babies.

You should tell anyone who handles baby not to smoke near him. If you are still smoking, consider quitting— is it the best option. Be sure to discuss this with your day care providers or babysitters as well.

Affirmation for Month Three

My baby develops at just the right pace.

While you can use soothing items, such as stuffed bears that play heartbeat music, you can also use a music player but remember not to have any electronics in the baby's crib or bed, and be mindful of the volume.

Experiment with the type of music your baby listens to until you find what works best. Experiment with the length of time you play music and whether or not your baby soothes when it's left on. We tend to think that babies sleep better when it is quiet, but the womb is a very noisy place. Some babies really prefer to have some background noise.

WEEK 13

Eat

Infant formula comes in three distinct preparations, including: ready-to-feed, concentrate, and powdered. Each has its own advantages and disadvantages in both preparation and cost. You will need to decide what works best for your family if you choose to supplement with infant formula.

Ready-to-feed infant formula can be fed immediately. You do not have to mix anything or add anything to the liquid. You can purchase it prepared in baby bottles with nipples already attached, or you might have to add it to your own bottle. Ready-to-feed is convenient because you don't have to worry about water or mixing. It is also a very costly way to feed your baby—the most expensive of the infant formula types, no matter which brand you choose.

Concentrate infant formula is a liquid. You simply add the liquid into a baby bottle and then add water. So if the instructions say to add half concentrate and half water, you would add two ounces (56.5 g) of concentrate and two ounces (56.5 g) of water to make a four-ounce (113 g) baby bottle. You can use concentrate to make "batches" of infant formula to feed over the period of a day or two, depending on the brand. This is the middle of the road in terms of expense.

Powdered infant formula is the easiest to carry for many, because it is stored at room temperature and does not go bad as quickly, until you add water. But you also must have a source of clean, drinkable water available to mix with the powder. This is also the least expensive form of infant formula.

One big issue with either powdered or concentrate formula is making sure it is mixed correctly. If you add too much water, your baby may not

Your baby likes warm milk. Be sure to prepare it in the safest way possible, meaning do not microwave. Every year, many babies are burned by hot liquids. Always test it to ensure it is not too hot for your little one.

get proper nutrition. Don't be tempted to "eyeball it." Measure your servings accordingly. You can measure before you leave home if need be. You can purchase items that allow you to store the water and infant formula separately until you are ready to feed your baby.

Sleep

Your baby is probably napping about five hours during the day around this age, and he might or might not be sleeping through the night. Many babies are still waking up at least once to eat at night during this month. While waking up at night to eat can be hard on you, it's a need he has at this point that he will likely soon outgrow.

If your baby does not need to eat in the middle of the night, there is no need to wake him up for feedings. If he can sleep, he will be able to nurse or eat more frequently during the day. This will make up for the lack of nighttime feedings.

Play

One item that seems to be sweeping the baby industry is a small chair designed to assist babies in sitting up. These chairs can help your baby look around without using a car seat, but they are often used too early and incorrectly. This can lead to dangerous consequences.

Be sure that your baby can hold her head up before attempting to allow her to sit up in a prefabricated chair. Remember that even if she can hold her head up, it should only be for brief periods of time. Trying to force her to sit in the chair for longer than this can be harmful to your baby.

MONTH
3

HELPFUL HINTS: SAFE SLEEP

The American Academy of Pediatrics recommends that babies sleep close to their parents in the first months of life. Some parents are ready by the end of the third month for their babies to sleep in their own space. This space might be their own room or it might be a room shared with a sibling.

Start slowly to prepare your baby for the move. First have your baby take naps in the room she will be moving to in the future. Then perhaps spend some other times in the room.

It is okay if you are not ready for your baby to move to another room. All parents have to make the decision that is right for their family. If your baby is still in your room, you will want to focus on safe sleeping habits. For example, the bassinet or cosleeper might need to be adjusted to accommodate baby's growing body or newfound skills. If you are cosleeping, you will want to continue to follow safe cosleeping guidelines whenever your baby is in your bed.

A cosleeper can help you settle in for a longer nights' sleep. Babies who sleep with, or close to, their parents tend to sleep better and quiet faster when they are awake.

The chair should always sit on the floor. Parents who sit the chairs on tables or counters risk having their baby topple onto the floor. These chairs are not weighted to hold themselves up and will fall with your baby inside if not used correctly. Ask your pediatrician if there is reason that your baby should not use one of these chairs. You may find that your pediatrician has reasons to discourage their use. Or you might find that for a specific reason, your baby should not be sitting before she can do so unassisted. A nice alternative is the bouncer, a seat designed to move with your baby's movements and support his head, neck, and upper body.

What to Watch For Explained

Not making eye contact is potentially problematic. This can be one of the earlier signs of emotional detachment or possibly autism-related behavior. While most babies will make eye contact while playing or talking to you, some babies actively avoid your eyes. While every baby does this occasionally, if you notice it frequently or constantly, it is something to have checked out.

Smiling when seeing a parent's face or hearing their voice is another developmental issue to watch for. Your baby enjoys hearing your voice and seeing your face, both of which are the first she will recognize. If your baby does not seem to recognize you, it is worth talking to your pediatrician about. You may have your child's vision screened or her hearing checked.

Reaching for objects is something that most babies are doing around this age. Sometimes you are asked questions about developmental milestones like this and you really aren't sure because you haven't been looking for specific things. Don't worry! Try offering your baby a fun toy while he is sitting near you. Does he look at the toy? Does he seem to see it or hear it? Does he reach for it? If you find that your baby does not reach out

for toys, it is worth asking your pediatrician to give your baby a check-up. Perhaps it's simply a matter of timing. Remember that developmental skills are on a curve. Some babies need more time, particularly if they were born prematurely.

Poor head control when sitting or being pulled up may be another developmental issue that you observe at this point. By allowing your baby the time and space to build these muscles you will most likely see an improvement in his ability to hold his head up. If you have been giving him time and you do not see improvement or even his willingness to try, it is time for a professional evaluation. Your baby's doctor can tell you if you need further evaluation, time, therapy, or just to wait and see.

Your baby should **calm to soothing sounds** if he cannot see you. A constant inability to calm just by words or music may indicate a hearing problem. Most babies are screened at birth for hearing loss, but perhaps our baby needs to be re-evaluated. There are other reasons for hearing loss which may be as simple as fluid in the ears or an ear infection. Your pediatrician can do a thorough physical exam to check for reasons that your baby's hearing may be affected.

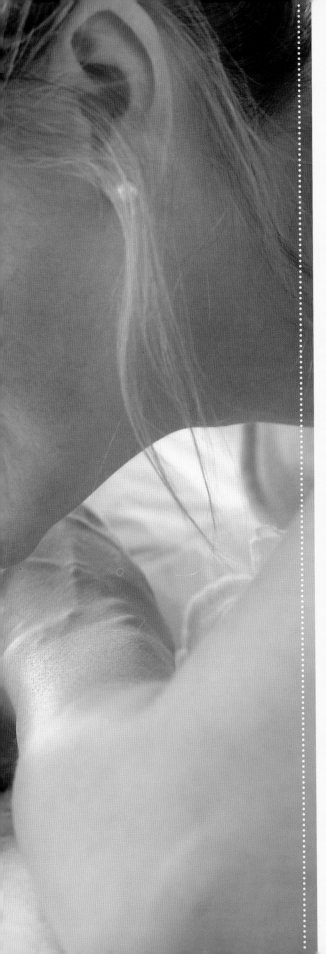

Week 14–17

Interact with Baby

√ **Checklist for Month Four**

- ☐ Find a playgroup or mother's group.
- ☐ Choose a baby carrier for your partner.
- ☐ Learn to deal with unwanted advice.
- ☐ Check your water heater.
- ☐ Chose baby toys wisely.

What to Watch For in the Fourth Month

- ☐ Signs of teething
- ☐ Fever
- ☐ Pulling at ears
- ☐ Not repeating sounds or babbling
- ☐ Reaching for objects

Baby Skills:

In the fourth month, your baby:

- ☐ Continues to work on rolling, perhaps all the way over to his back
- ☐ Has more relaxed hand movements
- ☐ Can use both hands to hold a toy
- ☐ Supports his body on his elbows when on his belly
- ☐ Might begin early stages of sitting
- ☐ Might show a preference to certain toys
- ☐ Can hold her head well, without support
- ☐ Continues to put weight on her legs when held in standing position
- ☐ Will have a "conversation" with you by babbling sounds back when you talk to her

BABY DATA

You are really on a roll now! Or at least your baby is trying to roll, if not succeeding. Mastering rolling in one direction might happen this month. This really gives your baby a new perspective on life, although it can also be frustrating when she does not quite understand how or why she got flipped over. She still needs your help.

Your baby might be more interested in toys this month. She will probably love the sounds and the sights now. She might even grab a toy with both hands and pull it toward her mouth, which is how she starts to explore everything. Watch out, because from this point on, she will try to put everything and anything she possibly can into her mouth!

New this month: the beginning stages of sitting. Your baby will begin tripoding, or sitting on her bottom with both of her hands on the ground in front of her. Even if she's really slumped over, this is the precursor to sitting. As you watch your baby beginning to move now, it can be hard to believe how much has changed in a few short months.

Feedings might be spacing out some. A good average will be every two to four hours, with one or two longer stretches in between feedings. (But remember, all babies are different, and breastfed

The fourth month is such a social time. Your baby is really coming out of his shell and enjoying those around him. Sometimes, you'll see his frustration about not being able to get around, but all that will change soon enough, as mobility is on the horizon!

babies especially might not always stick to a predictable feeding schedule.) Starting solids during this early stage of life is not a good idea in most instances due to the risk of allergies and just general inability to tolerate or physically handle food. A baby who is demanding massive amounts of calories might be an exception, though this demand might be masking a different issue, including the need for nonnutritive sucking. Your pediatrician can help you to make that decision, balancing your baby's caloric intake needs and family allergies. If you are formula feeding, stick to two and a half ounces for every pound (71 g per 453 g) of baby's body weight.

The good news is that you might be getting a lot more sleep at this point. It can be amazing how much different four or five consecutive hours of sleep feels from just two or three previously! Even better news is that while your baby might still be eating at night, you are probably only doing a feeding or two, rather than three or more feedings.

MONTH FOUR: Bringing Up Baby

Your three goals this month are simple:

- Learn to deal with people outside your family.
- Watch baby's new skills.
- Know what toys are safe for your baby.

TAKE YOUR BABY OUTSIDE

Sometimes it's so easy to stay inside. Mommy always has a million things to do inside the house, it seems. And indoors you can control the temperature. You can control the environment. No bugs, no grass allergies, no rain—sounds perfect, right?

It's easy some days to get caught up with doing things inside, but getting outside can really be a good thing for you and for your baby. Try putting her in a stroller and taking a walk a couple of times a week. While a stroller facing you gives her a lot of time to see your face, it still allows her some time

Hot Mama for Month Four

Nursing tops can make getting out and about much easier. They can provide you with confidence when breastfeeding in public. These tops come with a variety of openings, some of which you might like more than others. See if you can play around with a few borrowed tops before investing in your own. Most maternity stores and sometimes even large baby stores carry nursing wear now. You might try on a variety in stores and then search online for more variety once you find styles you like.

outside. She is benefiting from the fresh air, and she's also studying the world around her and learning more and more with every new thing she sees.

Being outside exposes her to new smells, sights, and sounds. She is also getting vitamin D from sunlight. Since you should not use sunscreen on infants under six months of age, you will want to take her outside at times when the sun is least intense, like late afternoon or early morning. But a bit of exposed skin at this point is great!

A blanket for playing outside is a nice idea. Even if all you do is lie under a tree and stare upward, your baby will be experiencing it, too. So remember, do not be concerned about what you do outside. Even running errands or shopping with your baby gets her out and about, and provides her with lots of interesting sensory stimulation in a variety of places, as well as interaction with you and other people! Use common sense, and avoid extreme temperatures and conditions. But get out and have fun!

Going outdoors to play is a good thing. Your baby can, weather permitting, really enjoy being outside. There are lots of sights and sounds that are interesting and different. A hike in a baby carrier can be a great change of pace for baby and for you.

CHOOSE A BABY CARRIER FOR DAD

In the beginning, you might have been a bit worried about letting anyone other than you carry the baby around. Or perhaps those around you were not interested in carrying a tiny baby. But now your baby is getting bigger and holding her head up better. This means she's ready to be a bit more social.

Baby carriers are great ways to help you carry baby without hurting your back, tiring out your arms, or filling your hands. You might already be using a carrier and, if possible, you have planned ahead and dad or someone else can also use it. If not, it might be time to look into getting another carrier that fits the body and personality of the other people who might carry the baby.

First, find a sling made with a fabric that is acceptable to the other person. Your hot-pink, flowered carrier might not work for dad, but a nice denim or khaki one is probably more his speed. You might also need to ensure that you have the right size of baby carrier. While some carriers are one size fits most, others are based on height and weight. Remember, the baby carrier you choose does not simply have to be a different pattern of your existing one. You might want to try a different style, so that you will have options. Consider whether your baby prefers a particular carrier style. This is where borrowing a carrier from a friend or using it for a bit in the store will work out in your favor.

Baby carriers are a great investment. They are durable and last for a long time. This means you can use them for multiple babies.

Remember that carrying your baby is a great way to bond with him. Babies need lots of close physical contact! Carrying your baby can also help reduce crying and keep him calm. You will be amazed at what you and others can get done with a baby in a carrier!

Getting dad his own carrier is important. This gives him a chance to be close to the baby and have a carrier that will fit better, and one he will be more likely to wear.

MONTH
4

LEARN TO DEAL WITH UNWANTED ADVICE

Having a baby often comes with unwanted advice. You probably already figured that out during your pregnancy. Somehow the sight of a baby makes everyone think they're experts.

When you are a new parent, you might be less confident in your parenting skills and theory. This can mean that unwanted advice makes you question what you are doing. Remember, unwanted advice is often unsolicited, as opposed to advice you don't like.

Unwanted advice is not fun for anyone. Remember most people are well meaning, they just don't have to live your life. You know what's best for your family—take whatever information is helpful for you, and forget the rest.

The best plan is usually to have a strategy in place before people come at you with advice. A simple, noncommittal acknowledgment works well: Just say, "Thanks!" If the person persists, you can also try simply placing the decision in someone else's hands: "After talking it over, my partner and I believe this is best." When dealing with really opinionated types, throw the ball back in your pediatrician's court. Feel free to start your response by saying, "Our pediatrician says . . . ." You can also change the word "pediatrician" to whomever else you'd like, as suits the situation: your mother, husband, and so on. If Mr. or Ms. Know-It-All still persists, do not hesitate to be firm: "Thanks, but we already know what we're doing."

Sometimes for new parents, it's reassuring to ask for guidance from those who've been there before you. The advice you get might be useful in whole or part. Be sure to take what works for you and your baby and use it. If nothing is useful, send it in one ear and out the other. Don't underestimate your own instincts, either! Remember, in the end you know what is best for your baby. It is not about knowing all the answers to parenting, but knowing where to find them and how to use them in a way that works best for your family.

CHECK YOUR WATER HEATER

Baths are always a relaxing, enjoyable part of baby's routine. At bath time, you might still be using a bathtub accessory or the infant tub to help bathe baby.

One of the biggest bath hazards, other than drowning, is burning the baby in water that is too hot. Normally you can mix the hot and cold water to find the perfect temperature. But if the hot water is excessively hot to begin with, you can easily burn your baby by accident.

To prevent this, you need to check your water heater. Turning the heater down to 120°F (49°C) can drastically reduce the risk of your baby getting burned. You should still always check the water temperature before allowing your baby to take a bath. Use your elbow to test the water first, because it is more sensitive than your hand or other parts of your body. You will be able to sense more easily if the water is too hot for baby's sensitive skin. Leave your water heater turned down for many years, because toddlers can quickly turn on a tub or faucet handle and scald themselves that way as well. Think of this as preventive maintenance.

CHOOSE BABY TOYS WISELY

You've probably been waiting anxiously for months to pull out all of those cool toys you got as baby gifts. As your baby gets more and more involved with playing with other objects, you will find that it is finally time to put all that stuff to use. If you're really excited at the prospect of your baby being able to play, you might also find yourself running out to buy toys for him. Don't go crazy; be selective! The perfect toy for a four-month-old baby is simple but graspable.

That said, be sure to consider safety issues when dealing with toys. Ask yourself a series of questions before making a purchase:

- Is the toy age appropriate? For how long will my baby use this toy?
- How will my baby use this toy? (Be creative, and know that it will inevitably end up in his mouth.)
- Does this toy allow my baby to put thought or effort into play? Or does this toy do everything for my baby?
- Is this toy easily washable?
- Is this toy easily replaceable?

Mama Moment

Do not panic if you are not back into your regular clothes yet. Remember, it took nine months for your body to change to have a baby, and it will take time to change again. Remember, it is not all about losing weight.

You will also need to work on reshaping your body and gaining strength. Exercise is probably more important than a super-strict diet. Be sure that you are taking in enough calories for your body to work effectively. Especially if you are nursing, you will need to make sure you are eating enough. Being active every day sets a great tone for you and baby!

TIP   **Put Toys to the Test**

In trying to figure out if a toy is the appropriate size for your baby to play with, use a toy tester, which is just a simple tube. If a toy passes through it, you should not give it to your baby for play. You can buy a toy tester; however, a toilet paper roll will function just as well.

- Are there small parts? Are there strings attached? These features can be serious choking hazards and are inappropriate for young infants.
- Is the toy made from products that are safe and tested? (No BPA or lead, for example.)

Safety is your first priority. Toys should be free of hazardous chemicals and free from known hazards such as small parts and strings. When in doubt, do not use the toy.

Toys should last a while and be easily replaceable should your baby fall in love with one and then lose it. You should also consider how long a toy will last: Can it continue to be used in later developmental stages as a plaything? Toys that grow in this way with your baby are an extra bonus!

Look for toys that spark your baby's curiosity and allow him to investigate and play. He does not want to sit and watch a toy do its thing; he wants to interact. Think of it this way: When your baby gets older, he will much rather push a lever that releases a rolling ball than sit and just watch a train go around the track. At this age, being entertained is not appropriate. Playing has educational value.

It is also okay if you do not have toys or if you have relatively few toys. Babies do not need a lot of toys. If you have two or three well-loved toys, that is perfect for your baby.

Toy safety isn't a laughing matter. Babies put everything into their mouths. You must decide which items you find acceptable; consider toy safety in terms of both design and materials.

WEEK 14

Eat

Your baby has the hang of mealtime! You have probably settled into a nice pattern of feeding that works for both of you at this point. This can mean a lot of pressure is off and you can relax and enjoy this time with your baby.

The trick is that many other things are competing for your time and attention. It is so easy to be distracted while feeding your baby and trying to do something else. While it is possible to get things done, like typing some emails or reading a book, remember to stop and smell the roses.

Watch your baby eat. Rub his head. Play with his fingers. Talk or sing to him. He probably enjoys the contact and you can see him smile, even with his mouth full.

Not only does this help stimulate his brain and give him the interaction with you that he craves, it is good for you. While it's tempting to multitask, this is time to stop and be with just him. Believe it or not, soon getting him to sit still and eat for a few minutes of quiet time will be a distant memory. So enjoy it while you still can; your email will wait.

Sleep

Your baby has probably outgrown being swaddled for sleep. Around this time, babies are moving much more and can squirm and kick their way out of swaddling. This can be a rough transition for him as he learns to sleep without being swaddled. If you have purchased special gowns and blankets for him to sleep in, you will want to choose new sleepwear.

Use sleepwear that is seasonally appropriate. This means is not too hot or too cold. Since blankets, in general, do not work well for babies and can be dangerous, other sleepwear items are available that cover baby without the need for a blanket, such as sleep sacks. They provide him the freedom to move and yet remain covered. But long-legged, and possibly footed, sleepers are also available.

Be sure your baby is still sleeping in the lightest amount of clothing possible. Overheating is uncomfortable for sleeping and can be dangerous as well, increasing the risk factors for SIDS.

Play

Does your baby like music? Try playing lots of different styles. Don't get trapped in the classical music or baby-friendly music ruts. You'll probably go nuts! Nearly any music is appropriate for your baby. Music can help stimulate growth and brain development.

The good news about using music you like is you are more likely to play it. The car is a great place for music. It can also help calm a baby who really does not like the car. Experiment with what your baby likes and doesn't like. Just as you have a preference for certain music at a certain times of the day, your baby might also. In general, use calmer music for calmer times.

MONTH
4

HELPFUL HINTS: BOWEL HABITS

You are probably still watching your baby's bowel and bladder habits closely as signs that he is doing well. You will still see about seven or eight wet diapers a day. However, you might notice that your baby stays dry for slightly longer periods of time. You should be able to see the same number of wet diapers whether you are using cloth or disposables, even though the disposables tend to hold more fluids before you can tell they are wet.

Your baby's bowel habits might have changed. She might have a bowel movement once a day or once every other day. This is completely normal. A few babies also go several days between bowel movements. This is not a problem unless the stool is hard and difficult to pass. Stool that comes out easily and is soft is not considered constipation and should not be treated as such.

If you feel your baby is constipated, you can talk to your pediatrician about what is causing the constipation. The most frequent culprits are infant formula with iron, vitamins, and cereals. You can talk to your pediatrician about switching brands, dropping feeds, or using baby enemas and other items to help relieve your baby's constipation. It is fairly unusual for a strictly breastfed baby to be constipated.

WEEK 15

Eat

If your baby takes a bottle, no matter what it contains, you will want to follow some commonsense safety rules with it:

- Check the nipple for wear and tear. Any damaged nipple must be thrown out immediately.
- Always use the slowest-flow nipple possible for your baby. A faster-flow nipple increases the likelihood that your baby will choke.

- Never prop a bottle up. It might give you free hands, but you may not respond well if baby is choking. It also removes important bonding time with your baby.
- Be sure to use proper storage guidelines for breast milk or infant formula.
- Do not put your baby to bed with a bottle.

Following these guidelines will help you have the safest bottle-feeding experience possible, whether you give one bottle a week or several bottles a day.

Play

Do not get stressed out about toys. Your baby is beginning to discover her hands. These are really cool toys that go with her everywhere. Have you caught her staring at them? Sometimes they even fall and drop on her face, causing her to startle.

You will have almost as much fun watching her find her hands as she has while playing with them. She will put them in her mouth and pull them out. She will open and close her fist in amazement as she tries to put together that they belong to her and that she is in control of them.

Sleep

Have you finally gotten a sleep routine? Great! The good news is that once you have a good pattern established, chances are you will stay there for the

Follow the feeding guidelines to make formula feeding efficient and safe for you and your baby.

HELPFUL HINTS: OVER AND OVER

Repetition is good for babies. It is one of the main ways babies learn and retain information. By repeating information, play, or songs you are giving your baby a chance to predict her world. Join along, and have patience. Just think about the repetition in terms of what your baby is learning. Every time she hears a song or does a finger play, she is learning that skill or action.

Reading the same book over and over or singing the same song over and over is probably not something to which you are accustomed. Consider finding a way to keep yourself involved until you can get feedback from your baby. So if your bedtime routine includes reading *Goodnight Moon*, perhaps choose a different book earlier in the day. If you greet her with a specific good morning song, know that the rest of the songs do not have to be a playlist, just varied songs.

majority of the time. Nevertheless, some babies will break out of their routines occasionally. Sleep patterns can sometimes be disrupted during periods of change or growth. Developmental milestones often bring sleep disruptions, as baby is so eager to practice new skills. When he begins rolling, sitting, or eventually standing and talking, he might have a hard time settling down to sleep or he might have trouble staying asleep. Sick or teething babies can also have a tough time sleeping well.

So if you have had good luck getting your baby to sleep at a regular time, and all of a sudden it seems to have gone completely crazy, do not panic. Even the best sleeper has rough nights or sets of nights. Try to see if you can pinpoint or change anything to help her get back into a good sleep pattern. Sometimes the issue simply has to work itself out in time.

WEEK 16

Eat

You can re-evaluate the baby cereal issue this month. If your baby is growing well and eating well, there is generally no need to start cereal. Starting any solids too early can be harmful to your baby.

Some babies experience intestinal discomfort when starting cereal and other solids. Some get constipated. Others have allergies, even minor ones that cause sniffling, runny noses, rashes, and other effects.

Talk to your pediatrician before starting any solids. Breast milk or infant formula should be all your baby needs for the first six months of life. Your pediatrician will guide you in altering this timetable, because some babies are also not ready at six months.

Sleep

How well your baby sleeps at night is tied to how well her day went. The two time periods are connected, even though they might not appear so. For example, if your baby had too many naps or slept for too long during her nap, she might not sleep as well at night. This might be the obvious example.

Also, an exciting day or a day with a lot of new activities can make your baby a bit more restless. Just as you might react to a busy day or have trouble "turning off your brain," a baby can have similar happenings with busy days or new activities. If this is the case, be sure to stick to your bedtime routine.

But before you do your bedtime routine, spend an extra few minutes really working on relaxation for your baby. If you use massage, consider it at these times, unless your baby finds it stimulating rather than relaxing. Sing or play quiet music, read a book—do whatever your baby finds relaxing until you visibly see that he is more relaxed.

Some days will always be more hectic than others. You might find that some babies are not bothered and simply go with the flow, while others are very sensitive, even to the slightest schedule change. You will know which one your baby is soon enough, and you can go from there.

Play

Your baby is beginning to roll over. He might be able to roll from belly to back or both belly to back and back to belly. Sometimes he might roll but gets an arm pinned under him. This is normal, and he will learn to overcome it. Feel free to assist him.

Use this playtime as skill building. Sitting with him on the floor, place your open hands palms-up under his trunk. Gently pretend to roll him over one way and then the other. Do this as you laugh and smile at him. Say things like, "Rolling over to the right . . . rolling to the left . . . ."

MONTH
4

This is a great way for him to connect rolling and playing. Rolling is one of the first big physical things your baby can do. It can be exciting and frustrating. Remember, never leave your baby unattended on anything off the ground like a bed, couch, or changing table. Babies can roll quickly, and you might not even know that they have this skill. Don't take the risk.

HELPFUL HINTS: TOOTH TIME

Some babies begin to get teeth around this time. This is considered early, though, and it's not a problem if your baby does not get teeth now. You might notice that he chews on everything or drools a lot more than he used to. These are signs of teething.

The hardest thing to realize is that the teething process can be very long. Some babies will drool and chew for months, and you will not see a tooth. Other babies might show teething symptoms for only days before a new tooth shows up. And other babies just wake up with teeth one morning. All of these are normal.

Rolling over provides a host of new options for your little one. Sometimes, however, inadvertently moving in a direction he didn't choose is both confusing and perhaps frightening. Rolling also means you need to step up the baby safety.

WEEK 17

Eat

Sometimes you might think your baby is showing signs of being ready to eat solid foods. Since the decision about when to start solids is based on physical ability to digest food as well as the capability to sit and eat, babies might range on a spectrum when it comes to eating. One thing your baby might be doing that is a near-ready sign is showing she is interested in sharing mealtime with you. Even if she is not quite ready to eat solids, there are ways to include her at mealtime with the family.

You can bring her to the table in a way that allows her to see most everyone. You might try sitting her in your lap or in a high chair if she has enough body control. Do not use a bouncy seat on the table—there is a risk it could fall. Placing a bouncy seat on the floor is also not ideal—it prevents her from participating fully at mealtime.

If your baby wants to eat when you eat, you can nurse her or feed her from a bottle during mealtime. You can offer an alternative form of feeding, such as breast milk in a bottle or cup. You might also offer her small amounts of water, since much of this will not be ingested. As a general rule, babies at this young age do not need water for nutritive purposes, as they get all of their liquids from breast milk or formula. Water for practicing with a cup is nonnutritive, especially since some babies refuse breast milk in a cup, water is a way to teach the skill.

Some babies simply crave the social aspects of a meal. A few toys might also engage your baby during mealtime. Consider letting her play with a bowl or a spoon. These tricks will help her learn to be a part of meals without needing the meal until her body is ready for it. Remember, starting solids early doesn't help her sleep through the night or grow faster. It can expose her to allergies and make digestion more problematic.

Sleep

At this age, it is still recommended that your baby sleep on her back. When you lay her down, be sure she is on her back. The trick around this age is that your baby might already be able to roll over. If she is not doing it now, she soon will.

This rolling over can send even the calmest parent into a tizzy. Before you decide to stay up all night flipping her back and forth, do not worry about it—there's no need if your baby can now roll on her own. If your baby rolls over, leave her. She might roll back onto her back on her own. The risk of SIDS, the reason you lay your baby on her back to sleep, begins to reduce as the year goes on.

Bringing things to her mouth, be it her hands or a toy, can be a sign that baby wants to eat. Catch this sign early, and feed her before she gets really agitated.

MONTH
4

HELPFUL HINTS: PROGRESS NOTES

Your four-month checkup is another chance for you to check on your baby's growth and development. At this visit she will be weighed and measured. She will also have a thorough physical exam with the pediatrician. Your pediatrician will ask you questions, and you should also have time to ask your pediatrician questions. This is a two-way street!

Your doctors will ask about certain skills your baby can do at home or things you have seen. These might include things like rolling from belly to back and back to belly. They will also ask about her eating and sleeping habits. If you are due for vaccinations, they will be offered at this visit as well.

Be sure to have someone write down the height and weight information for you. It's great for your baby book but also provides you with a way to remember it and keep track over time. While you think you will remember by the time you get home, you can forget. You might try writing it down on a calendar in your purse or in your handheld electronic device.

Try not to panic. The more your baby grows, the more likely you are to find that she is not in the position that you left her in. Babies love to move from this age on, and sleep is one of those times when they really seem to move around.

Play

"How big is baby?" is a very simple game that babies love! Here's how it works: With the baby lying or sitting propped up in front of you, take the baby's arms gently in your hands. Cross her arms over her body and gleefully ask, "How big is baby?" Swing her arms wide open and say, "Soooo big!"

Keep repeating this over and over. She will soon show you that she wants to play by crossing her arms over her body. You can personalize the game by using your baby's name instead of the word *baby*. The giggles and smiles you'll get from this game will bring you both lots of enjoyment!

Affirmation for Month Four

*My baby and I
make a great team.*

What to Watch For Explained

Signs of teething may abound this month. This can be anything from pain to drooling, pulling at the ears, and generalized crankiness. This can make everyone's life really difficult. If your baby begins to run a low-grade **fever**, even if you suspect it is due to teething, be sure to monitor it. While familial wisdom says that teething can cause a fever, research simply doesn't support this finding. If your baby has a fever and seems to be pulling at their ears, you may also consider an ear infection rather than simply teething. You should have your baby's ears checked if both of these symptoms occur together.

Pulling at the ears is nearly a universal sign for pain in the ears. Since your baby has more limited communications skills, this is something to watch for in infants. Pain can be cause by fluid building up in the ear or teething pain. Repeated ear infections or fluid behind the ear drum can lead to damage or a hearing loss over time. This is why it is so important to check with your pediatrician if you see these in combination.

If a baby is pulling on his ears with no associated crying, you may just have a child who is simply curious about their ears. You may also be worried if you find scratches on the ears from persistent pulling. If you are not sure as to why your baby is pulling on his ears, pain or not, be sure to ask your baby's pediatrician or other health provider to examine him. They can do an examination of the ear canal and tell you if there is an underlying problem and if you need to act.

Pulling on the ears can also be a sign of sleepiness for some babies. When you see this, take comfort measures—nursing your baby, snuggling, warm baths—whatever helps your baby to be calmed and soothed.

You may notice a lack of language development, such as **a baby who does not repeat sounds or babble**. At this stage, your baby should be babbling daily as well as repeating simple sounds that you make. This, too, could be a sign of hearing loss. Early intervention can reduce the risk and prevent permanent damage to your baby's hearing.

Reaching for objects is something that four-month-olds do. They are interested in their environment, and they want to get their hands on as much of it as they can. Your baby may not be successful in reaching for objects, but trying is the only way that they will learn. If you are not seeing your baby trying to grasp objects or reach for toys, you should mention it at your baby's next checkup.

MONTH
4

MONTH FIVE

Week 18–21

Watch and Wait

√ **Checklist for Month Five**

- ☐ Help your baby learn to sit up.
- ☐ Prepare to travel with your baby.
- ☐ Evaluate your high chair needs.
- ☐ Learn to clean baby toys.
- ☐ Choose good books for your baby.
- ☐ Learn to soothe a teething baby.

What to Watch For in the Fifth Month

- ☐ The ability to bear weight on feet when supported
- ☐ Signs of further development
- ☐ The ability to roll over in one direction
- ☐ Being more socially engaged
- ☐ Laughing or giggling

Baby Skills:

In the fifth month, your baby:

- ☐ Knows his name when called
- ☐ Can tripod, possibly even sit without support for a few seconds
- ☐ Tries to push up during belly time
- ☐ Looks around for people and toys
- ☐ Loves faces
- ☐ Follows voices to see where they are coming from
- ☐ Puts everything in his mouth, including hands and feet
- ☐ Talks more, using consonants repeatedly

BABY DATA

At five months, your baby will smile at you when you come into the room. He will also follow your voice and can hear when you're coming. This makes him quite the social creature. His new love this month is his name. The more you say it, the sooner he will know it is his name. Then he will actually look to see who said it.

His love of toys will continue. He will readily play with objects in his hands. He will hold things in his hands and still try to put them in his mouth. (Remember, this fixation with putting things into his mouth isn't going anywhere anytime soon!) Your baby has also found his toes by now. These will also go right into his mouth. Clean baby toes are fine for baby mouths, but be forewarned that he will do the same with his shoes and socks if you put them on him.

Your baby might do some face planting while tripoding. At first this will happen because he is unstable, but after a while it will happen because he is trying to reach for a toy while sitting up. The same can occur as he pushes himself up while on his belly.

Hopefully your family has a feeding pattern that is working well for you. With any luck, everyone is working together to make feeding time

New skills that are starting to emerge, such as trying to sit up, are fun. Try incorporating these skills into games you play with your baby.

more fun. You might even have moved him to a high chair to enjoy the family's meals, minus the food for him, of course.

Sleeping is becoming smooth sailing. You are most likely down to one nightly feeding, if you time the late-night feeding just right. Having your baby go to bed and then allowing yourself to stay up just a bit longer for some adult or alone time can feel great. If you feed him just before you go to bed, you can even have more time asleep.

HELP YOUR BABY LEARN TO SIT UP

As your baby has been learning new skills like rolling both ways, sitting up is right around the corner. But you don't just walk into a room one day to find your baby magically sitting up all by himself. You have to help him learn how to sit up.

As your baby learns to sit up, there is a great opportunity to add more fun in baby's life. Small toys designed to make noise are great at this age.

MONTH FIVE: Bringing Up Baby

Your three goals this month are simple:

- Learn the signs of teething.
- Watch for baby safety hazards.
- Know how to choose a good book for baby.

MONTH 5

It really all begins from the moment of birth. Your baby first learns to hold his head up. Then he practices holding his head up, gaining strength and control in those muscles. Tummy time is a big factor in learning to sit up as well, again because of all that head and neck muscle building. During the time his belly is down on the floor he will also be learning to do push-ups. Pushing himself off the floor with his hands and forearms will help him learn to sit up alone.

You can assist your baby in learning to sit up by giving him plenty of tummy time and encouraging him to practice sitting up. Hold him on your lap in an upright position. Allow him to lean back on you for support. Gradually he will gain enough strength to do so on his own.

You can also allow him to practice by sitting him up on his own. At first your baby will be very wobbly. You can start him in a tripod position to play on the strength of his arms. Sit his bottom down and with his body and trunk pointing toward his toes, separate his legs and place his hands on the floor in front of him. He will eventually begin to lift up, keeping only his lower half on the floor.

Your baby's early attempts at sitting will last only seconds. This is completely normal. As he continues to practice sitting up, it will last much longer. When your baby is older, his period of sitting will also include playing with toys. Since your baby lacks grace, when he is tired of sitting up he is likely to simply fall over. It is normal and not a problem, though it can be a bit rough on his body. Try to ensure that the ground near him is softer. Rugs are better than tile or wood floors during this period of early, unstable sitting. If you don't have rugs in your house, try to place baby on a cushy blanket if he is going to practice sitting. You also might try using a pillow for support at first.

PREPARE TO TRAVEL WITH YOUR BABY

At some point in your baby's first year, you might have to travel with her. This travel might be for fun or it might be work related. Having a baby can certainly change how you travel and with what you travel. Your child's age at the time of travel will generally dictate the type of preparations you have to make before you leave. But it's beneficial to know beforehand some general basics of traveling with a child under the age of one.

How will you travel? If you are traveling by car, you will have more control over the number of stops you make, as well as opportunities for feeding the baby and changing diapers. If you are flying, you might need to be a bit more prepared to work around someone else's schedule.

Consider how long you will be gone. You should pack more clothes than you think you will need for a baby. A good rule of thumb is two outfits a day.

Diapers can be tricky, but you can manage, even if you decide to keep your cloth diapers going. You will want to bring a wet bag to store your dirty diapers while traveling. Will you have a place to do the wash while you're away? If so, you might not need as many diapers as you previously thought.

For disposable diapers, simply pack a large package of diapers if possible. This will make more room in your bag on the way home, so it's a good excuse for souvenir shopping! If you can buy diapers at a store while at your destination, that is also an option. Either way, you have to have a minimum of diapers for the travel period, so be sure you have some in your carry-on for plane trips or in your vehicle for the road.

Breastfeeding on the road can be so convenient. The milk is always the right temperature and available all day, every day, no matter where you are. If you need to pump, consider purchasing a car adapter for your pump so that it can be used in the vehicle. You can sometimes use these even in an airplane as well.

Air Travel—Baby on Board

Rules associated with carrying breast milk or infant formula through airport security checkpoints have recently been revised. Mothers flying with or without their child will be permitted to bring breast milk or formula in quantities greater than three ounces (89 ml) as long as it is declared for inspection at the security checkpoint.

Nursing your baby during takeoffs and landings can help reduce the pain caused by popping ears. You can also use a pacifier or baby bottle.

Using bottles when traveling takes a bit more planning. How will you wash and sterilize the bottles? If you have access to a microwave for the trip, you can use the small bags that are reusable but still disposable. Bring along enough bottles to last a day, even with the ability to clean them. You will also want to consider how to make the contents warm. Car bottle warmers are available.

You will also want to remember to pack or consider the following items:

- Baby wipes
- Baby toys
- Baby blankets
- Car seat
- Stroller
- Baby carrier
- Baby toiletries
- Place for baby to sleep

Your first trips with baby are likely to feel a bit frantic. Good planning can help to lessen that feeling considerably. Try to stick to baby's natural schedule when possible and remember that babies are portable. Think outside of the box! If it's nap time, consider using the stroller or the baby carrier. The younger your baby is, the easier this part of traveling can be.

MONTH
5

EVALUATE YOUR HIGH CHAIR NEEDS

A high chair will be a great place for your baby to begin solid foods. But even before she learns to eat, it can be a great way to keep her safely in the kitchen. She can be with you but not in your arms as you cook, and not underfoot.

When thinking ahead for a high chair, you will want to think of your space. Do you have enough space to keep the high chair set up at all times? Or would you prefer a folding high chair? You can even find a booster high chair that fits on an already-existing chair in your kitchen or dining room. Or look for a high chair that slips onto the table, if space is tight. If your baby seems particularly eager to participate in mealtime like everyone else in the family does, seats that hook right onto chairs or tables can be a great choice.

All sorts of high chairs are available, with lots of fancy functions. Some have reclining seats while others offer an adjustable tray size. Do you need a place to store the trays? Or would you prefer a cup or bowl holder built into the tray top?

Safety is important, and it starts with the high chair's harness. The safest high chairs offer a five-point harness, much like a car seat. The straps go over the shoulders, around her waist, and meet in the middle between her legs to buckle. Some high chairs only belt around the waist.

A bar also extends to fit between your baby's legs. This is designed to keep your baby actually in the seat of the high chair and to prevent baby from slipping out in the gap. It can be anchored to the chair base or into the tray. Some types of high chairs also have it built in, with a small bar across it. These can be handy when you are trying to get the tray on and you only have so many hands.

Whatever high chair you get, it should be sturdy and washable. Some even have multiple tray covers that can go into the dishwasher. And the seat cover should also come off for easy washing, because your baby is going to get it very dirty! When shopping for a high chair, try it out. Give it the one-handed test to see if you are really able to take the tray off and on safely with one hand.

LEARN TO CLEAN BABY TOYS

Baby toys will get dirty. Of course, toys will also go into your baby's mouth. This means that you need to be able to rectify the difference between a dirty baby toy and your baby's mouth.

Baby has many opportunities to get toys dirty during the course of everyday life. Of course, they go into your baby's mouth and get yucky bits of food plastered all over them, not to mention all that saliva. Then too, they might go into another baby's mouth and get similar germs. Sometimes you—or more likely your baby—will drop them on the floor. Other times animals will try to play with them as well. This can make for dirty toys.

If you plan ahead, the toys you have will be easy to clean. Wooden or plastic surfaces are easy to wipe down. Many baby toys made of plastic can be washed in the sink or run through the dishwasher.

You can clean many baby toys without using harsh chemicals. Vinegar is one great option. Simply take some warm water and a bit of vinegar and wipe the toys down. This also works for plastic books and some board books—just use a damp cloth.

The ten-second rule—the theory that if something drops but you pick it up before ten seconds has elapsed—does not really work. But think about where the toy has dropped and use common sense. Dropping something on the floor at the doctor's office or in the street is probably vastly different from dropping it on your kitchen floor. Another way to clean your toys is simply to let them air out. The vast majority of nasty viruses will die within a few hours. Or you can use baby-friendly sanitizers.

Mama Moment

Have you figured out how to find some "me" time yet? It is important to find some time for yourself, preferably every day. It does not have to be something big or bold; even fifteen minutes to sit and read a book alone can make a huge difference in your mood. You can do scrapbooking, stamp collecting, whatever it is that you enjoy, for you and you alone. So what are you doing for you?

CHOOSE GOOD BOOKS FOR YOUR BABY

Love of reading starts early. You should strive to read to your baby every day. Not only will she love to listen to your voice, but she will also enjoy looking at the pictures. When you are choosing books that you will read to her, do not stress about anything as long as you are enjoying it. This means you can start by reading your favorite classics, even novels or poetry, to your baby. Throw in some good baby books for good measure.

She will also need to have a few books that are simply hers with which to play. These should be sturdy books. They will take a beating and wind up in her mouth. That is okay. Remember, your baby will explore a lot of things through her mouth, and books are no different.

A cloth book is a must for baby. Remember, everything goes into her mouth, including books, and babies will not hesitate to chew and eat paper. If the book is washable, that's even better.

Affirmation for Month Five

I know what my baby needs and I provide it.

Books specifically for her should have large, simple pictures. Words are optional, but if there are words, consider few words per page for when she does start to associate the words with the pictures. She probably still enjoys faces, so try to include some books that have lots of those.

Consider choosing some books that are made for bathtub use. These are handy, even if they don't go into the bathtub. They will take quite a beating. You can also get a book that is printed on a panel so it folds out. This is great to stand up in front of baby during tummy time.

LEARN TO SOOTHE A TEETHING BABY

Teething babies can be cranky babies. While some babies get through teething without a symptom, that isn't the norm. You might find your baby spends lots of time unhappy as his teeth begin to come in.

The teething process can begin well before you ever see any teeth. Around the five- to six-month mark you will notice that many babies are showing signs of teething, even if they do not yet have teeth. There will also be a few babies who have teeth at this age.

Symptoms of teething can include:

- Crying
- Increased drooling
- Chewing on everything
- Putting fingers in the mouth
- Poor sleeping habits

You might or might not be able to see white bumps under your baby's gums. Teeth can take a long time to work their way up through the skin, and often, movement below the gum surface can be just as uncomfortable as the final eruption through the skin.

Give your baby appropriate toys to chew on to help provide soothing pressure to sore gums. Some teething toys are specially designed to be chilled in the refrigerator. This can help to numb the irritated area. Sometimes, even just a washcloth wet with cold water might do the trick, especially if the texture is nubby and baby can really chew on it.

If teething toys don't help and your baby still seems to be in a lot of pain, talk to your pediatrician. Over-the-counter pain relievers can be used to soothe teething pain. All-natural teething tablets are also available over-the-counter. You might want to try those first and leave pain relief medication for really intense teething bouts. Numbing agents are also available, but ask your pediatrician before using these. Sometimes when babies' mouths are too numb, they can't feel anything and inadvertently bite their tongues or have difficulty swallowing, which can make matters worse. Talking to your practitioner will give you the latest scoop on which medications are the most effective and which dosages you can give your baby based on his weight and height. As he ages, different options will be available for him in the teething arena.

Your baby is likely to put his fingers into his mouth as he teethes. It's his way of putting pressure on a sore spot.

MONTH 5

Hot Mama for Month Five

Patterned shirts can be a real blessing for a new mom. You can hide all sorts of baby spit-up stains with a good pattern. Not to mention that a shirt is totally flexible. You can wear a shirt for everyday use and then add some accessories or a jacket to jazz it up, and you are ready to party!

WEEK 18

Eat

How is your breast milk supply? Be sure to watch your baby for signs of a drop in milk supply, such as weight loss. It is common for babies to lose weight if milk supply decreases. A number of things can cause the drop, including:

- Birth control pills containing estrogen (if you decide to use birth control pills, you should take those specifically designed for breastfeeding mothers, which contain progestin only).

- Significant weight loss in mother

- Illness or stress in mother

- Decrease in suckling at the breast (due to pacifier use or supplementing with formula)

Nursing is still your baby's main source of nutrition. Many mothers find it very handy when out and about to simply nurse their baby without the bother of carrying other forms of nutrition.

If you think your milk supply has dropped, you will want to figure out why. For example, the return of your menstrual cycle might diminish your milk supply slightly for a day or two every month.

Once you figure out the reason for the decrease, you will need to take corrective measures. Nursing your baby more frequently is a good way to boost milk supply. You can also use a breast pump, depending on your life circumstances. Often decreased milk supply at this point is temporary and short-lived. However, if your issue is longer term, you will need to seek advice from your lactation professional and possibly enlist other medical support. Your baby might need supplementation, though you will need guidance on how to do it without further affecting your milk supply.

Remember, your milk supply is an amazing thing. It can sense what your baby needs and when. Your body works with your baby to provide exactly the right amount of milk, made from exactly the right ingredients. Your body will go through changes, and you will notice that your breasts respond differently as you get further away from giving birth. This means you cannot gauge how much milk your baby is getting by the feel of your breasts alone. Many women notice that right after birth, their breasts feel quite full before a feeding and less full after a feeding. But this is not true after a few months of breastfeeding, as your body makes normal adjustments and your breasts begin to supply milk as baby demands it. So sometimes what might initially feel like a "drop" in your milk supply is really just your body becoming more adept and efficient at feeding your baby.

Sleep

Infant sleepwear is treated with a flame-retardant material. You will notice some outfits, which look similar to sleepwear, are marked "not intended for sleep." These warnings are designed to help protect your baby in the event of a fire. Some babies have reactions to this material, and it irritates their skin.

If your baby wakes up with red bumps or a rash over the parts of her body that were covered with the materials, you might want to be careful and avoid infant sleepwear treated with this chemical mixture. You can consider alternative purchases, including chemical-free organic sleepwear.

Play

As your baby develops better physical abilities, you can play many physical games with her. One baby favorite is when you lay her on her back on a soft surface. Have her grasp your fingers, but also wrap your other fingers around her wrist. Start with lifting her just slightly off the ground. She will get stronger and able to handle this exercise a bit better. Then you can pull her to a sitting position.

When you first start doing this with your baby, you might notice that her head falls backward a bit and she struggles to hold it up. Do not pull her so far forward that she can't pull her head up. Give her a chance to do so, although it might take her a second. This helps her practice holding her head up and pulling with her arms.

Make this a game and sing to her as you try it. She will delight in your voice, and she'll be excited because she's coming toward you. It's fun play, but she's also exercising the whole time!

HELPFUL HINTS: MIMIC CLINIC

Your baby can easily learn to recognize patterns. As you've just read, this is one of the many reasons that repetition is so great for him. But these patterns are particularly important when it comes to acquiring speech.

Your baby is listening to the patterns of your speech. He will often try to mimic them when he "talks" to you as well. One great thing to try is encouraging him to lead the conversation occasionally. Whatever he says, mimic it right back to him. Watch his face light up as if to say, "She really understands me!"

These pretend conversations are a great way to communicate with your baby. You are teaching him that you are listening to him, and you are responding in ways that you would like him to listen and respond. These first conversations are important in beginning to learn about socializing. Conversation, your baby will learn, has a pattern: Talk, wait, listen, respond, and so on.

MONTH
5

WEEK 19

Eat

As you begin to prepare for your baby to eat solids, have you considered what goes into baby food ware? For example, are you planning to use plastic utensils for your baby? If yes, are they free of bisphenol-A (BPA) and other potentially toxic chemicals? Does this even concern you?

Check out local stores where you can get more "organic" plastics, baby utensils, and plates. While glass is one of the safest in terms of leaching chemicals, when used in cooking, it is dangerous for your baby because of the potential for breakage. Some stores refuse to carry products that contain BPA and phthalates. Consider going on a fact-finding mission before the big change to solids comes your way.

Play

Repetition is one of your best friends in baby play. Do not panic and think that every time you play with your baby you have to do something new and exciting. Babies prefer repetition and learn best when something is repeated over and over. So when you sing the same few songs and read the same few books, your baby is learning. He learns patterns, cause and effect, and what to expect, not to mention that he loves having time with you.

Sleep

Crying it out: You have probably heard about this when it comes to infant sleep programs. While crying for long periods of time is not appropriate and is potentially even harmful to young babies, as your baby gets older, small periods of crying are less likely to be harmful.

This might make crying methods of sleep training sound appealing to you. Before you try anything, talk to other parents about various sleep-training methods that have succeeded for their families. Talking to a broad range of parents will give you a better look at the programs available. Start with families who have beliefs similar to your own with regard to parenting; they are more likely to have programs that will work for you.

While your baby isn't quite ready to eat yet, you should be preparing for the introduction of solids. This means finding safe materials with which to feed your baby, such as BPA-free plastics, metals, or wood.

Remember you do not have to do what doesn't feel right for you or your family. You can partially incorporate a program into your life and continue to try to find your way without a specific program.

Remember, as with many other parenting issues, there is no one right or wrong way to handle sleep—only what works for you and your family. If you and your baby are both happy and well rested, intervention may not be necessary. You might wish to look for other ideas if you are experiencing sleep issues. For some families this includes sleeping with the baby. For other families it means rocking the baby to sleep. But you still control what that sleep training looks like for you and your family.

WEEK 20

Eat

If you are using a breast pump with replaceable membranes or parts, you might find you need to replace them. They might not be damaged or look damaged, but many moms find even slight wear and tear will decrease their milk supply. If the amounts of milk you usually pump diminish and you can't explain it any other way, try switching out your membranes.

Not every breast pump has parts like these, but you should look inside your pump or in your pump manual to see about replaceable routine parts, such as the membranes. Many moms are surprised by how something so small can make such a huge difference.

HELPFUL HINTS: SAFE TOY FACTS

At this age, your baby is becoming interested in her environment. She takes in everything around her, from the sights to the sounds. She loves to grab anything she can get her hands on. She's probably also exploring the world by mouth, meaning whatever she can grab, goes into her mouth.

You need to be extra careful that her toys are age-appropriate. Look for toys that are:

- Nontoxic
- Age appropriate
- Designed for babies
- Durable
- See "Put Toys to the Test," page 110.

If your baby plays with toys anywhere other than your own house, such as a child care location or even at grandma's house, you will want to ensure that the same rules apply there as at your home. Safety should be enforced no matter where you are. You might have to bring a special bag of toys for your trips to grandma's house or ensure that grandma has her own stash of safe toys.

MONTH
5

Sleep

The importance of your baby's sleeping safely can't be stressed enough. This means periodically checking for crib recalls. If you purchased a new crib, there should have been a postcard to mail to the manufacturer. The card allows them to contact you with recall information. You can also check for recall information through various sites online.

If your crib has a recall, your first step is to talk to the company. Find out specifically what is wrong with the crib and what steps you need to take to fix the problem. Sometimes a company will simply mail you a part that needs to be added to the crib. Other times the whole crib must be returned. The company will let you know what your options are for fixing the crib.

Breast Pumps 101

Breast pumps have a variety of functioning parts, some more than others. Check your owner's manual to understand the workings of your particular pump before using.

- **a.** Silicone petal massager
- **b.** Pump cover
- **c.** Silicone diaphragm and stem
- **d.** Handle
- **e.** Funnel
- **f.** Pump body
- **g.** White valve
- **h.** Locking ring
- **i.** Bottle adapter
- **j.** 125ml/4 oz bottle or disposable bottle and bags
- **k.** Funnel cover/stand
- **l.** Dome cap
- **m.** Newborn teat
- **n.** Travel cover

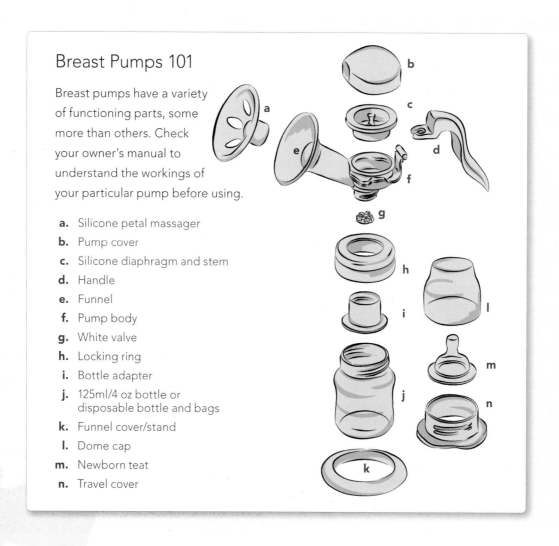

HELPFUL HINTS: DIAPER DILEMMA

You may have occasional trouble with leaky diapers. Leaks are common and could be because your baby is outgrowing her current diaper size.

Some babies go through diaper sizes quickly, while others stay in the same size for months. While disposable and cloth diapers both offer weight suggestions, they are only a guideline, simply because every baby is shaped differently. Two babies that each weigh fifteen pounds (6.8 kg) can look vastly different and need their diapers to fit differently.

If your baby has skinny legs, that might cause leaks. Try to tighten disposable diapers by crossing the tabs over each other. Cloth diapers are less of a problem for skinny-legged babies, but if your cloth diapers are leaking investigate using a gusseted cover.

Because babies are shaped differently, you might have to use a different-size disposable diaper than you would with cloth. Cloth diapers offer you more leeway, and usually expand with a series of snaps or folds. Going up a size does not always solve leaking problems. Some parents find that switching brands can help.

If you have a baby boy and the leak is coming from the top of the diaper, it might be because his penis is pointing upward and leaking urine. Be sure to point his penis downward in the diaper before closing it when you change him. You might also have this issue if his penis is not completely enclosed in the diaper from the side. Be sure it is well within the gussets of the diaper.

Consider whether you are leaving your baby in a diaper too long. Even if you have been changing your baby with the same frequency, if she is holding her bladder for a bit, there may be a larger volume of urine at one time, causing the leakage. This can also occur if the diaper is not being properly used. Be sure to open the diaper all the way and to open the gussets at the bottom of most disposable diapers.

MONTH
5

In the meantime, be sure that your baby has a safe place to sleep. This might mean breaking out or even borrowing a travel crib. This is a temporary solution, but hopefully the crib fix will be fast.

Play

You can use rhythm while playing with your baby. Rhythm is a great way to help her learn about patterns, which will help her learn other aspects of life later on, such as reading and math. You can incorporate rhythm very simply into your play.

To begin, just sing songs or read nursery rhymes to her. As you do so, tap on her body, trunk, or legs, or clap your baby's hands to the rhythm. Think of nursery rhymes that you might have long forgotten. Make up songs and sing them to your baby. Simply emphasize the rhythm on the baby by patting, clapping, or rubbing. This will reinforce the rhythm for her and help her start to feel it inside her own body.

Your baby is likely to enjoy these games thoroughly. Eventually, after enough repetition, she will show you that she wants to sing a specific song by mimicking the movements you do at play. Remember, this imitation is the sincerest form of flattery.

WEEK 21

Eat

Many babies around this age become distracted easily while nursing or eating. During nursing he may suddenly pull off to stare at something, and then happily go back to nursing.

Sometimes your baby might turn toward sounds or other people in the room. Other times the baby just seems to decide she would rather be looking elsewhere. No matter why she is pulling away from her food, it can be annoying for you.

Try to encourage her to simply eat. If distractions are a big deal, you may avoid them by feeding her in a quiet, distraction-free zone when possible. If it isn't possible or doesn't work, you can also just end the feeding and try again a little later. Some families report success with using a blanket or something else to keep the distractions to a minimum. Some moms even try wearing interesting necklaces or other jewelry to bring baby's focus back to nursing. But this can also cause some babies to sit up and take notice rather than eat! If your baby does start to get distracted when eating—and most eventually do—you will just have to experiment with which techniques work for you and your baby to help alleviate the issue.

Is your baby easily distracted while eating? This is very common. Sometimes, a quiet room helps, sometimes singing or reading to your baby during a feeding will work as well.

HELPFUL HINTS: PLAY IT SAFE

Around this time, you might begin looking at baby play yards, also known as playpens. The vast majority of newer baby play yards are portable and covered in mesh. They tend to fold quickly and easily and store in small spaces. They are designed for your baby to play in or sleep in. Some of the fancier models are also sold as bassinet/diaper-changing combinations for the earlier months.

You might also consider traveling with the play yard. Some families use it to contain their baby while they are cooking or working in an office, as it keeps baby off a possibly dirty floor. No matter why or how you use a baby play yard, you will want to consider safety factors:

- Wooden slats (for older models) should be no further than 2³/₈ inches (6.1 cm) apart.
- There should be no holes or tears in the covering mesh.
- All sides should be opened fully and securely to prevent collapse while in use.
- Remove parts intended for newborns as your child gets older.
- Do not leave your baby alone in the play yard/bassinet after she has reached the weight/developmental skills limits.

Your baby may enjoy some alone time to play. Just be sure she's in a safe environment.

MONTH
5

- Routinely check under the mattress for objects that might have fallen through or done damage.
- Do not tie things to the play yard.
- Do not place the play yard near electrical outlets, cords, or vents.

Play yards are great ways to keep baby safe and yet still near you. They can be super for sleeping when you travel out of town or spend nights with grandma. The only key, as with anything that you do for baby, is to ensure her safety.

Your baby will hopefully get the message quickly that it is time to eat and not to look around. Many babies will eventually figure out that they would much rather eat than play in these cases.

Sleep

Are you hearing from your friends that their baby sleeps better than your baby? Or perhaps you are getting advice about the right way to help your baby sleep at night? All of this can add to the stress you might be feeling about your baby and sleep.

Take a deep breath and relax. While most babies of this age can sleep between five and eight hours at a long stretch, not all babies can or do, for varying reasons. Some babies still need to eat in the middle of the night—examples include smaller babies with weight-gain issues or those whose stomachs still cannot hold large amounts of milk at once. Also, a baby who has reflux or other stomach problems often needs to continue eating more frequently during the night.

Remember that all babies are different. You are the parent of your baby and your baby alone. This makes you the ultimate authority on her. While others might tell you what their baby does or what babies do, you know what is right for yours.

Play

"Peek-a-boo! I see you!" This is one of the most common games to play with your baby. It is also so very simple. You can do it anywhere, and babies love it.

Peek-a-boo is a perennial favorite with babies. It's easy to do, but provokes such peals of laughter!

We all know the basic game: With your hands in front of your face, hide from your baby, then re-emerge and say, "Peek-a-boo!" You can elaborate on this old-standby by ducking behind the doorway or even using a piece of cloth or a scarf to hide behind. Babies also love the swirling rhythm and motion that goes with using scarves for peek-a-boo.

Some babies, at first, are very concerned about where you are. But once they know you are coming back, they are all smiles. This game delights babies of all ages. And before you know it, your baby will be "hiding" from you and saying "peek-a-boo!" too.

What to Watch For Explained

Your baby is growing by leaps and bounds. With these changes come new skills. **The ability to bear weight on his feet when supported** is one of those skills. This means that if you hold your baby up, he tries to stand up. He will wobble and only do so for a second or two at a time, but he is trying. Some babies love to do this and will practically insist on being in this position when you hold them while you are seated. This can make some of the older generation nervous because they grew up believing this can cause bowed legs. Never fear—that is nothing but an old wives' tale. While this exercise is good, talk to your pediatrician about the use of jumpers and exercisers for longer periods of time. Some can be harmful to your baby's developing legs if not age-appropriate.

Signs of further development in your baby are usually easily seen at this point. Sometimes it feels like your baby is learning a skill a day. Remember that all babies will develop at their own rate. Some babies are sprinters and others are in for a longer race. It can be difficult not to compare your baby, but avoid it whenever possible. You will want to report any lack of development, decrease, or back-tracking in development to your baby's doctor.

The ability to roll over in one direction is usually something your baby is able to do by now. If you are not seeing this skill, you can help your baby practice by being sure that he is getting plenty of tummy time. You can also help him by rolling him over halfway and seeing what happens. Many babies start by getting about half or three quarters of the way over, which can be frustrating for them. If you don't see your baby rolling or trying, discuss it at your next well-baby check up.

Being more socially engaged is the name of the game at five months. Your baby really enjoys interacting with everyone. Who can't help smiling and cooing back at an adorable baby? You can play with him and make silly faces or voices and get a great reaction out of your baby. **Laughing or giggling** is way he will draw people in. This helps your baby learn how to socially interact with others. Babies who aren't laughing, or actively drawing others in, may need to be evaluated by your practitioner. It can be that the baby is developing at a slower pace. Social interaction is an important part of their development, so your pediatrician will undoubtedly have plenty of advice on how to move forward.

MONTH
5

Week 22–26

Move On Up

√ Checklist for Month Six

- ☐ Decide if your baby is ready for solid foods.
- ☐ Plan your baby's first solid feeding.
- ☐ Remember what's important.
- ☐ Consider baby proofing.
- ☐ Check your medicine cabinet.
- ☐ Make your own baby food.

What to Watch For in the Sixth Month

- ☐ Interest in and the ability to sit
- ☐ Babbling to himself and to others
- ☐ Reactions to new foods
- ☐ Preference for one hand

Be Sure to:

☐ Schedule a checkup.

☐ Have six-month photos taken.

Baby Skills:

In the sixth month, your baby:

☐ Will try to crawl

☐ Will sit unsupported

☐ May have teeth on the bottom

BABY DATA

On the move! That is your baby's goal this month as she tries new skills. Sitting is becoming old hat, and she can most likely sit for at least a few seconds all by herself, without the support of her hands in front of her body.

Even more exciting, she might try to crawl while on her belly—or at least try to drag herself across the floor. Sad news for her: The toy she wants will remain out of her reach for a while, because most babies crawl backward rather than forward at first. This will lead to more frustration for your baby, because she is trying so hard!

Sleep time should be adjusting nicely. Most families have few sleep problems to report at this point. Even if he still does a nightly feeding or two, he probably does not stay awake or want to play. He probably gets right down to business, eats, and goes back to sleep. These, calmer, quicker night-time feedings are usually more bearable for parents. Waking in the middle of the night is easier to take

The first attempts at crawling are often quite funny. Many times your baby is just as shocked as you are at the success of her new movement.

when your little one isn't crying or difficult to settle. Do not panic if others claim that all babies should sleep through the night by now. Some babies don't do so yet for a variety of reasons. It is also important not to compare breastfed and formula-fed babies. The comparison is simply not valid because of the different nutrient content and feeding patterns. Just remember to do what feels right for your family.

As you consider introducing solids this month, you might have a bit of a time figuring out how to work food feedings in with milk feedings, and deciding what your baby needs and when. Solids at first should not replace breast milk or other feedings. They should be thought of as complementary.

DECIDE IF YOUR BABY IS READY FOR SOLID FOODS

Your baby is six months old. This means you are officially cleared to begin solid foods if your baby is physically ready to eat them. You need to look for a specific set of abilities, so consider these things:

- Has your baby stopped tongue thrusting (using her tongue to push everything out of her mouth as soon as it enters)?

- Does your baby seem to need to nurse or eat for long periods of time, like he did when he was having a growth spurt, only the need is very prolonged?

- Can your baby sit up without support for more than a minute or two?

- Does your baby enjoy mealtime with the family?

MONTH SIX: Bringing Up Baby

Your three goals this month are simple:

- Learn the basics of starting solids.
- Watch for baby to sit up.
- Know about changes in safety.

- Can she use a pincer grasp (her thumb and forefinger) to pick up food or other objects?

- Does she put objects, including food, in her mouth?

- Does she open her mouth if you are holding her on your lap and eating?

- Does she do well with a sippy cup?

If your baby is physically ready for solid foods, you should see all of these signs. If even one of them is missing, you should wait. While you might be eager to start solid foods, it is important to remember that not every baby is ready at six months. In general, most babies will be ready for solid food between six and eight months.

If you have concerns about your baby's readiness, talk to your pediatricians. They can give you advice on what specifically to watch for in your baby and how to make eating safe and happy.

MONTH
6

PLAN YOUR BABY'S FIRST SOLID FEEDING

Have you decided that your baby is ready to eat food? If the answer is yes, then you have some other decisions to make. Consider which food you wish to start with for your baby's first solid.

Many parents choose single-grain cereals. If you do this, rice cereal is often a good first choice. (Other grains, such as oatmeal, barley, and wheat, will follow subsequently.) But there is no reason that cereal has to be the first food; many infants start with fruits or vegetables. Aim for foods on the lower end of the allergy spectrum, such as sweet potatoes, bananas, squash, and green beans.

You should avoid certain high-allergen foods until your baby is much older. Some examples of these foods are:

- Peanuts
- Cow's milk and dairy products
- Eggs
- Tree nuts
- Soy
- Wheat
- Shellfish
- Strawberries

Also stay away from citrus for now, because all of that acid can be tough on baby and cause a nasty diaper rash!

While you can look for a general list of foods to avoid, know if any foods are personal allergens in your family. These should also be avoided. So if you are allergic to raspberries, skip them for now.

When you do introduce a new food, do so only one food at a time. Give your baby her first food and wait at least four days before introducing a new one. This allows you to watch for allergic reactions.

Allergic reactions are unlikely to be big, although they can happen. A major allergic reaction would include swelling of the lips, tongue, or airway. In such a case, you would need to call 911 immediately.

First solid feedings are adorably messy. Your baby has a lot to try to figure out like texture, taste, coordinating his tongue, and swallowing.

The most common food allergy symptoms are faint and hard to notice if you are not looking for them. A mild reaction could be something as simple as:

- Runny nose (Runny nose can also be associated with teething, which also happens around this time. But if you notice the runny noses only while feeding food X or if the runny nose is different in quality from what you usually associate with teething, this could be a sign of a food allergy.)
- Rash on skin or diaper area
- Loose stools
- Irritability
- Hives
- Gassiness

How you log this information is up to you. Some parents choose to write everything down, from the foods their baby has tried to any reactions they noticed. This is a great idea if you like data and if you are forgetful. Other parents are a bit more laid back and write something down only if there seems to be a problem. Or you could go middle-of-the-road and keep a running list of foods your baby has tried and how it went. You could alternatively mark a small X or other symbol near foods you do not wish to try again for whatever reason.

When giving first foods, keep in mind that you are feeding a baby. This means the serving size will be very small, and you will usually begin with only one solid food feeding a day. Don't get too caught up in how successful this first feeding is. You might get your baby to take a few bites, or he might love solid food and eat up to a couple of tablespoons. Then again, he might not like it at all. Don't be discouraged; sometimes it takes several tries for a baby to accept solid food. Whatever happens, just let your baby be your guide.

When getting ready for your first feeding, you will need a place for baby to sit, a bib, some food, a camera, and a spoon. Ready, aim, feed! Use a soft-tipped spoon for your baby's comfort. These are also

Mama Moment

As your baby grows and develops, so do you. Where you are as a mother has likely changed a lot since you had your baby. As you round the corner of the first half of your baby's first year, remember that changes will continue. If you have been the primary care provider for your baby up until now, whether or not you work out of the home, you are likely to find that others will be able to help you more as time goes on. Your baby will enjoy venturing out and you will get to see him blossom with others. Sometimes stepping back and watching your child from a distance can be just as wonderful as watching him up close. Remember to be open to these experiences.

Progressing with Solid Food

The following are some recommendations when offering your baby solids. They can be introduced in the order listed here:

1. Soft, sweet, mild-tasting fruits or vegetables—bananas, sweet potatoes, or avocados chopped or mashed

2. Protein-rich foods (meat or beans) cooked until tender in small pieces

3. Whole grain breads and cereals

4. Fresh fruits and vegetables (if canned, buy water-packed fruits)

5. Whole milk and other dairy products, eggs, and citrus products are not offered until one year of age

Remember, honey is not recommended until a child is at least one to two years old because of the risk of botulism spores. Many pediatricians also recommend not giving infants eggs, fish, peanuts, or any other nuts until they are at least one year old.

—Adapted from La Leche League/
The Womanly Art of Breastfeeding

usually a bit flatter than a regular spoon. Remember, small bites at first. Your baby will likely roll the food around in his mouth first, trying to decide what to do with it. Do not be surprised if your baby wears much of these first feedings all over herself. Just keep trying. Remember, at first, your baby is just practicing with eating. She does not really have a nutritional need for it yet, as breast milk and formula are still her primary source of nourishment. Real nutritional necessity for solid food comes later in the first year.

You might also find that your baby is not really ready for solids. If you are continually scooping the food up and trying to get it back in his mouth, only to be met by his tongue thrusting outward, it could be too early. Even a week can make a huge difference in starting solids. If it's too early, come back and try the same food again a few days later. Simply try waiting a bit for his body to mature. Remember, six months is an estimate, not a mandate.

REMEMBER WHAT'S IMPORTANT

Having a baby changes your life. There is no doubt about that. Around the six-month mark, hopefully your family is finding its new normal.

Have confidence that you know what you are doing as a parent by this point. You have made the changes that you need to make. You have incorporated the baby into your life, even though adjustments need to be made frequently as your family circumstances and your baby grow and change.

While more changes are still to come, you can feel good now about going with the parenting flow.

Now is the time to check in with yourself about where you are as a parent. Are you where you thought you would be when you started this journey? Have you veered from your original path? In what ways have you grown or changed?

If you find you're someplace different than you expected, that's fine. After all, there's no way to even imagine the changes that parenthood will bring to our lives until we actually become parents. The only caveat is that you are okay with where you are now as a parent. This doesn't mean you're making your parents, relatives, friends, or neighbors happy, just you and your partner.

So now that you have found your new normal, have you also figured out what is important to you? Do you know what you are doing when it comes to quality time? Do you feel the quantity of time you're able to share with your family is good? Stop

MONTH
6

Sometimes, it is so easy to get caught up in the cycle of a new baby. At the six-month mark many families are able to stop and breathe. Congratulate yourself on finishing the first half of an amazing year.

and count your blessings, and ensure that you are doing what you can to live in the moment. From six months on, your baby's growth accelerates drastically, so be ready to go from baby to toddler in the blink of six more months.

CONSIDER BABY PROOFING

You probably thought about baby proofing during pregnancy. You might even have gone as far as buying a couple of outlet plugs or other safety items to have around the house. But now that your baby is bigger and about to become more mobile, the time has come to get serious about baby proofing.

The first step in baby proofing is to realize the potential pitfalls in your home. You can read checklist after checklist and come up with some basic ideas. This is always a good place to start. Be sure:

- Outlets are plugged with child-resistant plugs.
- Cords are off the floor or shortened.
- Window-blind cords are safely stored or shortened.
- Chemicals are placed high up and are locked up (including medicine).
- Heavy objects are secured to the wall to prevent tipping furniture and appliances.
- Baby gates are installed at the tops and bottoms of stairs and other dangerous places.

However, you'll need to work out some more important details to have a baby-proof home. You will literally need to look high and low to see any potential hazard as your baby explores your home. You will likely more readily think about higher-up objects. Go through your house on hands and knees, just as your baby would, to spy things from her level.

Did you catch the plastic endcaps on the doorstops? Replace those doorstops with one-piece versions to prevent choking. Did you see some sharp corners that could use some padding as your baby begins to crawl, walk, and climb? What about some of the lovely breakables at floor or table level, such as vases and picture frames? Are there any floor lamps that might easily be tipped? See how this list could go on and on? The best advice is to check your house carefully, and continue to revisit your childproofing needs as your baby grows taller and more adept.

When in doubt, invite a toddler over to help you. With supervision, walk the toddler through the house and watch everything she does. Toddlers will go straight to the hot spots, and you can see how the mind of a small child works. After all, who would ever have thought to put the remote control in the DVD player?

When baby proofing, don't forget the plants. There are some that are dangerous and poisonous for your baby; but even plants that aren't poisonous can be risky when you consider that baby could pull a pot down to break.

To keep your family safe, you need to be aware of some other things you can't really see. For example, circuit interrupters can be installed near bathtubs and sinks. They will shut off your electricity should your baby try to drop an electronic into a body of water. If you have a toy box, be sure it has airholes in case your child accidentally gets shut inside.

The most frustrating thing about childproofing is, no matter how much you try to keep things away from babies, they always manage to get into everything! The challenge as a parent is devising ways to stay one step ahead of your little one as much as possible.

Also, don't underestimate your baby's developing pincer grasp. Once he figures this out, he will move around picking up every single microscopic item he can find on your floor. This includes lint on your rugs, stray bits of cat litter, dog food, string, and so forth. Your job, albeit an ugly one, will be continually following him around and thwarting him as he attempts to ingest these disgusting items. Each time you catch him, gently say, "Give it to Mommy (or Daddy)!" Hopefully all of the training will pay off eventually. But don't expect it to happen for a while. Much of parenting, during these early stages of baby's mobility and development, is repetition.

You will find that baby- and childproofing are monumental tasks, and are never quite done. Get the basics done now and patch things up as your child shows you where the danger lies when he moves around more and more.

MONTH
6

CHECK YOUR MEDICINE CABINET

Every few months you should make an effort to go through your medicine chest. Check all of the medications for expiration dates. As your baby gets older, you will also want to make sure you are stocked with age-appropriate medications.

For example, you would treat a baby's nasal stuffiness with a nasal aspirator and saline nose drops or a spray. As your baby grows into a child, you could add medications to that arsenal. Considering these changes in advance will also prevent middle-of-the-night runs to the drugstore for over-the-counter medications.

Be sure to have at least the following on hand at home:

- Nasal aspirator
- Ibuprofen
- Acetaminophen
- Simethicone (gas drops)
- Saline drops/spray
- Other medications as directed by your pediatrician

Keep these in a safe, dry, dark spot, as with all medications. Your storage spot should be easy for you to find, but difficult for children to find. You should also have an updated dosing chart available. Be sure to ask for one at your pediatrician visit this month.

MAKE YOUR OWN BABY FOOD

Making your own baby food can be a lot of fun. There are many reasons to do it, including your getting to choose exactly what goes into your baby's mouth. This is the most common reason families give for making their own baby food.

What you will need to get started is very simple:

- Food of your choosing
- Something to grind the food
- Storage containers (if you plan to make in bulk)

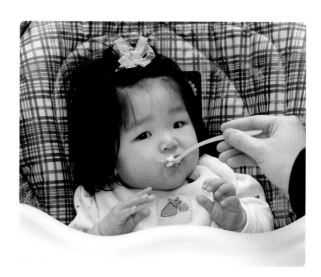

Making your own baby food is fun and cost-effective. Have your baby sample new concoctions before making a larger batch to freeze.

You can grind food in a food processor, if you have one. You can also purchase food mills specifically for this purpose. They range from $15 to $150 (£9 to £90), depending on what they do. You might not need a baby food maker that steams and grinds, so keep that in mind when you see the range. Don't forget, the baby food stage usually lasts for only a few months, because soon enough you will be able to start mashing actual table food for your little one to eat. With that in mind, there is really no reason to buy a super-deluxe baby food processor!

Some foods can be mashed with a fork, particularly if they are steamed. If you find this troublesome and time consuming, a baby food grinder can come in handy.

Different foods cook and grind very differently. So while one butternut squash gives you six or seven servings, three pears are only one or two servings. Baby foods freeze well, so if you make more than your baby can eat, you can freeze for later use. Covered ice cube trays work great for this purpose, and the cubes are just the right size for baby portions! (Just remember to avoid chemical hazards in the type of plastic.)

You can buy fruits and vegetables to prepare for your baby. Simply clean them off and cut them up. Some, like bananas or avocados, require no cooking, just mashing. Other vegetables and fruits will need to be cooked. Steaming works really well and preserves more nutrients than boiling does.

If the thought of chopping up food is more than you want to do, you can also buy frozen foods to cook and grind. Many organic options are available in frozen foods, if you require this for your baby. Many grocery stores also sell fresh fruits and vegetables presliced. You will pay a higher price for the prepared foods, but you'll be saving yourself time and effort.

As your baby learns to eat and becomes used to many foods, you can use the baby food grinder to grind up the family meal. This is also a great way to deal with leftovers from dinner. Simply grind and store them in the freezer, when appropriate, for a baby meal at a later time.

MONTH 6

Hot Mama for Month Six

Have you had a real dress-up date yet? If not, try to schedule one soon. Even if dressing up isn't your favorite thing to do, it will really lift your spirits and make you feel sexy. All mommies need this boost once in a while, after being covered in baby milk and dealing with messy diapers all day!

WEEK 22

Eat

As you begin solid foods for your baby, many other changes might take place, including the one place you probably don't want to deal with them: his diaper. Your baby's body will react differently to solid foods, and the new ways he processes solids will be evident there.

If your baby has been exclusively breastfed up until this point, you're probably used to non-offending odors and yellow mustard stools. With the introduction of solids, you are likely to see more formed stools that can be malodorous. This is perfectly normal.

Any baby is subject to constipation once solid foods are introduced, so be prepared for this. Make note of what foods tend to bind your baby up. Likely offenders are cereals, foods with iron, applesauce, and bananas. Try to space these foods out every few days after allergen testing, and then add in some less-binding foods like prunes on the days in between.

Sleep

The clothes your baby sleeps in can make a difference. When choosing what your baby will wear at night, you'll want to consider multiple factors, including safety, comfort, and purpose. You might also consider style, more for function than fashion.

Your baby's pajamas or nightclothes should be free of strings or decorations. These items could come off, and your baby could swallow them and choke. Some night clothing is also covered with a flame retardant. If you purchase clothing like this, be sure to wash it prior to use.

Your baby will also sleep better in comfortable clothes. Comfort is unique for each baby. Consider how hot your child is during sleep and what the weather is like when choosing a fabric. Also feel the inside seams for comfort. Tags can be uncomfortable for some babies, while they don't affect others. Keep in mind that your baby will be sleeping on her back. Avoid buttons or snaps that she would sleep on in that area.

Purpose and functionality are important as well. You should be able to reach your baby's diaper quickly and efficiently for nighttime diaper changes. Look for simple on-and-off clothing so that if you need to change her clothes at night, it can happen easily without waking her up as much as if you had to pull something over her head.

Play

Most sunscreens are meant for babies six months and older. Now that your baby is six months old, you can use some sunscreen on his skin. However, take precautions when choosing one. Sunscreens come in two varieties: chemical blocks and physical blocks. Use a physical block, such as zinc oxide or titanium dioxide. These work immediately and do not expose your baby to any unnecessary chemicals.

When searching for a sunscreen, be sure that you read all of the ingredients. Your pediatrician might tell you some things to look for or to avoid, given your baby's skin condition. You might want to avoid sunscreens that contain PABA. Most pediatricians recommend zinc oxide or titanium dioxide as the best blockers.

In general, you want to ensure that you have a broad-spectrum sunscreen that blocks both UVA and UVB rays. The sun protection factor (SPF) should also be at least 15. Don't worry about slathering the highest possible SPF you can find all over your baby. Sunscreens with an SPF over 30 really don't add much extra protection. Instead, just be sure to reapply sunscreen as needed—every few hours, and especially after your baby gets wet—because sunscreen does wear off.

MONTH
6

Sun protection is a must for your baby. In addition to sunscreen, a wide-brimmed hat and sunglasses are necessary.

HELPFUL HINTS: TIME FOR A CHANGE

Around this time your baby might start to dislike her diaper changes. It probably has nothing to do with the actual diapers. Rather, it's about the physical act of being changed. Some babies seem to be so into whatever they are doing that this diaper-change disruption is too much, and they become aggravated. Other babies dislike lying on their backs once they have discovered their newfound sitting or crawling skills. This can make your life a bit more hectic, as you scramble to tackle your little one and pin her down.

Babies at this age will wiggle and twist. They will try to squirm away. You will make a mess at some point. These antics can make diaper changing feel more like a wrestling match than a simple day-to-day task. Some mothers think removing baby's clothes can help to prevent these sorts of messes; that is for you to decide.

If your baby is getting squirmy when it is time to change diapers, you will really want to be prepared with all of the items you need. Think ahead. Might you need diaper cream? Get it before you start. Also consider moving your changes to lower ground. Just grab your changing pad and throw it on the ground for the actual change. You can easily move it back when you are done.

Another idea is to distract your baby during diaper changes. Have a special toy that she loves and let her see it only during diaper-changing times. This might buy you a few minutes of more cooperation to get the job done.

Thankfully, this wild and woolly changing time doesn't last forever. Once they get used to their newfound mobility, some babies settle back down into their normal, calmer selves for diaper changing, although some might continue to give their parents a run for their money for longer. If you can't manage to get your baby to settle and lie down long enough for diaper changes, just get creative. For instance, once your little one gets to the pulling-up stage, change her while she does so. Whatever the case, for now, be prepared and hold on tightly!

WEEK 23

Eat

When feeding your baby cereal, do not put it in a baby bottle. This is a choking hazard and should be avoided. Although there are bottles sold specifically for this purpose, with slits cut in the nipple, do not use these because altered nipples are dangerous.

Cereal in bottles is dangerous because babies nurse/drink at a bottle very differently than they eat. When your baby drinks from a bottle, he is expecting thin, easy-to-swallow liquids. When your baby is eating, he is prepared for foods that need to be chewed. A bottle that contains something thick is not what he is expecting. Hence, cereal in a bottle can surprise him, which might lead to choking.

Spending time with grandparents, even doing nothing special, is time well spent.

Cereal feedings should be done by spoon only. Even if you are giving your baby very thin liquids with only a slight bit of cereal, you should not place it in your baby's bottle.

Also remember that you should never prop a baby bottle. This is still true even though your baby is older. It can be very easy for your baby to choke. Even if you are right next to your baby, you might not be as quick to notice as you might believe. Remember, feeding time should be a time of close contact between you and your baby.

Sleep

If you find your baby is waking up more than once in the middle of the night to eat, you might want to evaluate whether or not he is really hungry. Perhaps he is simply waking up, and you are feeding him. The difference is subtle but can make a big change in how you deal with it.

When he first wakes up, first try alternative things to help him settle back to sleep. Most babies enjoy being patted or stroked. Try this without talking to him to avoid more stimulation, which can cause wakefulness. If the touch does not work, then move to shh-ing and murmuring. Calmly and quietly let him know you are there, without really talking. Think of it like, "Awwww, shhhhh." Saying these things in a quiet, soft manner can help him calm back to sleep.

MONTH
6

Sometimes babies wake up in the middle of the night and simply need to work on getting themselves back to sleep. This is not usually a problem, but it does take time. Helping your baby by giving him these skills is the best thing you can do.

If your baby is waking up multiple times at night and it is unusual, he might not be feeling well. Check his diaper. Check his temperature.

Could he be teething? Pat, cuddle, or rock him after treating any illness you may detect. Remember, we all have restless, sleepless nights, and sometimes a low-level illness can interrupt sleep patterns. Babies are no different.

Play

Your baby is beginning to understand cause and effect at this stage. Baby is learning that if you drop a toy, it falls. If you shake a toy, it rattles. These are big concepts for baby's brain.

You can help baby to develop this concept by playing with cause and effect. Hand your baby a toy. When he pushes the ball and it rolls, exclaim, "Oh, you rolled the ball!" Pass it back, and try it again and again. You will see cause and effect played out over and over from the high chair: Dropping things will quickly become a game for baby. He'll especially like the part where you continually pick up what he drops!

Cause and effect can also be negative. If you touch a hot stove (cause) then you will burn yourself (effect). Obviously, learning this concept in a positive manner is usually a lot easier. Hopefully, it will help prevent further trouble down the road.

Your baby will routinely drop things from the high chair. This is both learning and a game. Babies are playing around with physics, learning, "I drop the cup, and it falls." But they are also realizing, "If I drop the cup, Mommy picks it up."

HELPFUL HINTS: CARRYING SAFELY

Now that your baby is older and has more control of her body, your way of carrying her will morph as well. When she was a tiny infant, you most likely carried her facing inward. You always had a protective hand on the back of her head to keep her neck from flopping backward.

Now your baby wants to see the world. She also has really good control of her neck when she's awake. (All bets are off when she's asleep!) You should adjust how you carry her to meet her needs.

Consider carrying her facing outward. Simply place your arm around the middle of her body and pull her in to your body. While she is snuggled in your arm and held up, she can see out. You can carry her this way for short periods of time.

Your baby is also now old enough to try to sit on your hip when you carry her. Have her straddle your hip, on either side, with your arm on the same side, circling her waist. She can sit up or even lie down on you (not like in bed— she can lie against your body with her head on your shoulder, snuggling in close). If your arm gets tired, you can use both of your arms to support her weight. Should she fall asleep, slide her to your front, facing your body, grasping your hands under her bottom so you can support her weight.

When putting your baby down, apply a bit of caution. Watch that you are sitting her in a safe place. If she is starting to sit on her own, make sure she is stable before removing your hands. Look for small parts and other dangers near where you place her. Never place her in a car seat or chair that is perched on a table or counter—now that she can move, especially, she might be able to rock herself off a high place. Remember, no place but the floor!

MONTH
6

WEEK 24

Eat

BPA-free ice-cube trays, such as those made with silicone, make great storage for baby food. You can drop the food in when you make it and leave it in the freezer, removing only as many cubes as your baby needs. This makes serving your baby homemade food a lot easier.

You can heat these up with hot water. Microwaving is possible, but it can leave really hot spots, which can burn your baby. It can also destroy some of the nutrients in the food you have made.

You can place the food cubes into little glass jars or BPA-free plastics. These are portable and great for meals on the go. Day care centers can be very receptive to your bringing in your baby's food.

Sleep

When parents look to identify sleep problems, they usually start by considering what is happening around bedtime. While your baby's room, sleep routine, and sleeping location are important, there are other factors too. Some of them occur nowhere near bedtime.

One thing you can do to help establish good nighttime sleep is to stay consistent with a good morning routine. This means waking up at about the same time every day, all week. Some parents find that they can add about an hour on the weekends without too much disruption at night.

When it's morning, get up! You might need to wake your baby at first, but be bright and alert when you do so. Think just the opposite of your bedtime routine. Sing, dance, giggle, turn on the lights, open the blinds, and prepare for an active day. Modeling the behavior you want from your baby is the best bet. It could take a few days, but you might soon see the benefits of having a set waking time.

Certainly there can be times when sticking to a set sleep and wake time is challenging, particularly if your baby had a late night the night before, you are traveling away from home, or your baby has had an unusually busy day. And there might be times when your schedule does not go exactly the same way every single day, particularly if you already have older children with various, changing activities.

However, this is just one more tactic to consider adding to your arsenal in the never-ending battle when baby resists sleep. After all, as adults we've all heard that getting up at the same time every day and going to bed at the same time every night makes for the best sleep cycles. The plus with this technique is that it doesn't involve letting baby "cry it out," and it doesn't harm the baby. As all babies respond to different methods—sleep or otherwise—the key here is to try out this technique consistently for a few days before deciding if it does or doesn't work for your baby.

Play

Since your baby is working on or mastering sitting up, remember to use this playtime as practice time. Help your baby to sit up as you play. You can sit him up on your lap or use a pillow to help support him from behind. The pillow can also help with added protection should he topple over, which he most likely will do.

When your baby sits up, praise him! The praise might make him smile with his whole body, causing him to tip over, but help him to right himself and praise some more. While he is in an upright position, sing songs and play games. Patty-cake works really well in a sitting position. You can also try rolling a ball to him.

Take notice of when your baby gets tired of practicing sitting up. How long he sits up might vary with every session of trying. This can be because he has already spent a lot of time sitting up during the day, he's tired, or he's just not up for it that day. He might start to wobble or buckle. Simply help him to lie down and continue playing. Just as you would have sore muscles from learning a new skill, your baby does as well. So do not force him; lengthy periods of sitting are right around the corner.

MONTH 6

Helping your baby to sit up will help him to develop the muscles required to sit. Begin by practicing sitting for a few minutes each day, and then build up to longer periods of time. Remember, baby's muscles are just getting used to sitting up.

Affirmation for Month Six

My baby will sleep through the night eventually.

HELPFUL HINTS: PLAN YOUR VISIT

During this month you will have a well-baby checkup with your baby's pediatrician. Your doctor will ask you a series of questions about your baby's growth and skill set. Your baby will be weighed, measured, and examined. You will also be offered vaccinations per the schedule you have set up with your pediatrician.

This is also your chance to ask your pediatrician questions. You can ask about growth and development and what to expect in the coming months. You can also express any concerns that you have about your baby. Your next visit for a well checkup is normally scheduled at month nine, so this will be the biggest stretch between visits yet—three months!

You should plan to bring your questions already written down so that you do not forget them. Bring a change of clothes and a diaper, just in case. Consider bringing someone to help you juggle the baby while you ask questions.

WEEK 25

Eat

Once your baby is six months old, it is acceptable to give her fruit juice according to the American Academy of Pediatrics. Giving her juice before then has detrimental effects and is not recommended. However, when giving juice to your baby, keep in mind a series of recommendations. Fruit juice should be labeled 100 percent juice. Anything labeled fruit drink, cocktail, or mix is not all juice and might have added chemicals and sugars. Be careful when buying juice for your baby. You should also check the label to ensure you are getting only pasteurized juice. Unpasteurized juices can expose your baby to bacteria and diseases like E. coli, salmonella, and cryptosporidium.

You should never give juice in a baby bottle. This can encourage your baby to drink juice routinely, meaning the sugars that naturally occur will sit on the teeth. You should use a cup and offer juice only in a setting that is time-limited. Your baby should consume no more than four to six ounces of juice per day until the age of six or seven (113 to 170 g). It is imperative that juice is not used as a replacement for breastfeeding or for infant formula. Juice should be part of a snack offering and not a main course; otherwise, your baby could be at risk for malnutrition. Juice should not be given to console an unhappy infant or to a sick infant as a nutritional supplement. You should either nurse or give your baby an oral electrolyte solution instead.

Your best bets for juice are to offer it sparingly, if at all. (If you are hoping to teach your baby how to use a cup to drink something other than breast milk or formula, water in small quantities is a better idea.) Use a sippy cup, but do not give your baby juice at or near bedtime or when she is ill.

Sleep

Your baby has come a long way in the sleep department since her birth. While you will still find that night wakefulness happens, it is usually less frequent and tends not to last as long. One thing you can do to help get through night wakings is to realize that everyone wakes up at night, even adults. The big difference is adults have the skills to get themselves back to sleep.

So if your baby wakes up in the middle of the night, prevent yourself from rushing to the bedside. Let her stir a bit. You might be surprised to find that

Your baby's sleep habits have changed considerably since birth. Naptime rituals should be reassessed on occasion so your baby is getting enough sleep during the day, but not so much that it is effecting his nighttime sleeping.

she wants to play a minute and then goes back to sleep. Or she might talk or sing herself back down. These are great skills for her to have. However, she will never learn them if you are jumping up at every whimper.

Your baby is no longer a newborn who needs you to meet every need immediately. She is now capable of helping herself, even just a tiny bit. Minor stirrings are one thing, but you will want to step in before she reaches a full-fledged cry, because that is usually harder to come back down from once it has started. Remember, we're not talking about that here, just the chattering and singing that might happen during the night.

Should your baby need to eat, you now know when that typically is and how long it will take. See if she has a pattern of wakefulness before or after this period. How does altering her feeding help? Say she gets up at 3 a.m. to nurse, but plays for bit around 2 a.m. If you feed her at 2 a.m., does that give her a longer period of sleep, or is she still back up at 3 a.m.? Feel free to play around with this to see what works best for her and for you.

Play

Vocal play is really important at this age. Your baby is probably making all sorts of sounds. Ba. Ga. Da. Sometimes she might string these together: "ga ga ga ga" or "da da da da." She might or might not have attached any person to these words. If she hasn't yet, this is soon to come.

Encourage your baby's beginning sounds. Your baby will like using her voice. By "talking" in this manner she is exploring her voice, learning even more sound combinations, and figuring out the beginnings of talking.

Be sure that you respond to her. Chatter as you have in previous months, where you narrated her day or events. But also include baby talk. Repeat after her. If she says, "ga ga ga ma," you should turn right around and repeat it with a big smile on your face. Your reward? Watching her light up as she hears you repeating her.

Babies love to hear you talk, but don't forget to let them hear the outdoors as well. Depending on the weather, your baby may or may not have spent a lot time outside. Now might be the right time to hear the sounds of nature.

HELPFUL HINTS: SOCIALIZATION

Has your baby had plenty of grandma time? If the answer is no, it might be time to reconsider. Now is a prime time to let your baby get out and about with other adults who you trust.

Invite grandma and grandpa over for dinner or a walk. Let them take care of your baby while you are there. Remember, you might have differences of opinion about how to care for your baby, but these differences don't have to be negative. By this stage, your parents or in-laws have recognized you as a parent in your own right. Set the tone you would like to see reciprocated, and let them know what you need from them.

These little playdates might become more regular, with grandparents doing some babysitting if both parties are amenable to this idea. Remember, as your baby grows and develops, she needs to build relationships with others. This is a good thing. And, for the most part, who better than your parents or your partner's parents?

WEEK 26

Eat

As you enter the world of solid foods this month or in the coming months, remember that the tastes and textures of these foods are incredibly new and different to your baby. Do not be surprised if your baby resists a food or two specifically, or even foods in general. This is perfectly normal.

You should continue offering foods, even if you think your baby does not like them. The more exposure your baby has to a particular food, the more likely he is to develop a taste for that food in the future. Keep in mind that your baby does not have to eat a certain amount of food to try it. Offering a few spoonfuls of a food that he is refusing is good enough. Just try to offer the food a few times a week, even when served with other foods.

You should also be careful about which type of tableware you give to your baby. Early spoons are nearly flat, containing room for almost no food. This corresponds with how big of a bite your baby should take at a time, which is next to nothing. These spoons should also be soft on the end, to prevent hard metal or plastic from poking or jabbing his mouth. If that were to happen, your baby might resist eating or even be harmed.

Sleep

It's theorized that babies with sudden sleep issues might be about to develop new skills or could be growing physically and cognitively. Much as an adult might toss and turn before a big event, your baby could be doing the same thing.

This realization does not mean you will sleep any more than you have been. But it might make you feel less anxious about losing sleep if you can at least reason with your sleep-deprived brain about why it is happening. Remember that most things, including sleep disturbances, are just passing phases for babies, and that they change before you know it.

Play

Toes may be a favorite plaything. Who knew that something so simple could keep your baby occupied? He loves to look at them, taste them, and just wiggle them in general.

Your baby's flexibility is amazing as you watch him flip his body in half to extend his feet, comfortably, to his mouth. This is a great time to be sock free, for quick access to his toes. If your baby is wearing socks, be prepared for him to remove them. It may take a minute or two, but he'll be determined.

Remember, grandparent time is a good thing, so make the most of it! Your baby will love bonding with her grandparents, and other members of the family. All busy moms and dads need a break at sometime!

HELPFUL HINTS: TOOTHBRUSH TIME

As your baby gets teeth, you might have questions about dental care. As soon as you see teeth breaking through the gums, start a daily routine of cleaning them. This does not mean you will need to use a toothbrush and toothpaste yet.

In the beginning, it is often easier to take the low-tech approach. This means using a wet washcloth. Just wipe down the front and back of the tooth with the washcloth once or twice a day. Toothpaste isn't necessary. If your baby chomps down on your finger when you use the washcloth, then it might be time for a baby toothbrush. (For more on baby tooth brushing, see page 175.) You can help your baby get the fluoride she needs be ensuring that you prepare her food or infant formula with tap water rather than with bottled water. This will prevent her from needing a fluoride supplement. Most municipal tap water supplies are already fluoridated. You can check with your water company to find out for sure about your local tap water. This is also a good reason to drink tap water if you are breastfeeding.

Playing with your toes makes for a great stretch-ing activity. Have you tried it lately? (Now if only we were all still as flexible as our babies!)

Don't panic about dirty feet. Babies are rarely walking on the same surfaces that we walk on. Their feet are usually quite clean. A good bath might make you feel better. Just remember to thoroughly rinse out the soap between his toes.

Use his toes as play objects, since he wants to pay attention to them. "This Little Piggy" is a great toe game to play at this stage of development. You can even change the words up to make it more fun for you and/or him. For example, if you are a veg-etarian, instead of roast beef, you can have a little piggy eat tofu!

What to Watch For Explained

Your baby is all about physical movement these days! You may see that tripoding has developed into **interest in and the ability to sit**. Your baby has not mastered the art of sitting, so you will see a lot of bobbing and swaying. It's hard work to balance that body. If you aren't seeing your baby attempting to sit up by the end of month six, it's time to mention it to your family doctor.

One of my favorite things about this age group is listening to the **babbling to himself and to others**. These early language skills are fun to listen to and participate in. You might notice that he talks to himself when he is alone. Some parents wake up and hear noises on the baby monitor, only to realize that it is their baby! Be sure to talk back to him. This encourages his language development. If he hasn't started babbling yet, it could be due to an ear infection or other hearing issues. Be sure to point that out at your six-month check up.

This month you will need to watch your baby's **reaction to new foods**. Some babies are delighted. Other babies are more leery of trying new foods. Introduce foods slowly, one at a time, so if there is a reaction you will know which food is causing the problem. If you notice that your baby has an allergic reaction to a new food, be sure to report it to the pediatrician immediately.

Feeding babies at this age is a messy business. Don't stress over the mess—just use a bib and prepare for clean up. As you are feeding your baby, consider giving her a spoon to play with during meals. It will not only prepare her to feed herself at a later date, but will keep her hands busy. You may notice that she has developed a **preference for one hand**. You should always give her the choice of which hand she prefers. Offer toys by handing them toward her center, allowing her to choose which hand she uses to grasp.

MONTH 6

Week 27–30

Try New Things

✓ Checklist for Month Seven

- ☐ Consider a music class for you and baby.
- ☐ Learn to prepare for meals on the go with your baby.
- ☐ Dealing with a teething baby.
- ☐ Know about infant allergies.
- ☐ Get a baby teeth primer.
- ☐ Cope with bathing battles.

What to Watch For in the Seventh Month

- ☐ Stranger anxiety
- ☐ Not bringing objects to mouth
- ☐ Following sounds
- ☐ Eruption of teeth
- ☐ Interest in crawling or scooting

Be Sure to:

- ☐ Let other people hold your baby.
- ☐ Listen to the sounds your baby makes.
- ☐ Let your baby down to play alone.

Baby Skills:

In the seventh month, your baby:

- ☐ Will sit well alone
- ☐ Will use consonant/vowel combinations
- ☐ May use sounds that imitate conversations
- ☐ Can crawl around, backward or forward, belly on or off the floor
- ☐ Might be pulling up on objects
- ☐ Will beat two objects together
- ☐ Will possibly pass an object from hand to hand
- ☐ Will put weight on legs when placed in a standing position

BABY DATA

The big thing this month is you'll need to vacuum more frequently. Before you laugh, consider how much time your baby is spending on the floor. Add to the floor time his newfound love of pincer grasp, and you have a recipe for disaster. Your baby will eat any dust bunny, needle, button, or piece of paper he can on the floor.

Mobility has arrived! Now that he's moving around, your baby will want to play in different spots. Consider having a few toys in each safe area where your baby is allowed to extend the fun.

Your baby's ability to sit well makes floor time fun, and he is able to play with toys. Sometimes he might get greedy and try to hold two toys, one in each hand. From there, he might bang them together. Hold off on the drum set for now; this is typical behavior. He might even stare at objects and pass them from hand to hand.

Baby's developing verbal skills are even more fun. You will hear lots of babbling pouring out of your baby this month. It's great to chatter back and forth with him, but you do need to give him some quiet time to talk. He is less likely to talk if there is constant noise, be it from other kids, background music, or especially the television.

Sleep patterns might be interrupted temporarily as new skills emerge. Sometimes, when baby is learning to crawl forward and backward as well as possibly teething, some parents notice night wakings that have nothing to do with hunger. Calming and soothing is most likely what he needs during times of frequent waking.

You'll spend plenty of time thinking about baby food options. Perhaps you are making your own and enjoying the process of sharing foods you are eating pureed for your baby. Whatever is happening in the solid-food department, one thing's for sure: Watching your baby explore new food options is always fun and exciting. Sometimes your baby will shiver as he tries new foods. This doesn't necessarily mean he dislikes the food. Remember to follow the allergy testing guidelines for new foods: Try one new food at a time, allow at least four days between new foods, and don't be discouraged if it takes baby several tries to accept a particular food!

MONTH SEVEN: Bringing Up Baby

Your three goals this month are simple:

- Learn to deal with baby moods.
- Watch for signs of emerging skills
- Know how to feed baby away from home.

CONSIDER A MUSIC CLASS FOR YOU AND BABY

In case you haven't noticed, your baby loves music. Playing music around the house, in the car, and even at bedtime is a great start for your little music lover. Taking a music class designed for babies in the second half of the first year is something completely different. It allows your baby to move beyond listening and actually interact with the music.

A music class designed with babies in mind will usually be better than a generic music class. There will be age-appropriate music and playtime. Baby music classes also involve the parents. Parental involvement is so important as babies and young children are learning music, because just as with language, children learn music by modeling what they see in the people around them. Being involved in the class will also help you to learn skills to play with your baby at home.

MONTH
7

Most classes will begin with a circle time. Here you will sit with your baby and usually greet all the babies and parents with a "hello" song. You might also do some small-movement or finger-play songs while singing or with music: "The Itsy-Bitsy Spider," for instance, might be a small-movement song/activity option. These small-movement songs are meant to help grab and focus the children's attention.

Most classes will also include some large-movement, physically active songs. These songs will get you and your child up, dancing, and playing around the room. These times might include songs like "Ring Around the Rosie" or other circle dance songs.

Instrument play is another big hit in baby music classes. This might be structured differently depending on the class or depending on the ages and developmental ability of the kids in the class. These periods might involve free play-alongs to music, as well as some structured activities with instruments led by the teachers. You might have some time with small musical instruments like rhythm sticks, wooden blocks, triangles, shaker eggs, and other kid-friendly choices. You might also find things like parachute play, free play with toys, and other forms of play to entertain your baby.

Finding just the right class is important. You should enjoy the class just as much as your baby

Mama Moment

Now is the time to start thinking about calling up your midwife or doctor to schedule your next annual exam. While it has only been about six months since your postpartum visit, many practitioners book six months to a year ahead for annual exams. Calling now will give you a chance to get an appointment with the practitioner of your choice. This might also be the time for you to find a new practitioner if you weren't happy with the care you received when your baby was born.

Playing with musical instruments at home is great at this age. It gives your baby a chance to test out different movements and rhythms, not to mention it's a lot of fun.

does. If you are feeling comfortable and excited about the class, you will be more likely to participate and your baby will absorb more by watching you and the other adults around her. Feeling good about the class you choose will no doubt have to do with the teachers and the other parents. Can you have friendly conversations in between scheduled periods of class or during free play? Do you feel like you have things in common with the other parents? Is your baby near the same age or ability as the other kids?

Don't worry, incidentally, if you find a mixed-age class with kids from baby age up through preschool. This can be quite beneficial, as babies and young toddlers are especially enthusiastic about watching and learning from their older counterparts. Mixed-age music classes can make the experience even more engaging. Plus, if you have an older child, you can all attend class together if you'd like.

Most music classes will allow you to drop in and try out a class before enrolling. If you do enroll in a class and find that the group isn't a good fit, try to figure out why. Is there something that you can do to change that? Can you ask for help or feedback from the instructor? Or do you perhaps need to switch classes?

In between classes while at home, be sure to play songs similar to those you use in music class. Some classes will offer CDs of the music that you can play outside of class. You will know the class is worth it as you watch your baby's eyes light up when the music starts.

PREPARE MEALS ON THE GO FOR YOUR BABY

Beginning to feed your baby solid foods can feel like freedom and torture all at the same time. Freedom, because now you are able to try and experiment with other foods; torture, because now you have to feed your baby appropriate solid foods, and you might not always have them available.

The key is being prepared. Planning ahead is your best bet. Here are some items to remember when packing to go out:

- Bib
- Multiple utensils (for when they fall on the floor, or baby throws them)
- Baby food (homemade or in a jar)
- Napkins

Eating out with a baby provides a whole new meaning to the word. Being prepared for your day is always best, so you don't get stuck. Don't worry if you don't bring solid foods, you can always nurse while out and then feed solids later.

MONTH
7

If you tend to forget to put things in your diaper bag spur-of-the-moment, you might consider leaving a few jars of food packed for your next outing. That way, if you do remember the baby food, you have a spare, but if you forget, you aren't in trouble.

Plan ahead and think about how you will heat foods that you need to heat. An alternative is allowing frozen foods to come to room temperature. Make sure you will have access to hot water or other heating methods should you require it for your baby's food. If you're going to be on the road for a while without access to those sorts of heating options, consider packing an insulated Thermos full of hot water. Then, if you are stopping to feed your baby while in the car, outside on a picnic, or wherever, you can warm food easily.

Hot Mama for Month Seven

Do you like high heels? When you were pregnant, you probably felt a bit tipsy on your feet in heels. This was due to the relaxing in your body and your shifting center of gravity as your belly grew. Now that you're no longer pregnant, you're probably steady enough on your feet to wear high heels again—at least when you aren't carrying the baby. You might need to get a new size if your feet grew in pregnancy.

Worst case scenario, if you are out and have forgotten the solid foods you had intended to feed your baby, you can still nurse your baby or give him a baby bottle. This will keep the baby fed and you can give the solids at a later time.

Don't stress too much about traveling with baby food. Remember, this baby food phase doesn't last very long in the grand scheme of things. Soon enough, as your baby progresses and she can eat a larger variety of food and foods that are not pureed, you will manage to find things on menus for your baby to eat more easily. In most homes or restaurants you can find one or more of the following:

- Banana
- Plain baked potato
- Avocado
- Plain beans
- Sweet potato
- Plain pasta
- Hummus
- Lentils
- Various vegetables, like green beans, cooked to be soft and chopped up finely

When eating out and ordering foods for your baby, be sure to ask how they are seasoned to ensure that you are okay with the cooking methods. For example, are the green beans flavored with pork? And, when ordering out, always remember to taste the food yourself first—you wouldn't want baby to gobble down an overly spicy bite by accident! Your options will continue to expand the older your baby gets.

DEAL WITH A TEETHING BABY

What might come as a surprise is that your baby can bite you even before she has teeth. Think about this biting in terms of pressure being a pain reliever. Your baby is teething and trying to relieve pain on his sore gums. Biting toys, furniture, or people solves that problem.

The big problem is that, teeth or not, it hurts! When you get bitten, you might be really surprised. You might even yelp in pain. This will usually surprise your baby and he might begin to cry. What a tough situation to be in as a parent.

Although this biting is painful and aggravating, take a deep breath and realize what is going on. Your baby is not trying to hurt you, he's merely trying out new teeth or doing what his body is telling him to do. The vast majority of babies will stop as soon as they realize their actions are eliciting adverse reactions from the adults they love. These instances might be their very first lessons in learning about what hurts people, and that others have feelings too! When your baby does bite, be sure to show him clearly through your voice, facial expression, and body demeanor that biting is not a good thing. Then be prepared to hand him an alternative teething ring quickly!

Teething rings come in all shapes and sizes. You can also purchase teething rings that are made to retain cold, which can be an added comfort. Be sure to use objects that are meant to be put in your baby's mouth. Right now, as you've learned by this point, your baby will put almost anything in his mouth.

Be careful about yelling at your baby when she bites you. (This isn't to say that if you yelp in pain you are doing something wrong—that is a natural reaction. Just don't actually scream at the baby for biting.) Also, you should never bite the baby back. Far from teaching her a lesson, it can start a negative cycle. Preventing biting is usually the best strategy.

All nursing mothers fear their babies biting while on the breast. Yes, as they first get teeth babies do occasionally bear down with their teeth. But don't worry, this will likely happen only once or twice before baby realizes she can't get any milk if she bites down at the breast. In fact, a baby who is actively nursing cannot bite. This is because she would bite her own tongue, which is extending over her gum line as she latches and drinks. Babies who

Teething leads to biting. All babies do it, but that doesn't mean it's acceptable. They will bite anything, from toys to their own fingers. Typically, once it progresses to that latter stage, they start to understand the cause and effect.

MONTH
7

bite usually do so because they have stopped nursing or because you are not paying attention to them. Watch for signs that your baby is starting to lose interest in a nursing session, and then pop her off the breast. Sometimes a baby will protest and want to nurse more. If your baby was merely falling asleep while drinking, this might wake her up enough to resume nursing properly. Remember, like other biting instances, biting while nursing is not something that your baby plans on doing.

If your baby bites you while nursing, pop the baby off the breast and say, firmly, "No." You can resume the feeding, stopping again if the baby bites. Your baby might cry if you say no, but be firm. You need to show him that biting is not acceptable. If you are nursing and the baby bites more than twice, end the nursing session. Do something else for a bit and then finish nursing later. Stopping the bothersome activity and using redirection are usually enough to deter the baby who is a persistent biter.

KNOW ABOUT INFANT ALLERGIES

Allergies are certainly no fun. And you are probably hoping that if you have allergies, your baby does not get them too. You can help reduce the risk of infant allergies by breastfeeding, and hopefully you have avoided starting solids too early or too quickly. Signs that your baby has a type of allergy can include:

- Coldlike symptoms, including a runny nose, sniffles, or cough
- Dark circles under the eyes
- Frequent ear or respiratory infections
- Eczema or skin rashes

Your baby is likely to exhibit these symptoms if he has an allergy to something to which he's been exposed. This can be something environmental, like animal dander, dust mites, or mold spores; or it can be food based, such as cow's milk proteins, wheat, or corn. If your baby has any of the above symptoms, you will want to talk to your pediatrician about what to do next.

An allergist, a special physician who treats only allergies, can test your baby for allergens. You might even be able to locate a pediatric allergist, who specializes in treating children with allergies. Blood tests are available to check for IgE antibodies in your baby's blood, but these tests are not very accurate. (These antibodies are found in people's skin and mucous membranes. Often someone with allergies has a high level of IgE antibodies, which causes their allergic reaction.) Skin tests can also be used for infants and older babies. However, if your child has not had enough exposure to a particular allergen, you might have false negatives. Your allergist can tell you when or if retesting is needed.

You can also try to figure out some of your child's allergies on your own. For example, does your baby seem to have a stuffy nose earlier in the day, but it clears up as the day goes on? Your baby might be allergic to dust mites. Perhaps when you go on vacation, your baby feels better when the family dog or cat isn't around. Pets and dust mites are common household allergens.

You can buy special items to help reduce the amount of allergens your baby is exposed to in your home. You can purchase mattress covers at specialty stores, but you will want to avoid plastic covers, as they might be harmful for your baby and they do not breathe. More frequent vacuuming can help, particularly if you have a vacuum with a HEPA filter to help prevent dust mites from getting back into the environment. Some families find that hardwood or vinyl flooring helps them to reduce allergies.

Nurseries are also dust-mite magnets. All of those adorable stuffed animals and fluffy toys? They harbor tons of dust mites. You might consider ditching all but a few. You can wash them in really hot water or dry them in a hot dryer to help kill the dust mites. The same goes for bedding, which should be washed at least weekly in hot water. Some allergists even suggest putting toys in the freezer overnight for the same purpose if they can't be washed or dried.

If you and your partner have allergies, your baby has a good chance of having them too. If both of you suffer, the chance for baby is about 70 to 80 percent; less if it is just one of you. Since your baby might seem to be fine at first, you might think you have avoided allergies, but they can show up later in the first year—your baby needs to be exposed to the allergen for a period of time before showing symptoms. For seasonal allergies, when your baby is exposed for a few weeks at a time, it might take years for your child to show adverse signs of exposure. If you do discover at any time that your child has allergies, your pediatrician can help coordinate all of the care you will need.

GET A BABY TEETH PRIMER

Many parents tend to ignore baby teeth, beyond whether or not their baby has them. You need to ensure that you protect these tiny teeth, even though they are not permanent. From the first tooth, you need to begin good oral care.

You will actually want to wash or brush your baby's teeth. He might not like this at first, but add it to your daily ritual and do not give up. You can either purchase a finger toothbrush or use a washcloth to do it.

A finger toothbrush is like a miniature glove that fits over your finger. It has an area with tiny bristles meant specifically for baby teeth. You can clean your baby's teeth with this toothbrush.

You can accomplish the same thing with a baby washcloth. With this method, you just wipe down the front and back of your baby's teeth. However, it becomes more problematic as she gets more teeth, particularly in the back. In fact, as baby gets more teeth in general, you might consider switching to an actual handheld baby toothbrush, because she might begin chomping down on your finger when you place it in her mouth!

You will also need to decide if you want to use toothpaste. Regular fluoride toothpaste can be dangerous for babies if swallowed. Babies get all the fluoride they need from tap water as they begin drinking it, as well as through their mother's breast milk. Too much fluoride can actually stain teeth or poison your baby. Some baby- and toddler-friendly toothpaste is available without fluoride. When in doubt, ask your pediatrician.

MONTH
7

The vast majority of dentists and pediatricians will recommend that your baby have a dental checkup around his first birthday. You can always go sooner if you have questions or concerns. Your visit can include oral care questions, as well as questions about pacifiers and thumb sucking. If your baby uses a bottle, this visit is a check for baby-bottle tooth decay. You'll also receive some prevention information, like avoiding bottle use at times other than feedings, avoiding bottles in bed, and not giving juice in the bottle. With any luck, at this young age your child will have a positive dental experience that will set the tone for future visits.

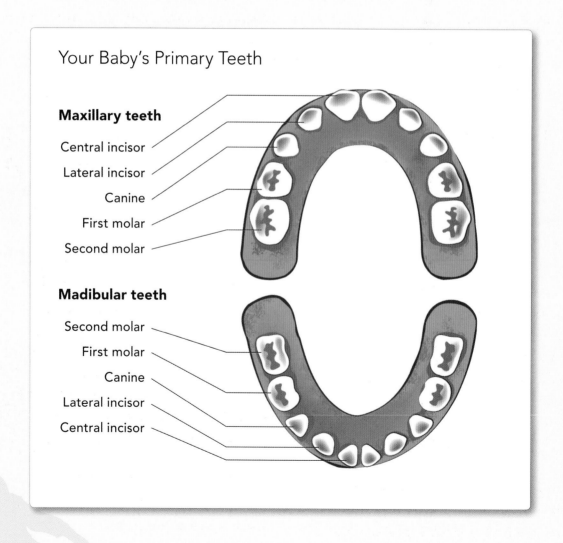

Your Baby's Primary Teeth

Maxillary teeth

Central incisor

Lateral incisor

Canine

First molar

Second molar

Madibular teeth

Second molar

First molar

Canine

Lateral incisor

Central incisor

While teething might start as early as three months, most babies do not usually get their first teeth until around six months. So even if your baby begins the teething process, you might not see teeth for a while; this is not a reason to panic or worry.

Your baby will most likely get her lower, middle teeth first (central incisors), followed by the upper middle teeth. The lateral incisors and canine teeth are next. Then you will see the first and second molars. All in all, your baby will get twenty teeth by the time he is two or three years old. Some babies follow this pattern to a tee, others do not. Some babies do not get their first teeth until after their first birthday.

COPE WITH BATHING BATTLES

If your baby previously has enjoyed the bath but suddenly decides bath time is not as much fun as it used to be, you can have a real battle on your hands. Your baby might show his displeasure by crying, kicking, wriggling, and just downright doing anything he can think of to avoid being bathed. This can leave you tired and frustrated, not to mention dreading bath time as well.

Take a step back and remember that you need to approach bath time calmly. Do not get tense and nervous, anticipating a fight from your baby. Your attitude can actually go a long way toward making bath time tolerable.

Think about what changes you can make to bath time to prevent or lessen the woes you and your baby are dealing with. Why does your baby dislike bath time? Does he sense it means bedtime is to follow? Does he hate being naked or wet?

One thing to consider is how you are bathing him. Are you still using the baby bathtub you got as a shower gift nearly a year ago? It might be time to give him a more "grown-up" version of a bath, where he can sit up.

You can do this with a special bathtub chair for use in regular tubs. This allows your baby to sit up and play while being bathed. Babies love to splash, so perhaps incorporating a few minutes of playtime might also make him more amenable to the idea of

Bath safety is not a joke. As your baby gets older and develops more body control, it can be easier to think that she is safe for a minute while you get a towel. Remember, it is never safe to leave your baby unattended in the bath.

a bath. Do know that the bath chairs are not a substitute for adult supervision. Do not leave your baby alone in the tub for even a moment.

Another alternative is the sink. Many a baby has enjoyed baths in the kitchen sink. Some parents even prefer the sink because it is less painful for their backs. Simply stop up the water and use the faucet to fill your clean sink with water, then allow your child to splash around. Sink baths are also a nice photo opportunity, if you have someone else to take photos while you're doing bath duty.

Is your baby frustrated with bath time because he wants to play and you are a no-nonsense kind of bather? Try giving him a toy or two to play with, or encourage him to splash about for a bit. This might help ease him into bath-time fun.

Perhaps he's experienced some rough bathing techniques. If he seems to be fearful of the water or the noise, run the water before he is near the bathroom, so that he can enter it while it's calmer and quieter. If he is already showing signs of hating to have his hair washed, consider wrapping him in a towel like a baby burrito and washing his hair in the sink. This really works for getting the hair clean but also helps prevent soap in the eyes.

Basically follow your baby's lead when it comes to bath-time woes. Try to figure out why there is an issue and see what you can do to overcome it. You might have to try multiple things, but eventually you will find a solution that works for both of you.

WEEK 27

Eat

You will still want to avoid feeding your baby certain foods at this point. The first on that list would be anything that you or your family members are allergic to now, or as children. Remember, there can be a familial trait to similar allergies. Some foods, such as soy, cow's milk, peanuts, corn, and wheat, are also higher in allergens.

Eggs fall into an interesting category. After eight months it is considered safe to give your baby egg yolks, but not egg whites. Egg whites are a higher-allergen food and should not be offered to your baby in any form until after the age of one.

Along with allergies, other foods are dangerous for babies. Honey is a good example: Given prior to the age of one, it leaves your baby susceptible to infant botulism. So you will want to avoid honey at least until baby's first birthday. You should ask your baby's pediatrician for other advice specific to your family.

Play

At seven months, your baby is eager to get around and explore his world. He is limited, however, by his lack of mobility. Consider showing him around. Walk him around the house, outdoors, wherever you are, and show him different things.

You can hold him up to look at a tree and even allow him to touch the bark if he reaches out. You can lower him to the ground to play in the grass. Allowing him to touch and explore what is safe is a great way to expose him to different things in his life. Use your common sense here: Obviously you would not hold him up to an electrical outlet, but you might show him the family portrait on the wall as you name the members of your family.

Try to make a game of this activity. You can show your baby something, point to it, and name it. Your baby will smile and provide you with directions to continue or do something differently. Most babies really enjoy this game.

Sleep

Are you working with your baby to help him sleep better at night? Music can really work well. Perhaps you already have some music you have been using. If it is not working, you might wonder why.

Some music, while it might calm an adult, could be distracting for your baby. Music that frequently changes beats, or becomes softer and louder, can confuse your baby and keep his brain awake trying to listen. The goal of music at night or nap time is to calm and soothe. Your baby is used to noise from the very beginning, but that music or noise should be calm and predictable.

While many sources will tell you that classical music is good for your baby's brain, they neglect to tell you that it isn't a great choice for the night. Classical music is too complicated for most babies to sleep with. So if you have been pumping classical music into the bedroom or nursery, consider a change of pace. Other genres of music that are poor choices for nighttime music include jazz, marching band, and the like.

Music that works really well is usually meant for relaxation or sleep. It can also be designed for baby specifically, such as a set of baby lullabies. If you are not sure if something will work, consider borrowing a CD from a friend to try for a few nights. Find what works for your baby and then make your purchase.

Include your baby in your daily activities. Even something as simple as gardening can be a big adventure for him.

MONTH
7

WEEK 28

Eat

Breastfeeding in public should be getting easier at this point, because your baby and you are both nursing pros by now. This might not always be the case if your baby decides he does not like to have his head covered by a blanket or nursing cover. This does not have to be the end of discreet nursing—just a note that you need to try something new for him.

Nursing is something you should be a pro at now. But some babies go through a period where they are not as cooperative as you might like when it comes to nursing, but it is temporary.

You might consider nursing clothes, even at this stage. If you have not tried them yet, they will make nursing more discreet by keeping you as covered as possible, even when your baby has pulled away from the breast to look around. Another trick some mothers use is to put a big hat on the baby's head. This covers the breast area while allowing him to control the coverage of his face. A breastfeeding hat cover is also sold for that purpose.

Another trick is to keep a small cloth or blanket close by to cover up when baby has pulled off the breast. Some mothers also limit nursing if the baby continually would prefer to pull off to play rather than eat, noting that they must not be that hungry. This does not mean that your baby will go hungry. Some babies have become more efficient nursers, getting the same amount of breast milk in less time; others will have longer, more thoughtful feedings in quieter settings.

Play

Since your baby will practice talking to help learn words and conversation patterns, it shouldn't surprise you that she will chatter frequently. You might hear her talk to you throughout the day, often joining a conversation already in progress. What might surprise you is when she talks to herself.

Most parents first notice a baby talking to herself when it comes through over the baby monitor. It might be early in the morning, the middle of the

HELPFUL HINTS: ON THE MOVE

A crawling baby can be lots of fun. Many babies will be crawling by this month. The problem is that not every baby crawls in the same manner. This is not something to be concerned about for your baby.

You might notice she is really good at the army crawl, flat on the floor, pulling herself with her arms. You might also see her doing the inchworm: lifting her middle section, then going flat and repeating until she gets where she is trying to go. All methods of crawling are acceptable. The goal here is for your baby to get where she is going.

You might also notice your baby is trying to crawl to reach an out-of-range toy. The problem comes when she tries to move forward to get the toy and actually goes backward. This can be even more frustrating for her, but she doesn't know how to change directions. Do not panic. You can't really do much except wait; she will figure it out.

You might also notice your baby rolls to where she is trying to go. Or perhaps she scoots sitting up to reach objects. Or maybe your baby hasn't decided that crawling is worth the effort yet. Remember, every baby does things slightly differently. If you are concerned about your baby's lack of crawling or style of crawling, talk to your pediatrician. In the meantime, grab the video camera to capture some of these fancy first moves.

MONTH
7

night, or nap time. First you will hear your baby's familiar stirrings. You will probably brace yourself for the cries that signal your baby is ready to get out of bed. But then you hear her talking.

Your baby is happily babbling to herself. Perhaps she's talking to the baby she sees in the mirror. She might even be explaining life to her toys. But

Your baby loves to imitate you. You might not even notice, but see what happens when you hand your baby a keyboard or a phone—she knows just what to do!

she is most definitely having a conversation and holding court. This is usually a sweet thing to listen to and should be encouraged.

Consider recording these sounds for your baby's video album. Sometimes if you can do it just right, you can film from the door of the room without the baby seeing you do it. If you have a video baby monitor, that also might work. Or a simple voice recording done with a handheld recording device might also be workable. These baby chats make a great recording to put on your baby's blog or send to family and friends who are not nearby.

Sleep

Since your baby is now more mobile, you might find he does not sleep in the same position all night. You might lay him down on his back, only to go in and find him nestled in on his stomach. This can be very disconcerting for parents who want to protect their babies. Do not panic.

When you put your baby down to sleep for a nap or for the night, simply lay him on his back. He is probably going to move during sleep time, and if you don't turn him over when you see him, he will probably choose some position other than back sleeping. Some babies choose side lying, some look like they were crawling and fell asleep, others sleep sprawled out on their bellies. Odd positions are fairly normal and nothing to worry about for your sleeping baby. Just make sure that baby's sleep environment is safe.

HELPFUL HINTS: NAIL CARE SAFETY

Cutting your baby's nails at this age can be quite the challenge. Your baby might not want to have her nails cut at all. This can mean trouble, particularly when your baby has sharp nails that cut into your skin as your play or nurse. You might also notice that she still accidentally scratches her face.

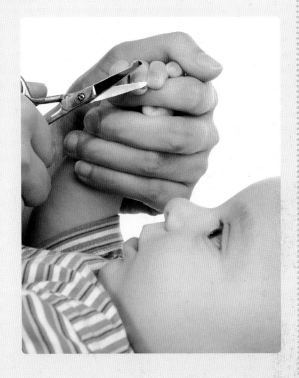

When your baby is nursing, you can clip one side of her nails, and then as you switch sides, do the same. You might want to enlist your partner's help here, to make things easier. If your baby will not even stand for this, you can try to wait until your baby is asleep. This can wake your baby up if she is not asleep deeply enough. So tread lightly about the timing of your stealth manicure.

You might also choose to use a baby nail file. This prevents your accidentally clipping her skin while trying to cut her nails. When all else fails, have someone else hold her while you do the cutting. Immobilizing the hand you are clipping is the most important part. Also keep her other hand still, because if she takes a swipe at you, it could interfere with the clipping. Clipping an upset baby's nails can be frazzling, but take a deep breath and try to get through it! Just remind yourself that she is upset from being held and having the clipping done, not because you are hurting her.

MONTH
7

WEEK 29

Eat

Your baby is probably interested in feeding herself now. She might grab at the food you are trying to feed her as it goes into her mouth. She might try to take the spoon away from you. This can be a messy and unhelpful proposition. Don't worry—there are ways to increase the amount of food she ingests and decrease both of your frustration levels.

Letting your baby feed herself is a big step for both of you. Be prepared to clean up. For your baby, it will be a full sensory experience.

Consider offering her very own spoon to hold while you feed her. This can give her the feeling of feeding herself without all of the actual mess. She is likely to have a lot of fun banging the spoon around in between bites of food. You can also give her a chance to feed herself with her spoon or hands at the end of the feeding. Simply save a bit of the food in the bottom of the bowl and let her have a try, with help.

This independence is likely to increase. Soon she will be ready for more finger foods. Then you can offer finger foods while you control the messier foods. But be forewarned: Ultimately, everything gets messy when a baby begins feeding herself. Try a little damage control, and place a plastic mat or towel under her chair at home. This way, cleanup will be at least a little bit easier.

When practicing self-feeding, consider where you are and what is practical. If you are at a restaurant and you have to feed your baby, you might be less inclined for her to help you than if you are at home. You might consider bringing some bigger bibs. The other alternative is to strip your baby down to the diaper for self-feedings. Then just make bath time the next step. You can even just dip him into the kitchen or bathroom sink quickly to rinse off!

Play

Raspberries, the tongue noises that your baby makes sometimes, might or might not be accompanied by bubbles. This sound is fun for your baby to make, and babies usually do it often once they figure out how they did it the first time.

Some parents dislike this noise while others think it is the most adorable thing they have ever seen. The good news is your baby will most likely grow out of it quickly, so if you are annoyed, don't panic. If you think it's cute, simply repeat it to your baby or praise him when you see him doing it. It is really just him learning to play with his mouth and not a sign that he is displeased with anything.

Sleep

If your baby has become a wiggler at night, you might find that the sheets are getting disturbed. A crib sheet should fit tightly on the crib mattress to prevent your baby from becoming entangled in it. If your baby were to become entangled, he could be harmed.

HELPFUL HINTS: SHAMPOO SOLUTIONS

Around this age, your baby might decide she doesn't like having her hair washed. It's not clean hair she is opposed to, it's the whole idea of the water being poured on her head. Water drips in her face, and soap may get in her eyes. It's important to get hair washing right from the beginning, to prevent her from having an unnatural fear of the whole experience.

To prevent her from getting water in her face or eyes, you can try a couple of techniques. First, use special products made to prevent water from going anywhere but in her hair. You can buy shields that look like hats, or special pouring devices with built-in barriers. Another technique would be to lay her down on a towel, facing upward, with her head over the sink. Support her neck with your hands. This way, the water will run down into the sink and nowhere near her eyes. An alternative to this position is to hold your baby on your lap while washing hair. This can even be done while you are taking your own bath.

Do not force your child to have her hair washed. This can make the experience much more frightening for her. Don't surprise her and wash her hair when she thinks you aren't going to pour water on her head either. That is only setting yourself up for a negative experience, which might haunt you for years to come.

MONTH
7

The crib sheets that have worked for all of these months might now not be working as well because of your baby's movements. You can try to get sheet keepers that will hold the sheets on a bit more tightly. They fit on the underside of the mattress. Some families have also found that bag-like sheets for the mattress work well for them.

WEEK 30

Eat

Babies love the thrill of drinking from a cup all by themselves. Let us just agree that babies are also not very neat about drinking from cups. To help prevent the tons of spills that can happen as your baby is learning to drink from a cup, consider how much liquid you are putting in the cup. This will limit spills.

You can use spill-proof sippy cups for your baby's first cup to help limit spills as well. These cups do not have valves, but lids with openings that discourage spills. If you have questions about which sippy cup is best for your baby, do not hesitate to talk to your pediatrician. (For more on sippy cups, see Month Eight.)

Sleep

Young babies travel well. You can take a baby almost anyplace you need to go. And when they are little, they can sleep almost anywhere at any time. However, once your baby is over six months of age, it is a different story.

The value of juice into your baby's diet is debatable. If you do offer juice, limit the amount and consider watering it down. It should never be given at bedtime or nap time.

If you have been taking your baby with you to meetings, the movies, or out to dinner, you might need to stop in order to preserve bedtime. Not every baby is as sensitive to this, but if you have been having issues with your baby not going to bed well or waking up early, check your social calendar and see if nights out and wakefulness are related.

HELPFUL HINTS: HIS FIRST HAIRCUT

Some babies have a lot of hair by this stage of development. Other babies have not so much hair. Both extremes are normal, and there is no need for concern. If you have a baby with a lot of hair, you might be wondering what you can do about it.

If your baby is a girl, it is okay to use hair bows and things to pull her hair back out of her face. However, you will want to ensure that whatever you use is not something that she can get out of her hair and swallow. Avoid hair accessories that could be choking hazards.

You might also be contemplating a first haircut. Yes, it is possible to have a young baby's hair cut, although you might have to shop around for someone who can fit the bill. You might consider calling stores that work specifically with children.

Some families decide to try to cut their baby's hair themselves. Unless you have some hair-cutting skills or the job is very minor, this would probably be a mistake. Babies move so fast and are so wiggly that even trimming the bangs yourself can be risky—all it takes is one slip of the scissors! Remember, you don't want your baby to end up with a chop job!

If you decide to go with a haircut, be sure to take photos. Save that first lock of baby hair! It makes for a really nice keepsake.

MONTH
7

This might mean you'll need to hire a sitter for nights when you would like to have dinner out with your friends. Or it may mean that one of you stays home to make sure that your baby's nighttime routine is kept. And some families choose to hold off on going out for a while. There is no one right answer. But chances are good that keeping your baby's nighttime routine makes the difference in the number of hours both of you sleep, and how restful your night is.

Play

Your baby might enjoy standing up on her feet. You may notice that she tries to stand on your lap. It is okay to help her stand there for a bit. This might worry you if she is not walking yet. Don't be afraid that you're putting too much pressure on her little legs. This is not the case at all. In fact, in "standing" on your lap, she is practicing for the real thing.

You can help hold her up and assist her by providing support. She will allow her legs to buckle and fall when she is done standing. Catching her and preventing the fall is the best thing that you can do. She might start by simply standing and then move to bouncing and dancing while you hold her hands. Always allow her to lead the standing efforts and never force her.

Helping your baby to stand up is perfectly fine. In fact, once you start, you might not be able to stop her.

Affirmation for Month Seven

My baby's growing independence is a good thing.

What to Watch For Explained

Stranger anxiety is a normal occurrence for most babies. You may see anything from a slight hesitation to crying loudly. This can be frustrating for you, your baby, and the others who are trying to help, particularly if the strangers are his care providers. Doing your best to calm your baby is the best approach. Most babies will calm shortly when they are distracted by a toy. You may experience stranger anxiety on a short-term basis when changing a care provider, moving, or other life transitions. This may affect sleep patterns and cause some finicky eating. Don't be discouraged. If you feel that your baby is not able to cope with stranger anxiety, you should speak to your pediatrician for reassurance.

If your baby is **not bringing objects to his mouth** by now, it could be problematic. Most babies will do this, particularly if it relates to food. Place food items in front of him on the table and watch as he grasps for them. If your baby is not bringing toys or food to his mouth then you should discuss this with your pediatrician.

One new task that babies master at this age is **following sounds**. Your baby may have been able to do this before, but now they are able to follow with their whole body and not just their eyes. If you don't think that your baby is hearing well or following sounds, be reassured by requesting a hearing check.

As your baby's **teeth begin to erupt** around this time you both may be uncomfortable. Your previously happy baby is now a fussy one. You may also see changes in eating and sleeping habits. This can be a tiring and confusing time for some babies and parents. You can try to use comfort measures, such as teething toys, cool cloths, and the like. Your medical advisors may also recommend other things to try.

Now that your baby is gaining physical control of his body, you will notice that sitting is no longer enough—your baby has an **interest in crawling or scooting**. This technique may be very different form baby to baby. Some babies crawl backwards. Some babies slide on their belly. Other babies invent their own version of movement—whether it is a half-crawl or a half-walk. The important fact is that you are seeing a desire and an effort toward motion. Try placing toys just out of reach and watch your baby try to get them. Sometimes this is frustrating as they learn, but you should be seeing an effort, if not an ability. Write notes about this progression on your list of questions to ask you baby's doctor at your next appointment.

MONTH
7

MONTH EIGHT

Week 31–34

Make It Work

√ Checklist for Month Eight

- ☐ Decide if it's time to introduce a cup.
- ☐ Learn about stranger anxiety.
- ☐ Cope with baby's growing independence.
- ☐ Listen to your baby talk.
- ☐ Diagnose and treat constipation.
- ☐ Encourage your baby to crawl.

What to Watch For in the Eighth Month

- ☐ Ability to sit alone
- ☐ Using sounds to draw you in
- ☐ Broaden your baby-proofing
- ☐ Consider cup safety

Be Sure to:

- ☐ Expand baby-proofing efforts to include the floor.
- ☐ Not compare your baby to others.
- ☐ Contact your pediatrician with concerns about developmental delays.

Baby Skills:

In the eighth month, your baby:

- ☐ Will begin to babble sounds such as *da-da* and *ma-ma*
- ☐ Will try to pull up on objects
- ☐ Crawls backward or forward
- ☐ May get around by scooting
- ☐ Can't get down from a standing position
- ☐ Can anticipate events; she may know that her book comes after her bath
- ☐ Can understand some words
- ☐ Passes objects from one hand to another
- ☐ Can use pincer grasp

BABY DATA

Moving, moving, moving! Your baby is all about getting around. She might be crawling—sometimes just for the sake of crawling; other times she'll crawl with a purpose—like following you or getting to a toy. She might even crawl to furniture in an attempt to pull herself up.

The signs of cup readiness vary, as does the age at which your baby is ready for a cup.

Pulling herself up can lead to problems such as falling, as your baby is not yet adept at it. She is also likely to fall as a means of "getting down." So it is time to address the new dangers that require baby proofing.

By now, your baby is using her pincer grasp for everything—the good, the bad, and the ugly. She might sit in a high chair and use her newfound dexterity to pick up her food, but she is equally likely to use it to eat dirt. She might have found some favorite foods by now, but give her a variety of foods.

Sleep is usually going well by now, except for the occasional wakeful night due to an odd thing like an ear infection or a new tooth. Remember to keep everything quiet and calm as you work to get her back to sleep.

DECIDE IF IT'S TIME TO INTRODUCE A CUP

Chances are you have played a bit with a baby cup by now. If you have not yet done so, now is the time to try. Parents often think they should wait until a baby can hold a cup and not spill it or drop it, but that is a long way off. For now, be content with the fact that most babies spill or drop cups, and that a large selection of spill-proof cups is available.

Your first step is to decide which type of cup you want your baby to learn to use. Some families choose to go with a standard, open nonbreakable cup. The benefits are that your baby will learn to use a cup and learn that fluids come out of the top. This can be messier than teaching with a spill-proof or spill-resistant cup in the beginning.

MONTH EIGHT:
Bringing Up Baby

Your three goals this month are simple:

- Learn how to cope with baby anxiety.
- Watch for signs that your baby is ready for a cup.
- Prepare for mobility.

Other families choose to use a spill-proof or spill-resistant cup right away to minimize mess in the beginning. People who advocate for other methods say that once children learn to use a cup with a lid, they are completely surprised years later when they drink fluid that comes straight out of the top.

If you choose a spill-proof or spill-resistant cup, you will also need to select a style. You could use a cup with a lip that allows liquid to pour through at a very limited rate. Or you might choose cups with straws and lids. Some families also choose cups with valves that prevent fluid from leaking unless the child is sucking.

Once you decide which type of cup to use, you will need to decide what you will put in it. Hands down, water is the best thing to put in your baby's cup. This is particularly true as your baby is learning to drink from the cup, because spills aren't sticky, just wet. As your baby gets a better idea of how to use a cup, you can add other things to it; but other than water, breast milk, 100 percent juice, or

MONTH
8

infant formula, your baby shouldn't have much else. Do not put liquid foods such as applesauce or soup inside your baby's cup.

LEARN ABOUT STRANGER ANXIETY

Your baby has spent a lot of time with you in her life. When she was younger, you could pass her around at family gatherings and not think a thing about it. But now, she will shy away from anyone but mom or dad, and sometimes only one of you. Her once-loved grandma now sends baby into tears. She might cling to you, crying in fits and sobs. This can be hard to watch.

Stranger anxiety might begin to rear its head at this point in time. Don't panic. This phase, like others, will eventually pass.

At these instances, try to calm your baby down. Hug her and love her. Talk to her softly. Try to give her feelings words. "It is okay. This is grandma. Grandma loves you." Give her time to make the adjustment to being with the new person.

This anxiety toward others can happen with lots of people. Some babies have greater difficulty with stranger anxiety than others do. Some become upset when they encounter people they do not know well, while others get upset around even close relatives. Suddenly your baby might not want anything to do with siblings, relatives, or even day care workers. Believe it or not, this is a normal stage and it will pass.

A new caregiver might be especially frightening to your baby during this stage. If you do need to use a new caregiver, show your baby you trust this person. Smile at her and talk to her in a kind way, while holding your baby. Have this person interact positively with your baby while you are there. Gently ease your baby into understanding that having other people assist in his care is not a way of separating from him.

Remember, when your baby gets anxious about being with another person, above all, do not force her into the arms of a stranger. Let your baby warm up to the person and get to know them. And remember to give her lots of love and snuggles, so that she knows she is safe and she feels secure.

COPE WITH GROWING INDEPENDENCE

As your baby gets older, he will gain independence. This can be a good thing, but even a good thing can be painful at times. Remember, you have been preparing him for this growth since birth.

All the cuddling and loving you gave your baby as a newborn was meant to instill in him a sense that you were there for him. When you answered his cries in a timely fashion, you showed him that you were dependable. And as you met his needs, he saw that life was right.

At this point in your baby's life, he is ready to be a bit more independent. He is able to crawl away, but he'll also turn around to ensure you are still there, watching him. Your baby might enjoy playing peek-a-boo, but only because he knows

Your baby will light up when he sees you. You are his favorite person in the whole world.

you are still there. As the rest of this year plays out, you will see that he can go farther away from you, confidently.

And so begins the developmental dance of testing independence, and then turning back to mom and dad for reassurance. All the new things he experiences are exciting, but after approaching unfamiliarity, your baby will probably want to check in with you, the person with whom he feels safest.

LISTEN TO YOUR BABY TALK

Sometimes our days get really busy. We have places to go and things to do. Listening to the baby repeat the same sounds over and over might be placed on the back burner. But it is important.

Your baby has been learning to talk since before birth, starting with listening to you talk and sing. It continued as you talked to her after birth by reading and playing, and simply by being around her. As your baby has gotten older, she has also started to play with her own voice.

Now she makes sounds. *Da-da, ma-ma, ba-ba,* and *ga-ga* combinations are typical at first. These initial sounds are probably used indiscriminately, and they do not yet indicate any one particular person or thing to your baby. She will also start repeating patterns. She has been listening to conversations and picking up how a conversation goes. She recognizes that one person talks, then one listens, and then roles are reversed. She has been paying close attention.

You can help your baby in her quest for language. First, continue what you have been doing all along. Read to her, talk to her, and describe her day. Play games that involve words, singing, and patterning. Ask her questions: "Who is that in the mirror?" Then answer the question: "It's baby!" (You can also use her name.)

Sometimes it is important to be quiet and to let your baby talk. Listening can be just as much fun as joining in.

Also give your baby quiet time. Quiet is something we don't often have in our lives. But it is actually important for your baby. Give her some time each day without sounds. No radio, no television, and no real conversation other than hers. This undistracted time is important for her to develop language skills. You might also find that you like the relative quiet more than you knew.

DIAGNOSE AND TREAT CONSTIPATION

Constipation, or the inability to pass stool, is really uncomfortable. As you change your baby's diet and add solid foods, you might notice that he has fewer bowel movements. He might also have hard stool that causes him pain to pass. It may even cause a bit of rectal bleeding. You might see that your child is straining as he tries to have a bowel movement. This might be normal for him and not a sign of constipation without the other symptoms. If he is straining and crying, constipation is the most likely culprit. To assist him, lay him down and bring his knees to his chest. This simulates a squat, which will help him to pass his stools more easily.

Treating constipation through prevention is the best bet. Know which foods are likely to cause constipation, such as bananas and applesauce. Foods that contain iron, such as infant formula and baby cereal, are also culprits. Pair these foods with nonbinding ones, such as those high in fiber (prunes, pears, apricots, etc.). Together, these varieties of foods can create an appropriate balance in your baby's diet.

You might also try adding more liquids to your baby's diet. This might mean nursing more, particularly if you have decreased the amount of nursing due to the added solid foods. You can also add water to baby's diet.

If constipation continues to be a problem, mention it to your pediatrician. She might be able to help you pinpoint other issues or help you find better solutions. Sometimes solutions can include:

- Making dietary changes
- Adding juice
- Using glycerin suppositories
- Giving medications, including enemas

Most of the time, simple changes to baby's diet work just fine. Remember to be aware of baby's bowel movements as you make changes to her diet. This can help save you both a lot of trouble.

ENCOURAGE YOUR BABY TO CRAWL

Babies are usually eager to learn to move around. Now that your baby has a better grip on sitting, the next logical course is moving. You can help your baby by encouraging him to crawl.

To begin, place him on a comfortable area of the floor. It should be clean and padded, so carpet works well. If you have hardwood floors or tile, consider laying down a blanket for padding. It works best to lay your baby on his belly. Then take a toy he wants and place it just out of reach. Encourage him verbally to go get the toy. You can repeat this game as often as he will play with you. Just be sure he does eventually get the toy and has some playtime

Mama Moment

Trying to fit exercise in with a newly mobile baby can be very difficult. You will have to be creative with how you get time to exercise alone or find ways to work around your active little one. One really good way to work out is to incorporate the baby into workout.

You can do several yoga poses and exercises while holding a baby. Some companies actually sell entire workout programs involving this concept. You can try doing aerobics with your stroller, either in a class or alone. And you can even do a low-impact aerobics workout, using your baby sling. Again, some videos are available in this topic.

with it. Never getting the toy makes the pursuit of crawling not worth the reward—the toy.

As your baby gets a bit better at moving around, you can also encourage him to crawl by playing games with him. Consider crawling races as a fun activity for both of you. Place a toy at one end of the room, and both of you can start crawling from the other end of the room. You can encourage him

The park is a great place for an outing. Have a blanket picnic, and try out some of the baby swings.

to crawl and say, "I'm going to get the toy! Is baby going to get the toy? Hurry, get the toy!" Make sure you are laughing and smiling. This is supposed to be fun, though you will quickly find out what hard work crawling is for adults!

It is recommended that you allow your baby to crawl wherever he wants, as long as it is safe. This exploration will help to expose him to different textures and touches. A good example would be allowing him to crawl on carpet, hardwood floors (after some experience), grass, and so on. You can also make a baby obstacle course when he becomes adept at crawling. Place laundry baskets down for your baby to crawl around and set up items she can crawl over, like blankets, soft toys, and pillows.

Remember, not every baby will crawl at the same rate or pace. Some babies seem to love to crawl and crawl a lot. Other babies are content to just sit there and not go anywhere. If you are concerned about your baby's crawling ability, your pediatrician can help you decide if there is a problem or if your baby simply dislikes crawling.

WEEK 31

Eat

Your baby might very much enjoy eating. Previously he has gotten all of his calories by drinking, so eating is still a fairly new concept to him. Some babies really like the new tastes and textures, while others do not want to eat a variety of foods.

Affirmation for Month Eight

My baby loves me, and I love my baby

Once you have a set of foods that you know your baby is not allergic to and will eat, you can continue to use those reliably. Adding new foods is advisable, but you should do it slowly. You can even offer a combination of foods at a meal. So if you are feeding your baby pears for the first time, you might want to start the feeding with some familiar apple-sauce. Sneak in a few bites of pear to see how baby reacts. This comforts some parents because they know that their baby is not going hungry.

Do you have a problem choosing which foods to offer? Some parents have a schedule. For example, you might always serve a fruit at breakfast and a vegetable for dinner. This is perfectly acceptable but not necessary. If your baby eats two fruits one day and two vegetables the next day, that is fine, too.

Your baby is becoming more adventurous each day when it comes to new tastes and textures.

Hot Mama for Month Eight

Is your body still showing some signs of baby? New earrings, a brightly colored scarf, or a new belt can really add some-thing to your outfit and help you feel great—all while directing attention away from your trouble spots. Try something bold and brave! This works for casual or dressy occasions.

Play

Babies of this age love to be tickled! Even pretend-ing to tickle your baby will send her into fits of laughter. You can usually get some good giggles by lightly tickling her on her neck, under her arms, or on her side.

Watch her face for signs of fun, as sometimes tickling can go too far. As long as she's laughing and playing in between tickles, it should be fine. If she starts to pull away or act cranky, you will know your baby has had enough tickling. Also be careful in letting younger kids tickle the baby, only because they might not be able to see when it is time to stop the tickling session.

MONTH
8

WEEK 32

Eat

Some parents choose to give their babies juice. The benefits of juice are questionable, because you remove some of the best parts of the fruit. Babies do not need juice; their primary liquid need continues to be breast milk or formula. However, most nutritional guidelines say that if given appropriately and without added sugar, some juice is okay.

Tickling is something babies love. Sometimes, you can even pretend to tickle them, and they begin to howl with laughter. Just be careful not to overdo it.

If you are giving your baby juice, remember never to use a baby bottle, because the sugar will sit on baby's teeth. Juice should always go into a cup, where liquid does not just drip out. Juice can also be diluted with water for most babies. This can help cut down the amount of sugar. You should also brush your baby's teeth after giving juice to help reduce the sugar left on the teeth.

Sleep

Teething can wreak havoc on nighttime sleep for your baby. Sometimes you might find that your peaceful sleeper has become inconsolable. So what is a parent to do when this happens?

First you need to figure out what type of pain relief works best for your baby. Is it chewing on cold things? Do teeth gels rubbed on his gums do the trick? Does your baby simply need some comforting? If you are breastfeeding, does some extra nighttime nursing give him comfort? Occasionally pediatricians will recommend acetaminophen for pain associated with teething. Once you have figured out how to deal with the pain, you can quickly come to the rescue should your little one awake with teething troubles.

Play

Babies at this age love to crawl in and out of things, and you can create some great baby games by piquing this interest. Try getting a small basket, just a few inches tall. Look for one that is about twice the size of a shoebox.

HELPFUL HINTS: MOMMY'S LITTLE HELPER

The next time you are in the kitchen and need to work, try having a helper. Your baby will love to play on the kitchen floor right next to you as you work. Simply give her some small kitchen pots, measuring cups, and spoons to play with.

She will have fun banging the pots with the other items. She will drop the spoons inside and take them out again. She will mimic your motions and cook up a creation of her own.

This is a good time to create a small area in a lower cabinet to store her safe play items, but it also means more safety measures should be taken in the kitchen. Be sure you have all chemicals, even dish soap, high up where baby can't get to them. You should also employ baby-proof locks on cabinets you do not want her to open.

This is the perfect-size basket for your baby to climb in and out of. You can also give him rides, pushing him around on the carpet in the basket. Your baby will no doubt also find other ways to play with the basket. When not in use, it's perfect storage for baby toys.

Laundry baskets are great fun for babies at this age. Let your baby knock it over and climb inside.

MONTH
8

HELPFUL HINTS: VITAMIN FACTS

Vitamin D is essential to your baby's health. It was recently discovered that babies have not been getting adequate vitamin D from sunlight exposure, due to reasons including:

- Area where they live (weather, cloud cover, etc.)
- Skin pigmentation
- Sunscreen

For this reason, the American Academy of Pediatrics recommends that a baby be supplemented with 400 IU of vitamin D per day. This can be found in most multivitamins made for babies and young children. Many formulas are also supplemented with vitamin D, making additional supplementation unnecessary. Some pediatricians also recommend some sun exposure, if you cannot or do not wish to use vitamins. You will need to discuss this with your pediatrician.

WEEK 33

Eat

You might find that your baby gets gassy as he tries new food. This can make him very uncomfortable. You might know because you can hear him passing gas. Your baby might also fuss, kick his legs, or try to "stand" up, or his belly may feel hard.

You can try gas drops to alleviate the pain. Certain strokes from your infant massage class can also help him pass the gas and feel better. These strokes are commonly referred to as the "I Love You" strokes.

You can do these strokes any time your baby has gas. You can also try to keep a food diary to see which foods are causing the gas. Common offenders include carrots, broccoli, products containing cow's milk, and others.

Sleep

Some babies wake up at night more than others, and continue to do so longer than other babies. Our society has become so fixated on newborn sleep, we've nearly driven ourselves mad thinking about it and analyzing it.

As a parent, instead of obsessing about how much your baby is sleeping, you have to understand and accept night waking for what it is: a protective mechanism that helps your baby live. When babies fall into really deep sleep, they are not as readily able to take their cues to feed or breathe or respond to their environment. This can be dangerous for a baby. Waking up is the protective measure; it is not a punishment for bad parenting.

Bear in mind that your baby could be waking up for many reasons. He might need to eat. Some new developmental milestones may be affecting his sleep. Perhaps he is in pain from sore muscles after practicing a new skill or even just from plain old growing pains. He might be testing out some newfound independence during the day, which

prompts him to wake because he craves the emotional security and reassurance of your presence during the night.

These realizations can be hard to remember or even contemplate, particularly when you are utterly exhausted. Do not beat yourself up over your baby's lack of sleep. Try to find a solution that helps meet everyone's needs, including yours. Could you switch off who gets up at night? Does your baby sleep better in one place or another?

I Love You (ILU Strokes)

The strokes depicted can improve digestion by moving material through the baby's colon.

1. Imagine that your baby can look down and "see" a letter U on his tummy.
2. Stroke your baby's left side from below the rib cage to the top of his left hip with the flat part of your fingers. The baby "sees" the letter I.
3. Illustrate the letter L by stroking below his rib cage on the right side, moving across his tummy to the top of his left hip. He can "see" the letter L.
4. Now show your baby the letter U by starting at the right hip, stroking up his right side, across his tummy, under his rib cage and down his left side to his hip.

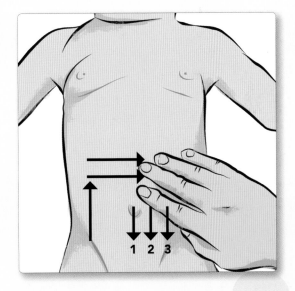

Some experimenting might be helpful. In general, just remember, you cannot really control infant sleep effectively without risking harm. And while some babies sleep through the night sooner and others do it later, one thing is for sure: Eventually, all children learn how to sleep better! Even if it feels like you have the worst sleeper in the world right now, one day you will wake up and realize you are all rested and sleeping well.

Play

Your baby is still thrilled with placing items in a box and taking them back out. Many baby toys are based on this concept. But you can also make your own version.

Take a small laundry basket or the basket mentioned in the previous section and place a few of his favorite toys inside. Show him how to pull the basket over to get the toys back out. Going back and forth with the toys will keep him very busy. Do watch for your baby trying to pull up on the laundry basket. It is most likely not sturdy enough to support his weight. This can cause him to topple over.

HELPFUL HINTS: SAFETY FIRST

Your baby might decide that the car seat is not her friend. She might twist and bend and fight just to avoid going into the car seat. Staying out of the car seat is not an option, but unfortunately you cannot rationalize with your baby.

You can take a couple of approaches to get the baby into the car seat. Hold her close so that she can't see the car seat. As you get nearer to the seat, bend over and lean in as close as possible until you sit her in the seat and the buckle quickly. You can also try distraction. If buckling baby in is a grueling experience, hang in there. She will probably settle down soon after you climb into the driver's seat. Most babies are fine once they are in the car seat, but the act of being placed in the car seat is what baby dislikes.

Your baby will love playing with a ball. You can roll it, chase it, or simply watch it for hours of entertainment.

WEEK 34

Eat

Since you have been giving your baby solid foods for a while now, it might be time to introduce high-protein foods. For many families this will include meat—poultry such as turkey or chicken, or other meats such as pork or beef. Remember, though, that beans are also a great source of protein.

Your baby's digestive tract is ready to tolerate these more intense proteins. And skill-wise, your baby is ready to handle the texture and consistency of meats with less risk of choking. You will still want to grind up these meats for a while as your baby gets used to the taste and texture. If you are giving your baby beans, they should be well cooked and at least slightly mashed to break the skins and prevent choking.

Feeding your baby a variety of foods is a great idea. The exposure can help them experience a greater number of tastes at an earlier age.

Your baby may or may not like proteins right away. Give your baby a sample. Don't force new foods on him. He will let you know what he likes. Remember, new foods should be offered many times before you decide that your baby truly does not like something. Proteins may take longer for your baby to accept because of the new texture. Consider giving proteins mixed in with something else he likes to eat already, such as chicken and apples.

Play

Babies love balls. At this age, your baby will really love playing with you and a ball. Simply sit her down on one side of the room, a few feet away from you. Take a ball and roll it to her. This will make her smile and giggle.

If you miss, she is likely to try to chase the ball. Her idea of chasing might not be pretty, but it is effective. She might topple over in the direction of the ball and scoot her body until she is near it.

The help of an older sibling or child can be beneficial, as long as they understand the goal is to get the baby to play. Another alternative is to have another adult sit with the baby and "help" her roll the ball back to you. This makes for lots of great fun!

Sleep

It is important to remember that sometimes your baby will be a great sleeper, and then, all of a sudden, her sleep might take a turn for the worse. Sometimes it is because she is not feeling well.

MONTH
8

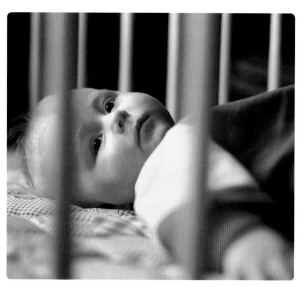

Sometimes, your baby will want to simply lay awake in the crib or bed without crying. This is fine and should not cause you alarm. Consider how often you simply lay in bed before falling asleep.

Perhaps she is teething or dealing with seasonal allergies. Your baby might also be having a tough time dealing with all the changes she is making, such as becoming more mobile and vocal.

This is not a comfort at 3:00 a.m. when you are up with your baby for the second time. But the same rules still apply. Be calm and quiet. Keep the lights dim. Feed her only if that is what she really needs, though nursing for comfort might be what she really needs. Keep distractions to a minimum. This is a phase and it will pass. How long it will last is a guess. Some babies have a few nights like this every month, while others do a single, longer period of night waking.

HELPFUL HINTS: LEARN CPR

Infant safety and cardiopulmonary resuscitation (CPR) is a great class for any parent or child care provider to take. Your baby is going to be exposed to more items that can cause harm as he becomes more mobile. This makes taking a CPR class a really good idea.

If you took a class in preparation for your baby's birth, that's good. Find your handouts and manual and give yourself a refresher course. Some parents find that starting over fresh with a CPR course is a great idea.

You can usually find CPR classes in a variety of places. Try calling your local Red Cross. You can also look for classes through a birth network or you can ask at your local birth center or hospital. If all else fails, try to find a community group willing to help you sponsor a class. Being prepared in an emergency is very important, because minutes and even seconds count.

What to Watch For Explained

The **ability to sit alone** is one that brings much joy to the lives of babies and their parents. By this point your baby should have mastered the milestone of sitting. This major skill is one that has been evolving for a long time. Expect some spills and tumbles along the way. These are to be expected. You need to alert your pediatrician if your baby is unable to sit without assistance at this point. That can mean that the stomach muscles aren't strong or your baby has balance problems, perhaps from ear infections.

Using sounds to draw you in is a skill that your baby learned early, though the first sounds were cries which brought you to meet your baby's needs. Now your baby has developed the ability to get your attention without crying. Your baby may even try calling you by a name over and over. If you really want to see him smile, repeat the name that they try to say. Acknowledging that they are calling out to you is as simple as saying, "I hear you calling me!" The smiles that are returned will melt your heart.

Broaden your baby-proofing as your baby becomes more mobile. As the early days of crawling are upon you, you will begin to notice new problem areas. Your mother's group or friends who have older babies will tell you some of the common pitfalls that you might not have thought about until now—such as your coffee table. Your pediatrician may also have a brochure on baby-proofing and contact information for your local poison control center. The simple fact is babies get into things faster than you can watch. An ounce of prevention is worth a pound of cure!

Consider cup safety when making choices concerning your baby's drinking habits. Not only will you want to consider what the cups and utensils are made of, but also the individual parts of the cup. Some cups are said to be spill-proof or leak-proof. This means that they have small parts that create a barrier to trap liquids inside. If your baby is having trouble with ear infections or other ear problems, the suction needed for these can be detrimental. You may be able to remove these parts and use the cup without them, but some cups have the parts built in. If you are using a cup with small parts, be sure that your baby cannot remove them and accidentally swallow the small parts that make up the interior of the cup.

MONTH
8

MONTH NINE

Week 35–39

So Big!

√ Checklist for Month Nine

- ☐ Introduce finger food.
- ☐ Learn to use redirection.
- ☐ Rethink your bedtime routine.
- ☐ Check for anemia.
- ☐ Brush baby's teeth.
- ☐ Know how to cope if baby is sick.

What to Watch For in the Ninth Month

- ☐ Capability to pass objects from one hand to another
- ☐ Babbling with change of tone
- ☐ Ability to bear weight on legs alone
- ☐ Choking hazards and prevention
- ☐ Crib safety

Be Sure to:

☐ Schedule a pediatric appointment

☐ Have baby's nine-month photos done

☐ Evaluate your home for lead-based paint

Baby Skills:

In the ninth month, your baby:

☐ Sits well

☐ Probably crawls

☐ Might stand for a few seconds or when hands are held

☐ Might pull up

☐ Babbles

☐ Tries to engage you in conversation

☐ Moves toys from one hand to another

☐ Knows her name

☐ Engages pincer grasp

Three-fourths of your baby's first year is behind you. Some days, it probably seems like just yesterday she was a tiny infant, and other times it feels like many sleepless nights ago.

BABY DATA

Your baby is enjoying being verbal. He might even chatter back and forth with you in a pretend conversation. This patterning of conversation helps him learn to talk. You might find him practicing by talking to himself, and this is fine.

Your baby still loves toys, but he also enjoys games now. Your baby might like when you play hide-and-seek with his toys, for example. Peek-a-boo will really get him smiling and probably even laughing. Try combining the two by hiding behind a doorway, calling his name, and as he looks over, jumping out and saying, "Peek-a-boo!" This will really bring on the giggles.

This month might be a culmination of sleeping frustration, particularly if your baby has not been sleeping well. Many parents say that their own unmet expectations are behind these frustrations. It's

hard to continue waking up during the night when you believe your baby should be sleeping soundly at this age. Sleeping doesn't have a magic age. Some babies grow into their ability to sleep calmly at a young age, while others take much longer to settle into peaceful, unbroken sleep patterns. Remember, your baby is an individual. That means you, as the parent, need to figure out what works best for him and the family.

Be sure to include baby at mealtimes. Have his high chair near the family to watch and learn to mimic the flow of a meal. New foods might have a thicker consistency, and you might be experimenting with small finger foods. Remember not to go too quickly. Some babies at this age are ready to have one feeding replaced with solid foods. Some babies still need every liquid feeding of breast milk or infant formula; that is, your baby might want to nurse or have a bottle in addition to eating solids, as opposed to a solids-only meal. Let your baby be your guide.

INTRODUCE FINGER FOODS

Now that your baby has some experience eating solid foods, you can explore more food options. Finger foods are next on the list. Your baby should be able to sit up well and bring the food to her mouth on her own before attempting this type of food.

Choose a food your baby likes as a first finger food. The food you choose should also be fairly mushy or easily dissolvable in baby's mouth. Tiny bits of banana work really well as a first finger food.

MONTH NINE:
Bringing Up Baby

Your three goals this month are simple:

- Learn the basics of baby dental care.
- Watch baby for sleep changes.
- Know about your baby's well checkup: skills and all.

You can purchase small jars of fruits and vegetables for this purpose. Snacks generically known as puffs are also made as finger foods for babies. Think of these as tiny rice cakes. They are small bits of grains, flavored with fruits and vegetables. They dissolve fairly quickly inside your baby's mouth. Puffs are great for a take-along snack that doesn't go bad in your diaper bag.

You don't need to buy anything special when you're ready to start finger foods. There are plenty of options at home. You can feed baby many of the things your family is eating, provided the food is soft and diced up into small pieces. Variety of options is the key here. Your baby will enjoy feeling the different textures. Pears and cereals are grainy. Peaches and peas are slippery. Some foods mash easily in the fingers, like bananas. Your baby will probably use dinnertime as a chance to play with food textures. This is a good thing.

MONTH
9

Playing with the textures might involve smashing or rolling food between her fingers. She might also roll the food around in her mouth. Perhaps your baby makes faces and plays with the food on her tongue. This sounds messy and it can be, but that's why you have bibs. All this food play does not mean your baby is going to be the food-fight queen in middle school; it is simply a way for your baby

Finger foods tend to thrill babies. The joy of self-feeding, all the new textures—what isn't to love? For parents, the clean up seems much better, until you've crunched a few into the carpet.

to explore her world. While not every meal can be a big ordeal or messy event, be sure to allow your baby some time to play with her food—think of it as a learning experience.

Just watch giving your baby foods that are easy to choke on. Top offenders are foods with pits (like cherries or olives) or round ones that might obstruct airways, such as grapes. If you feel these are important foods for baby to eat, you can give them skinned and chopped into tiny bits. The skins on these foods might be harder for your baby to mash with baby gums, making choking more likely.

LEARN TO USE REDIRECTION

No matter how you intend to discipline your baby as she grows up, you will need to think about how to handle the baby years. Discipline for a baby helps to set the stage for years to come. Discipline is also a way for parents to communicate their desires for their child.

Babies learn to get around at different rates, and as they learn to move, they start to get into everything. Once that happens, you will have to think about how you will handle telling them what they need to know about staying safe from harm, while still allowing them to explore their world.

Enter the word *no*. No is something you'll find yourself saying a lot more as your baby learns to explore. No is an important word for your baby to learn. You should use it as needed to let your baby know that you do not approve or that an activity is dangerous.

The problem with the word *no* comes in its frequency of use. There might be times when nearly every other word you say is no, which can be disheartening as a parent and for your baby. You can encourage your child to explore in other ways, without feeling like a negative Nelly all the time.

Redirection is the easiest way to alleviate this problem. For example, if your baby wants to play with the electrical cord outlets, you can redirect her attention by moving her away from the socket and saying, "We don't play with outlets. Let's play over here." Usually the change of location will be enough to distract her into playing with something else.

Sometimes the change of scenery is not enough. You might have a tenacious baby who will crawl back to the object or activity that is enthralling her over and over. You can continue to move her and offer her something else as a distraction. You might turn her around and hand her a favorite toy or something fun to explore.

Redirection does not replace the use of the word *no*. It does allow you to give your baby a chance to learn what no means and the importance of the word without hearing it every five seconds. It can also help you feel better as a parent for not always saying no. Redirection is an effective tool in your parenting arsenal, and it can be used for many things throughout your parenting career.

Mama Moment

As your baby gets bigger and heavier, you have got to watch your back. Remember to bend at the knees when leaning down to pick up your baby. You should also remember to kneel rather than bend when possible: Think bathtime for baby. This can save some strain on your back.

As your baby gets bigger, your back might hurt more. This could be because of the added weight or the way you carry yourself when carrying your baby. Consider choosing different holds with your baby sling, such as a hip carry, or even using a baby backpack if your baby has enough skills for this. For severe or recurrent back pain, you should seek your practitioner's advice.

RETHINK YOUR BEDTIME ROUTINE

Just when you think you finally have sleep time down pat, your baby changes the bedtime routine. You had the perfect schedule that your family loved. You did part and your partner did part, and your baby went to sleep and stayed that way.

Many parents find that around nine months of age, sleeping is still an issue, though many babies are sleeping better during the night, and once asleep, they frequently stay asleep. However, getting them to go to sleep can be a bigger problem. This is a signal to change up your bedtime routine.

MONTH
9

Sometimes you simply need to start a bit later or a bit earlier. Play with the times that you lay your baby down to see if you are having any luck in making a timing switch. Sometimes your baby is ready for bed a bit sooner because of more active play, and sometimes your baby simply wants to be awake a bit longer.

You might also need to look at the routine itself. Are all of the parts of your routine still working for you? Does your baby still seem to become relaxed after a bath or a massage? Does your baby enjoy a book?

Sometimes simple changes like adding or removing a massage are all that is needed. If you find that your baby is no longer getting that sleepy look

after a massage, maybe it is time to move it earlier in the day. Or maybe you just need to change how you are doing the massage. Maybe, for instance, you've discovered that rubbing your baby's face is stimulating, but a limb or trunk massage is not.

Is the book you're reading helping your little one to fall asleep? Or do you find that the book wakes him up and engages him? Definitely nix all activity books, including books that make noise or involve pop-ups, finger plays, or lifting flaps. Instead, shoot for rhyming books that are slow and melodic to help enhance relaxation. Save the other books for playtime.

When making bedtime-routine changes, do so slowly. Try one small change at a time and watch for differences. You might need to watch each change for more than a day or two to gauge its effect. Do not try to completely overhaul your baby's bedtime routine. For instance, if you haven't been doing a bedtime routine at all, you wouldn't want to institute a six-step plan. Or if you have been doing a six-step bedtime ritual, you shouldn't drop to a quick bedtime story and peck on the cheek. Such a drastic measure is rarely needed at this age.

Once you have figured out what helps your baby to sleep better or fall asleep faster, you are set. The next time your baby has issues, just return to the same process. Looking first at the timing is always helpful. Then give what you are doing a good review and determine if it is still working.

Is it time to redo your nighttime routine? Remember to double check it as your baby grows.

CHECK FOR ANEMIA

Anemia occurs when the body does not have enough iron in its system. Your baby is said to be anemic when the oxygen-carrying red blood cells can't carry as much oxygen as they should. This is also known as low iron, and it can cause physical and motor deficits in infants and toddlers.

At your baby's well checkup this month your baby might be screened for anemia if he is at risk for it. Risks for anemia include feeding of cow's milk (this is the most common factor) or low-iron infant formula, low birth weight or prematurity, or high blood loss. Your baby can also become anemic if you are anemic and you breastfeed him.

Babies will get iron from nutritional and supplemental sources. These can include:

- Dark-green leafy vegetables (spinach, kale, etc.)
- Whole grains
- Beans
- Fortified infant cereal
- Iron-containing infant vitamin supplement drops
- Infant formula

Your pediatrician can test your baby for anemia with a finger prick. This will tell the doctor how much iron (hemoglobin) is in your baby's blood. If your baby is iron deficient, you can give him iron supplements or work nutritionally to increase the amount of iron-containing food he eats per day. Nutrition labels can help you figure this out as you feed your baby.

Once you have been treating your baby's anemia, either with food or iron supplements, your baby should be retested according to your pediatrician's instructions. Sometimes this test might happen at the next visit, but often it will occur approximately three to six months after the original diagnosis. Some babies tolerate the nutritional forms or treatment better than the supplements, which can have a nasty, metallic taste. Infant cereals and even some plain breakfast cereals contain large amounts of iron and work really well for infants.

Infants who are consuming iron-enriched formulas should not take iron supplements. Too much iron can cause constipation and even poison your baby. Talk to your doctor if you have concerns.

BRUSH BABY'S TEETH

Once your baby has teeth, they need to be brushed. This seems like it would be common sense, but many parents neglect these first teeth. Even though your child will eventually lose her baby teeth, these teeth do matter!

You do not need to brush your baby's teeth the same way you would brush your own teeth. As already mentioned in Month Six on page 164, if your baby got his first teeth before he was able to sit up alone, hopefully you were able to use a clean, wet washcloth to wipe down the front and back of each tooth gently but firmly. Now that your baby is older and is sitting up better, you can switch to a baby toothbrush. The easiest is a tiny, soft rubber toothbrush with very small bristles that fits over your finger. This type of toothbrush gives you more control of what you're doing, which is important when brushing your baby's teeth. As with wash-cloths, however, over-the-finger toothbrush styles can be tricky once your baby decides it's fun to start chomping on your finger!

Hot Mama for Month Nine

It took nine months for your body to change during pregnancy. It can also take at least nine months to even try to get your body back into some sense of order, so don't be too hard on yourself if you're not exactly where you'd like to be just yet. Now that you've hit the nine-month mark, you've had the same amount of time in gestation as you have had after it. Where are you? If you're not where you want to be in terms of getting back into shape, now might be a good time to take stock of what you need to do to get there. Work out more? Eat less? Maybe a combination of both? If you haven't done so already, consider carving out some time at least once a week that is just for you—join a gym, take an aerobics or yoga class, or even just take a walk by yourself.

If that is the case, baby toothbrushes are also available. They have soft bristles with short handles. Always use a toothbrush designed for an infant. And never give your baby the toothbrush to play with while walking around, for fear of falling on it.

Your baby doesn't necessarily need toothpaste at first. Toothpaste might complicate tooth brush-ing if your baby doesn't like the tastes and textures. Just getting him used to having his teeth brushed with water will be easier on your baby. You can always add toothpaste later.

When you do choose toothpaste, be careful. Stores provide many options. Avoid toothpastes that contain fluoride. It is fairly easy for babies to get too much fluoride, which is poisonous. Many toddler and infant toothpastes are fluoride free. These are the best bet. Switch to a fluoride tooth-paste only when you are sure your child will spit all of the toothpaste out rather than swallow it. This does not come until children are much older.

Once your baby has a tooth, the American Academy of Pediatric Dentistry recommends that she see a dentist. Other professionals recommend waiting until your child is one or two before the first dental visit. You should call your dentist for advice on when they feel your baby should come in for a checkup. Consider going sooner if your baby has problems or if you have concerns.

KNOW HOW TO COPE IF BABY IS SICK

Having a sick baby is absolutely no fun. Depending on what type of illness your baby has, you might be changing your routine quite a bit to help care for him. If your baby does get sick, hang in there and don't worry. Some illnesses pass relatively quickly, or baby feels better when medicated, which can be a welcome surprise for parents.

While you can't plan ahead for illness, you should have a plan in place to help you keep your wits about you when your baby does get sick. Try to have a backup plan for your daily responsibilities, whether that be working, caring for other children, or simply doing daily tasks around the house. If your baby is in day care, what is the plan? Will you stay home? Will your partner? Do you have emergency child care? Sometimes family members work out well here, particularly if it's a short-term deal.

Some babies will need a bit more attention or cuddling when they aren't feeling well. For other babies, particularly if medicine makes them feel better, they might rather play as normal. Be sure to follow your own baby's lead and whichever the case, offer an extra cuddle or two.

If your baby has a fever you are treating with medication, be sure you are giving him the right amount. Be very careful with medication droppers. Be sure to read the label and check for the correct dose before giving it to your baby. Always look for the fill lines rather than giving an entire dropperful of medicine. Many medicine droppers are marked with more than one fill line. Dose accordingly, depending on your baby's age and weight. Again, your pediatrician will be able to give you updated dosage instructions. It is also very important to always use the medication dropper or dispenser that came with the medication, as various droppers are measured and marked differently.

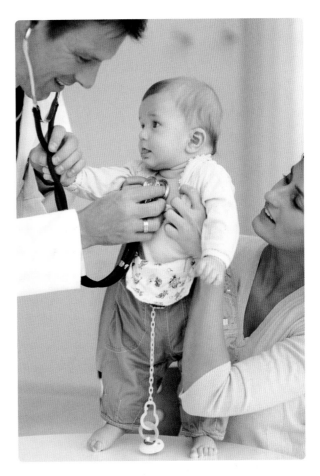

A well-baby check-up is usually fairly simple, but as your baby is growing, you might have a few rough spots with stranger anxiety. Show your baby that you trust your care provider and that you will stay with her.

If baby is agreeable, try to keep your regular routine as much as possible. Keep in mind that your baby might not be as hungry, particularly for solid foods. When they are sick, some babies will resort only to nursing or drinking from a bottle. This is not worrisome, as long as they are drinking and not showing signs of dehydration. Some signs of dehydration include:

- Dry mouth
- Chapped lips
- No wet diaper for more than six hours
- Strong-smelling urine
- Dark-colored urine
- Sunken-in soft spot on top of head
- No tears when crying

Dehydration can occur particularly with vomiting or diarrhea. If you think your baby is dehydrated, call your pediatrician for advice. You should not give your baby fruit juice, sports drinks, or soft drinks. Your baby might need special fluids called electrolyte-replacement fluids to help get him back on track. Since babies are small, they can dehydrate quickly.

WEEK 35

Eat

Your baby might be eating a lot of food, between solids plus nursing or bottles. Your baby might also still be exclusively nursing or drinking formula. There are wide eating variances at this stage of the game.

With the help of your pediatrician and your preferences, you can decide what is best for your baby. Some babies simply eat more or more frequently than other babies. Some babies do not eat as much or as often. Let your baby's weight and development be your guide. If these are on track, your baby is doing exactly what is right for her.

Sleep

At the age of nine months, most babies have a sleep pattern. They usually sleep for two periods during the day. These naps are generally an hour or two long. The biggest chunk of sleep is at night. This period of sleep could be anywhere from ten to twelve hours long. However, sometimes babies still wake up briefly during this long stretch. Though many are not eating, some still might be.

Your baby's sleep patterns should generally be something similar to the above, with individual variances, naturally. Some issues that might cause your baby to break from the sleeping routine, include illness, teething, pain, discomfort, or even noises. Remember, you are probably having fewer sleepless nights at this stage than in the past, and things will only get better over time.

Play

Babies love balls! Nothing is more fun than watching your baby's face light up as he spies a ball. You will want to ensure that any ball you give your baby to play with is safe. It should not be so small that he could choke on it, nor should it be so big that it causes things to fall over if touched by the ball. Sit your baby across the room. You can sit a few feet away. Gently roll the ball to him. Clap when he tries to get it. If you have him spread his legs into a V and you open yours the same way, you can usually prevent the ball from rolling too far away. Eventually he will begin to try to roll the ball back to you. If not, maybe an older child would enjoy the fetch portion of this game until then!

WEEK 36

Eat

Choking can be a real concern as your baby begins to eat more solid foods, especially since some babies of this age like to shove whatever pieces of food they can grab into their mouths very quickly. You

HELPFUL HINTS: BABY TALK

At this stage, your baby is beginning to understand simple words. Be sure to use plenty of them. In addition to taking tours of the house, reading to your baby, and narrating your baby's day, use as many simple word commands as you can. Then you can add more to the simple phrases to explain.

So for example, you might say to your baby, "No. We don't touch the stove." You have given him a simple command; in this case, "no." Then you've told him why you said, "no." This allows him to put together simple commands and actions. Other simple words he might understand at first would be:

- Yes
- Wait
- Eat
- Drink
- Playtime
- Naptime
- Please
- Bye
- Hello
- Stop

Starting with simple one-word commands will help your baby to grasp language. It will also help your baby to understand his role in his world. This is part of communicating with your baby.

MONTH
9

should always stay with your baby while he is eating, even if he is in his high chair and secure. This is true even once he's been eating solids for a while. Babies can choke quickly and without warning. Signs that your baby is choking are:

- Difficulty breathing
- Inability to vocalize or cough when trying
- Weak cough
- Wheezing sound when breathing in
- Blue-tinged skin
- Loss of consciousness

If you think your baby is choking, pick him up quickly. Look in his mouth to see if you can see the object. If you can, flip him over, lay him on his back, then try to sweep the object out with two fingers.

If this doesn't work, flip him over. With his head lower than his body, and face and jaw supported by your hand, give him five forceful thrusts between his shoulder blades with the heel of your hand. If this doesn't work, flip him to his back and give him five thrusts to his chest with two fingers just below his nipples. If this does not dislodge the object, call 911. Repeat the series of front and back thrusts until emergency crews take over or until the object is dislodged.

Do not start first aid for choking if your child can cough or breathe well. Either of these are signs that your baby is working to clear his throat on his own. Starting first aid too soon can actually cause more harm.

While you can read these instructions, it is much better to take a hands-on class for first aid. You can sign up for these at any community center or Red Cross center. Many childbirth classes also have information on finding an infant first-aid class.

Sleep

Teething is one reason your baby might not be sleeping as well as usual these days. When a tooth starts to come through, it can be painful, but your baby will have a hard time communicating this pain to you. Think of how frustrating this must be for a little one! To spot signs of teething, watch for your baby to drool more frequently, chew on things more often, and generally focus on her mouth.

A sleepless night is still possible, even with a nearly one-year-old. Thankfully, they are more likely to be a rarity. Hang in there; life changes, teething, and new skills can all bring about sleep disruptions.

If your baby spends a lot of time doing these things, try soothing her prior to bed. This might mean giving her a cold toy to chew on before bed or giving her a gum massage while you wipe down the teeth she might already have. You can also talk to your doctor about medications for pain, such as acetaminophen. Be cautious of numbing agents: Some practitioners do not recommend these because of the potential it has to numb your baby's gag reflex.

If your baby awakens in the middle of the night, try similar comfort measures. It might be a bit more difficult for you to remember when your baby wakes, so try to remind yourself of this potential issue before bedtime. Sometimes, just the comfort of nursing or being touched is enough to help babies calm enough to go back to sleep.

Play

Your baby is ready for a greater variety of finger foods now, and you have a lot of options. As mentioned on page 211, small bits of readily digested cereals and fruit—or vegetable-flavored puffs—are becoming quite popular. Place some of these on your baby's high-chair tray to keep him entertained while you make dinner.

These snacks tend to be very low in calories, which makes them a good snack in the sense that they are not dense. Just be careful that your baby is not filling up on puffs as replacement for more nutritionally dense foods.

WEEK 37

Eat

You can buy baby-feeding devices that look like mesh bags on the end of a stick. The premise is that you can put food inside the bag and attach it to the stick-like base. Your baby then can chew on the bag, extracting bits of the food. Think of food items like bananas, cooked sweet potatoes, peas, and so on.

This is one way to introduce less-strained solids into your baby's diet with a lower risk of choking. The bags are messy, however. They are supposedly washable, but they need to be washed right away. Or you can buy replacement bags and use them as disposable items.

Sleep

Do not be afraid to put your baby to bed slightly awake or even fully awake. Some babies need to put themselves to sleep to sleep well. By helping them into a drowsy state, you can give them that chance to finish the job of falling asleep.

Some babies can do this easily, while others struggle. The bedtime routine can be helpful, but so can loving parents. Ease your baby into this transition and be responsive to her needs. Watch your baby for signs of tiredness and follow her lead by guiding her to sleep. Responding promptly to your baby when she wakes at times when she is supposed to be asleep can help her to fall back to sleep sooner.

MONTH
9

Play

Rough play is a staple in many families. It might come more frequently from the men in a given family, but you will frequently see it. By rough play, we mean tossing your baby in the air, tumbling around on the ground, and generally pushing the physical safety limits.

Remind people who care for your child that you want your baby to play, but safely. This means you do not want to risk brain damage or other physical injury to your baby by having him tossed in the air. Be sure to show them other ways to play physically with your baby like crawling races, ball tossing, and more. This provides the physical, loving outlet babies are looking for, without the risks of overly rough play.

Dads tend to be the ones who play rough more often than moms. Good thing for daddy time—babies love to rough house!

HELPFUL HINTS: UPDATE THE CONTENTS

Have you checked your diaper bag lately? As your baby grows, your diaper bag needs change. Remember to switch out old clothes that are out of season or no longer fit. The same is true for diapers that might be too small. Nothing is worse in an emergency than finding out you don't have the right equipment, or even what you thought you had!

As you go through the diaper bag, you might realize that you can also switch diaper bag sizes. Most babies at nine months do not have the same needs as a newborn. So you might be able to switch to a smaller diaper bag. Some basic things to consider carrying include:

- Diapers
- Wipes
- Change of clothes (one bodysuit)

Other than these items, your list is optional. Some families choose to carry some snacks, such as containers of food. You might also have a toy or a book. If you are looking to pare down your list of baby-care items that are rarely used, simply go through and remove everything you haven't used in six months.

WEEK 38

Eat

Your baby will eat almost anything at this stage, food or not, so make sure your home is safe. Most people know they should have household chemicals, medications, and poisons locked up and out of baby's reach. But you might not think about some other risks when it comes to household dangers.

Be aware in your garden. Babies can be attracted to pretty flowers, and they will put them in their mouths, so watch carefully.

Certain common household plants can be poisonous, for example. At baby's eye level or even just on a table, a plant looks like a delicious treat. You might certainly find your baby munching on a plant without much warning. Check that all plants and the soil they are in are not poisonous before leaving them in your home. Consider seasonal plants as well, like poinsettias.

It is probably better to move the plants to higher ground or take them out of your home. This can prevent potential poisoning if your baby inadvertently eats the plant. But it can also save you from cleaning potting soil up off the ground.

Sleep

Double-check your crib for safety hazards this month. Your baby now sleeps differently than in previous months. This means she is moving around and rolling more.

As she's developing new skills, your baby might also be climbing up and standing on the crib mattress. Be sure that your crib meets the current safety standards. Remove all of the toys or crib bumper pads that might be in the crib. Your baby could step on these things and eventually climb out of the crib. These items are also not recommended in earlier months because of the risk of suffocation.

If you have decided to cosleep, you will also want to refresh the safety rules in your mind. As your baby becomes more mobile, falls can be more likely, particularly from high surfaces or when baby is sleeping alone. At this point, a crib or pack-and-play at least for naps can be helpful. You might also consider putting a mattress on the floor for naps.

MONTH
9

HELPFUL HINTS: SAFE SPACE

Your baby enjoys playing on the floor. This provides him with a sense of space and wide-open areas in which to crawl and explore. But being on the floor is a double-edged sword.

You might enjoy watching your baby playing on the floor and crawling around, but safety risks come with this type of play. You'll need to vacuum more frequently to remove small parts that may be potential choking hazards.

A blanket can help to cover up some small things that collect on floors. Carrying a blanket with you in the stroller or in your car might allow you to let the baby down to play when you're out without having to worry about what he's crawling on! But, he might try to make a quick getaway off the blanket.

Make a quick check of rooms for lightweight furniture that your baby could easily pull over when he's trying to stand up. You should also look for outlets and cover them with outlet covers. Cords that are dangerous should be placed out of reach or removed.

Play

Body parts are particularly fascinating to your baby. You can expand on the "Where is baby?" game by asking, "Where is baby's mouth?" Then show baby where his mouth is and where your mouth is too. You can do this for all of the body parts, but the parts on the head (eyes, ears, nose, and mouth) are the most common to start with for baby. Then you can add limbs, like legs and arms. From there you can break it down into smaller parts like fingers, toes, knees, elbows, and so on.

Once you have progressed to bigger body parts, think of the well-loved children's song "Head, Shoulders, Knees, and Toes." Try singing this with your baby for fun. You and your baby will enjoy the time together as well as the excitement of singing and playing around with new words. Don't be surprised if he wants to show everyone not only where his eyes are, but where their eyes are as well!

Facial features were meant to be named and tagged by baby. Just be careful when you play this game—you—might get your eyeballs poked and your nose popped before you know it!

WEEK 39

Eat

Bibs are certainly a good idea, although sometimes your baby does not agree. By this age, your baby might easily rip off simple Velcro bibs. Instead, you can use bibs that go over the head or that fasten behind the neck. While some have ties, the hook-and-fastener types work much better on babies who are on the move or are reluctant to leave a bib in place.

In theory, at least, bibs are meant to keep your baby a bit cleaner while she explores her food. Most times, however, small bibs are no match for the big messes older babies make when eating. Keep in mind how your baby eats when you're choosing a bib. Some bibs are very tiny, and work more as "drool" bibs. You can find larger bibs, including some bibs that are more smock-like, with small trays to catch spare food that falls. You can even buy a bib that completely covers your baby's arms—think of a shirt.

If your baby is hesitant to try a particular bib, consider alternatives. You can buy products that turn simple napkins into a bib. These are handy for travel, as you can dispose of the mess rather than wash bibs. You can also try the old T-shirt method: Just let your baby wear one of your old T-shirts while eating. This might work well particularly as your baby grows into toddlerhood. At that point, the boost of wearing mom or dad's T-shirt might be enough incentive to sell the idea! Never let your baby sleep in a bib. Even when your bib has a quick-release fastener, your baby can still choke.

HELPFUL HINTS: SAY NO TO TV

As your baby gets older, it can be increasingly tempting to allow her to watch television. The American Academy of Pediatrics states that babies under the age of two should not watch television. This means not only regular programming, but DVDs and other programs aimed for younger children.

The American Academy of Pediatrics takes a hard line on television and babies for a good reason. Studies have shown that infants who watch television develop language skills more slowly than their non-television watching counterparts. This is true even of television in the background. Try to limit your television time to when the baby is not awake or near you.

Affirmation for Month Nine

I enjoy every stage of my baby's development.

MONTH
9

Sleep

At this age, if your baby is in a crib, she is likely to be on the move. She will often crawl around the crib. If she can pull herself up, you might also find her standing at the rail. These are all normal behaviors as she explores her surroundings.

Don't be surprised if you put her down for a nap on one end of the crib only to find her completely turned around at the other end of the crib. Again, being sure you've checked the crib for safety measures is important, particularly as she becomes more mobile.

Play

Musical play is always fun for your baby. Consider making a small investment into baby-appropriate musical toys. Egg shakers and mini-pianos often are baby's favorites. These small toys allow your baby to shake and bang with the best of them.

You can help your baby by guiding him into rhythmic play. Place the shaker in your baby's hand and then gently help him to hold and shake the egg. You can do the same with the piano keys. Just remember, things might get a bit loud, because wildly shaking and banging also has its place in your baby's play!

These types of toys are sure to bring a smile to your baby's face. Just be sure that your baby is not playing with toys meant for older children. Those toys might have smaller parts that are dangerous for your baby.

Expose your child to music and musical instruments from an early age. Do not be dismayed by banging—baby is just exploring.

What to Watch For Explained

The **capability to pass objects from one hand to another** seems like it should be a simple task. It is a skill that most parents are not looking for in their child. This skill is at the heart of your baby's brain and body working together. Controlling one side and then the other is a very important skill. If this ability isn't developing, your pediatrician may recommend testing. Being ahead of the game and watching for it is optimum. Hand your baby a toy in their less-favored hand and see where it goes; chances are it will be the other hand.

Babbling with a change of tone means having a mock conversation. You may notice that your son or daughter will "talk" to a toy changing the intonation of their voice. You can hear a pattern of conversation. This is one of the reasons that it is so important to talk to your baby even right after birth, because learning to converse begins at this point.

The **ability to bear weight on legs alone** is beginning. You may only see this skill if your baby is cruising around holding onto the furniture, but some babies are beginning to take a few steps. Walking is not a skill that many babies have at this age, but your baby should be able to accept all of their weight on their legs. Your pediatrician will be looking for this skill during their well-baby visit.

Choking hazards and prevention begins at home, but needs to extend everywhere. You should look around the house and baby-proof. Also check any vehicle that your baby rides in. You may find bits of food or small toys that have been left or accidentally dropped into the car seat. Mealtime can be a time for choking hazards. This can be because we over estimate what foods our baby can eat well. Small, round objects or hard foods, are dangerous for babies at this age. This is true even if you are sitting right there or if your baby has teeth. If you want to feed your baby grapes, for example, divide them into quarters or smaller, and skin the grapes to make them easier to eat.

Crib safety is something that you may not have given a lot of thought to up to this point. If your baby has just moved to a crib, you may be more aware of the risks involved, but if your baby has been in a crib for a while, you may have become complacent. Ensure that your baby cannot climb out of the crib over toys, music boxes attached to the sides, or even the bumper pads, which are generally not thought to be a safe idea. Ensure that the crib is not near a window with blinds or near anything that dangles and could harm your baby. Check this monthly as your baby's skills change. Never underestimate your baby.

MONTH
9

MONTH TEN

Week 40–43

A Mind of His Own

✓ Checklist for Month Ten

- ☐ Decide about shoes for baby.
- ☐ Cope with a nursing strike.
- ☐ Wait for your baby's first words.
- ☐ Figure out how to use household items as toys.
- ☐ Change how you give your baby a bottle.
- ☐ Keep a check on your baby's mobility.

What to Watch For in the Tenth Month

- ☐ Reaction when you call baby's name
- ☐ Letting you know when he is happy or sad
- ☐ Ability to make multiple consonant sounds
- ☐ Understanding the meaning of "no"

Be Sure to:

☐ Let your baby practice feeding himself.

☐ Give your baby a cup of water with every meal in the high chair.

Baby Skills:

In the tenth month, your baby:

☐ Is probably crawling

☐ Might have teeth on top

☐ Might pull up

☐ Might try to take steps

☐ Might be cruising

☐ Will practice talking

☐ Can understand the word *no*

☐ Likes to put things in her mouth, including finger food

BABY DATA

Welcome to the tenth month. Your baby is likely to be very eager to move right now. You might also feel similarly, perhaps for different reasons. You might be anxious if you feel she is not mobile enough, and might even feel that her mobility is problematic. While nearly all levels of movement are normal at this age, if you are concerned you should talk to your pediatrician. If nothing else, your doctor can ease your mind and help you to see what to look for in terms of problems and normal ranges.

If your baby is still working on her top teeth, she might be unhappy and biting at everything because she is in pain. Offering cold foods and even a cold, wet washcloth can be helpful. As in months past, talk to your pediatrician about remedies before trying anything new. Remember, some pediatricians do not recommend over-the-counter numbing medications because of their ability to numb the back of the throat, making it easier for your baby to choke. Consider using a fingertip toothbrush to massage the area if your baby will let you.

Be mindful of the furniture this month. As your baby begins to move around, she might use furniture to pull herself up. While the big couch is not going to tip over, that unsteady table you've been meaning to get rid of for years will fall over, and the lamp will drop right on her head. The same goes for furniture with table skirts that come off—these are easy for your baby to pull down, which could cause her and your furniture harm. If you have lightweight furniture that you must keep out, such as bookshelves, night tables, and TVs, consider bolting them to the wall or tying them to a sturdier, adjacent piece of furniture. This way, they won't be dangerous.

Also watch for furniture corners! As your baby pulls up, she'll most likely be using tables to do so. Since she will still be unsteady on her feet, she's apt to take a lot of falls. Cover coffee and end tables with padding, if need be. Rubber protectors are made for other sharp corners, such as fireplace hearths.

DECIDE ABOUT SHOES FOR BABY

Baby shoes are really cute. The problem is, many families receive tons of shoes as gifts for a baby who doesn't touch the ground that often. It's even possible that as a young infant, your baby didn't like wearing shoes all that much! But as your baby starts to get down on the ground more, shoes become more of a necessity.

Nothing gets past eagle-eye these days. Your baby is watching and learning from everything you do.

MONTH TEN: Bringing Up Baby

Your three goals this month are simple:

- Learn about baby foot care.
- Watch for verbal changes, including babbling and words.
- Know how to handle a nursing strike.

Before you make a spontaneous purchase, first ask yourself some questions:

- Does your baby need the bottoms of his feet protected?
- Does your baby need the tops of his feet protected?
- Are you using the shoes for decoration or protection?
- Will the shoes allow him flexibility and mobility?

At this age, babies need shoes for lots of reasons. Protection can be a huge issue. Ask yourself what you are protecting your baby from: Perhaps it's the weather, or from someone stepping on his toes as he's learning to walk. Some believe that being barefoot also helps your baby learn to walk, because he is able to feel the floor and surface better, making his footing surer. Many pediatricians say that shoes are not needed until your baby is over one year of

MONTH
10

age. So perhaps the shoes are simply something you like, which is also a perfectly legitimate reason to have them.

As your baby starts to crawl, the tops of her socks will get really dirty. Sometimes they might snag on things on the floor. Soft shoes made of flexible leather can be the answer. They are easy to put on for you, but hard for baby to take off. These can be worn with or without socks. A crawling baby in thicker shoes might destroy the tops very quickly. Plus, it is cumbersome to crawl in heavy shoes!

You might want to consider shoes with more of a sole once your baby is walking well. You can choose a tennis shoe, a walking shoe, or even a dress shoe. Whichever the style, the bottoms should be nonskid to help your baby retain his grip on the floor when possible. Look for safety issues, like pieces of the shoe that come off and might

Socks and shoes will get dirty as baby learns to crawl and even as baby begins to step and walk. Feel free to take them off and let her go barefoot.

be swallowed. Also know that you'll have to retie lace-up shoes often, so consider alternatives such as Velcro or buckle shoes.

In the end, the decision to shoe or not to shoe is yours. There might be medical reasons to help you make your decision, so be sure to ask your pediatrician for advice. Just remember to let your baby be barefoot at least occasionally.

Mama Moment

Enjoying your baby is not hard to do these days. So many new things are happening developmentally for your baby, and it is all so much fun to watch. So it might surprise you if some people in your life have started to say, "I bet it's about time for another baby . . . ."

Remember, you're on your own timetable and no one else's. The physical strain of having a baby lasts for quite a while. Add to that the fact that you're probably enjoying being the mother of your little one right now, and you're probably not thinking ahead to another baby just yet. That's perfectly fine— there's no rush!

COPE WITH A NURSING STRIKE

Nursing strikes occur when your baby decides that she is not going to nurse for a while. This can be fairly frightening and worrisome for a new parent. But nursing strikes are not uncommon. If your baby is refusing to nurse at times, consider if the strike has a pattern. Does your baby nurse only in certain positions and not in others? Is she uncomfortable while nursing? It might be an ear infection. Teething issues can cause discomfort during nursing as well. Other issues, such as switching deodorant or soaps, or even being out of familiar surroundings or routine can cause nursing strikes. Sometimes they happen just because.

Partial nursing strikes at certain times during the day are also common at this age. Is your baby so excited about her newfound mobility and ability to explore that she forgets to nurse frequently during the day? If so, you might notice that she will make up for those episodes by cluster feeding more frequently at other times of day, such as when she first wakes up in the morning, around nap time, or before bedtime. Sometimes babies will nurse less one day, and then make up for it the next. All of these things are quite normal! Rarely does a nursing strike mean that breastfeeding has come to an end.

So what should you do about a strike? You can just try to wait it out, and when your baby does decide to nurse, simply be there to nurse her. Continue to offer nursing opportunities to her frequently, but don't force her or stress too much about it. Remember, under most normal circumstances, a baby will not starve herself! Some mothers suggest nursing or trying to nurse the baby when she is sleepy and less likely to resist. You can even try this while your baby is asleep—sometimes, if baby stirs during a nap, for instance, it can be a good opportunity. Since babies are easily distracted and sometimes find it hard to focus at this age, catching them at drowsy times like these can help to work around nursing strikes!

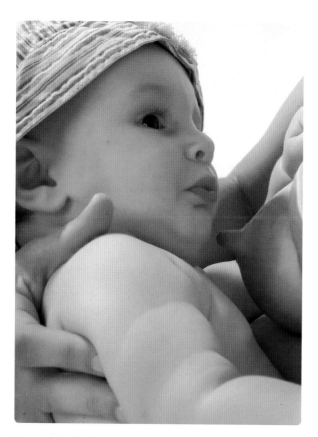

Let your baby decide when is best to nurse if you are having issues with nursing strikes. These can happen, but they typically resolve shortly. Be patient.

Some tips to get your baby to nurse include:

- Keep in close contact with her.
- Offer the breast frequently.
- Act like you don't care if she eats. (Getting too upset about it can make matters worse, as nursing is never easy for mother or baby when both are stressed out!)
- Try skin-to-skin contact when you can.

While your baby is striking, you will want to maintain your milk supply. You can do this by hand expressing or using a breast pump. This will also help you to stay comfortable.

Most nursing strikes only last a couple of days. You should call for medical or lactation support if you think an illness such as an ear infection is causing the nursing strike. You should also ask for help if the nursing strike continues for longer than a few days.

WAIT FOR YOUR BABY'S FIRST WORDS

If you are like most parents, you are anxiously awaiting your baby's first words. You have invested a lot of time and energy into helping your baby prepare to talk. You have been singing and reading to her and doing lots of other activities that encourage her to speak her mind. Now she's nearly ready.

Babbling was the first step. You would hear it in the back of the car, you would hear it from her bed. Now you are just waiting for her to make some sense of all those consonants and vowels. Most parents will hear the "da da da da" and "ma ma ma ma" sounds as words. At first these are probably not. But the praise you heap on your baby when she says it will help her learn to associate these sounds with the people involved. In fact, many parents miss the first words their baby tries to say. Your baby is not likely to say a word clearly and distinctly the first time she tries it. So you might spend days hearing her say "nur" or "nu" before you realize that she's asking to nurse, just as "duh" might be *dog* and "ba" might be *bottle*. It takes time to string all of the syllables together into a complete word.

Encourage her by acknowledging that you understand her words. Praise her and ask her to repeat herself. You will be rewarded with a huge smile, because babies love it when they realize you understand them. You'll probably hear the word again and again.

Some babies will begin to say their first words well before their first birthday. Other babies won't begin to try to say words until after their birthday. If you are concerned about your baby's speech, ask your pediatricians. They can do simple things like look at your baby's developmental history, review the medical records, and even consider a hearing test if there is concern.

As her first options, your baby is most likely to pick words that she uses every day, like *mama, dada, baby, nurse, bottle, dog,* and so on. Listen for her to call something the same thing over and over, even if it is not quite right. And don't forget to write it down in her baby book. Believe it or not, you will forget!

Hot Mama for Month Ten

Have your makeup colors redone to give yourself a fashion boost. Remember, makeup goes bad after a while. If you haven't done so in a long time, use this as a good excuse to get some new cosmetics! Don't worry if you don't have a lot of time day to day to do your makeup fully—some blush and a little lip gloss can go a long way toward helping you feel a bit more polished. Then you can pull out your entire makeup collection for special occasions.

USE HOUSEHOLD ITEMS AS TOYS

Baby toys are cute. But they can also be expensive and needless for the most part. Babies, when presented with a box of baby toys or a box of household items, will choose the household items the majority of the time. This might be because they see their parents using them and are trying to emulate them. Whatever the reasons, babies love household items such as:

- Measuring cups
- Small laundry baskets
- Pots and pans

MONTH
10

- Wooden spoons
- Boxes
- Old phones
- Old remote controls
- Empty food cartons (milk jugs, egg cartons, butter tubs, etc.)

This is not to say that you should give your baby anything and everything he wants. Allow him to keep a few items you have checked thoroughly for small parts, like the milk jug cap, splinters, and so on. Then let him have at the toys at playtime.

A bowl and a spoon are near-perfect toys. You can pretend to cook like dad, bang a drum, or invent any number of creative ideas.

Think of the great band you can have with a couple of wooden spoons, an egg carton, and a milk jug! Your baby will have a blast.

Some parents keep these types of toys in a kitchen cabinet for baby. Your baby could then play with them while you are in the kitchen cooking or cleaning up. The noise helps you focus on where baby is and what he is doing, which is much more of an issue now that he is mobile.

Don't throw away your baby's toys just yet. There is certainly a time and place for well-tested and loved toys. These other items are just another way to entertain your baby.

CHANGE HOW YOU GIVE YOUR BABY A BOTTLE

As your baby gets older, you will need to begin to think about weaning him from the bottle. This is a slow process and needs to begin before his first birthday. This is when the American Academy of Pediatrics and other professionals recommend that your baby stop taking a bottle. This is for several reasons including the decreased need for sucking. Babies of this age have developed other ways to get nutrition into their bodies. And bottles do cause ear and tooth issues, although no-spill sippy cups can aggravate ear issues as well.

To simply show up on your baby's first birthday and not give a bottle can create a big problem, not to mention prompt your baby to throw a huge fit. Start changing your baby's bottle routine well before the year is out. The first step is to find a cup that your baby likes.

All sorts of sippy cups and regular cups are available. Sippy cups are usually nonspill or low-spill to help prevent your baby from making a mess when the cup inevitably falls or gets turned upside down. Some of these cups work with a valve that blocks the liquid from coming out. Be sure to check with your pediatrician about whether or not these are okay for your baby. Some babies with frequent ear issues can have trouble with the vacuum these valves create. Other sippy cups are designed with narrow spouts or wells that make it more difficult for liquid to escape. And then some parents go straight to a nonbreakable cup.

To start, give your baby a cup to play with and try out when she is not thirsty. Use whatever you would normally put in a bottle, be that breast milk, water, juice, or formula. Start with a tiny amount to prevent wastage and spillage.

TIP Beware of BPA

If you are concerned about bisphenol-A (BPA), a chemical that can leach into your sippy cups if used, be sure to check your sippy cups to ensure that they are BPA free. BPA is thought to mimic estrogen and cause potential reproductive issues, such as early breast development, as well as learning disabilities, diabetes, and more.

Once your baby is comfortable with the cup, replace one daytime bottle feeding with the cup. If you work during the day, this drink from the cup might happen during day care hours. Do not put your baby to bed with a cup or a baby bottle. Eventually work your way up to replacing all daytime bottles with a cup. Remember, your baby gets comfort from sucking. So giving up the bottle is about more than just food and nourishment. This is a slow process, and you should follow your baby's lead.

MONTH
10

Be sure the plastics used in your baby's dishes and cups are safe. This is important, because these are what actually go into your baby's mouth.

CHECK ON YOUR BABY'S MOBILITY

Your baby probably loves his newfound mobility. The ability to get places without having to be carried is certainly a wonderful freedom. The problem is that all of this mobility presents a whole new host of issues for parents. These issues center mainly on safety.

As your baby becomes mobile, continue to scan your home and places that your baby frequents for danger spots. These could be stairs, staircase and chair rails, lightweight furniture that tips over easily, or other items that might come crashing down on your baby's head. Where possible, gate off dangerous areas, like the tops and bottoms of the stairs. Also check out the spaces between the guardrails on walkways: Are they large enough for baby's head or body to fit through? If yes, get a cover designed to protect baby from climbing through or getting his head stuck.

While your baby is down on the ground and mobile, watch closely. Before you know it, he will crawl into the other room to find a toy or to follow the family pet. That means he is in danger of getting into something he shouldn't get into, or that he could fall or pull something over on himself.

To your baby every object looks like a good one to pull up on, be that the couch, coffee table, garbage can, or floor lamp. He has no ability to judge the strength of an item to hold his weight. This can send him and the object crashing to the ground.

If you can't watch your baby, do not leave him unattended. Consider placing him in the high chair while you cook or in a play yard when you are getting dressed. This will keep him safe while you are occupied, which is a part of life.

Stairs are particularly dangerous for your little one. Be sure to place gates at the top and bottom of staircases in your home, to be sure she does not explore stair climbing when you are not there to watch her.

WEEK 40

Eat

Your baby will be ready to eat about five or six meals per day at this age. These meals will be a combination of solids and breast milk or infant formula. Most families also end the day with a nursing session or with a baby bottle. You will also want to add in snacks. These can be either solids or liquids.

This is a guideline. You and your baby might be more comfortable with more liquid feedings, and that is fine as well. The goal is simply to allow your baby to get the nutrition needed, in whatever way works best for your individual baby. What is also important at this stage is encouraging your baby to develop her new abilities to chew and use the pincer grasp to pick up smaller bits of food like smashed banana, sweet potato, and so on.

If you are using baby food in jars, you might have moved from the first-stage foods made for brand-new solid food eaters to the second- or third-stage jars. The only real difference in these foods is the consistency—they are chunkier. If you make your own baby food, you are probably doing less pureeing and more chopping. At this age, babies are actually quite capable of eating a variety of foods straight off the family dinner table, as long as bites are cut up quite small to prevent choking.

Play

Your baby is learning to clap and love it! You might find she loves to watch herself clap and watch others clap for her. This is perfectly normal and age appropriate.

You can help her by playing clapping games with her. Patty-cake is probably the most famous clapping game. You can sing the song with the usual words, or you can switch up the words and invent new rhymes.

Babies will love to grab items that are sturdy and close to their height. Walking between these items is called cruising.

MONTH
10

HELPFUL HINTS: PRACTICE MAKES PERFECT

Your baby might be trying to stand up all the time now. No matter how you try to make her sit down or place her in any other position, she might straighten her legs and refuse. This is simply her way of exercising her legs and preparing to walk.

You might be concerned about her putting weight on her legs, but if she's doing the standing, she is ready for the weight. Remember to follow her lead on how long she wants to stand. The bad news is that your baby still does not yet know how to sit down gracefully. So she either falls over or collapses when she is done standing. This can lead to bumps and bruises, so be careful.

It is not as much of problem if you are holding her hands and she is standing on your lap. But if your baby is standing up and holding on to a toy or piece of furniture, she can actually hurt herself on sharp corners or edges. Keep this in mind when letting her stand, and watch carefully.

Consider playing "Itsy-Bitsy Spider" as well. Simply take your baby's hands and clap them together, as you recite this nursery rhyme. Your baby is sure to squeal and giggle with glee.

Another simple yet fun activity is to count your baby's fingers and toes. You can just smile as you grab each individual digit and say something like, "Lilah has one toe! One, one toe!" Move to the next toe and repeat. This game starts to introduce your baby to the concept of counting, while also getting in some fun playtime with you.

Sleep

Most babies this age need nine to eleven hours of sleep at night, plus two naps during the day. Sometimes these naps are each an hour or two. Other babies choose to have one long nap and one short nap during the day.

Is daytime napping the problem with nighttime sleep issues? Too much as well as too little sleep at noon can be problematic.

Naps might actually be more of an issue for you during this month than nighttime sleep. For example, your baby's short nap might happen in the car while you are running errands or picking up other kids from school. This can be disheartening because you were probably hoping to use that thirty minutes to do something constructive, such as paying bills or taking a shower. As baby gets older and more active, a few quiet, free minutes of sleep during the day mean a lot to parents!

If this is happening, you can gently mold the timing of a nap without causing a lot of trouble. For instance, if you have to leave at 3:00 p.m. to go get kids, you can slowly pull that nap back to 2 or even 2:15 p.m. Do this by trying to give your baby a nap fifteen minutes sooner each day. So on the first day, you would put your baby down at 2:45 p.m. In a few days, nap would begin at 2:30 p.m. Now these naps might be shorter or get a continuance in the car while you are in the process of trying to move them back. But it will still eventually give you your thirty minutes back, even if all you want is a nap yourself!

Affirmation for Month Ten

My baby is unique and has an individual personality.

WEEK 41

Eat

You might find your baby really likes to eat—when you sit him in his high chair and serve something, he cleans his plate and asks for more. More, more, more, he signs!

Some babies have big appetites, but few babies will overeat if allowed to eat to their will. Look at it in terms of spreading the calories around. A smaller lunch or snack might mean a bigger dinner. Your baby might also be making up for burning a lot of

Your baby is approaching the age when you can experiment with new finger foods. Just be present to make sure they can handle new textures and have enough teeth to chew properly.

MONTH
10

energy by crawling. If the food is healthy and his appetite is good, let him eat as much as he wants; he will stop when he feels full.

You might see your baby do this often or just occasionally. This is not typically an issue with weight. If you are concerned, your pediatrician can show you your baby's growth curve to look for problems or other issues. Most of the time, a hungry baby just loves food and needs lots of calories for crawling and playing.

Sleep

If your baby is up at night and needs help going back to sleep, you are probably tired in the mornings and might even be cranky at night. If this has become a habit and your previous efforts to encourage your baby to sleep better at night have not worked, it is time for a change.

Consider sending in the reinforcements. This means you can let dad or your partner go in for a change. This is not a punishment for your baby or for your partner. It might simply be that your baby is too used to your presence and "knows the drill," so to speak. By sending in a fresh face, it is also a signal to your baby that something is different.

You might or might not get different results. But sharing this side of baby duty might help you and your partner feel a bit more calm about those wakeful moments when neither of you is forced to deal with all of them.

You might also play with your bedtime routine. Perhaps your baby would like to listen to some music at bedtime. This can be one very nice way

to calm down. You can also consider adding music in her room for the night. Some infant/child music players are available. Some parents just set up the mp3 player, hit repeat, and let the music play all night in an attempt to keep their baby sleeping. Or if their baby wakes up, the music might help with self-soothing.

The biggest thing is to remember that you will not solve any sleep problem in one night. You might not even solve your issue in a week. Go at the pace that seems right for you and your baby.

Play

Whether your baby can move a little bit or a lot at this point, he is taking full advantage of mobility! Help your baby learn to build his muscles by encouraging his movements and giving him new experiences.

Remember to let him crawl on various surfaces, such as grass, carpet, hardwood floors, and so on. You can also help your baby by building mini-obstacle courses in your home.

Think about setting up things like small pillows or folded blankets, soft toys, the piano bench, and various other things that he has to navigate around. This can mean crawling over, under, or even through things. These are fun activities to encourage your baby to move and think. He will come to the toy and have to decide, "Do I go over it? Do I go around it?" These small steps will help him to develop his analytical thinking skills as he gets older, even though these might seem like very basic thought processes at this point.

If you decide to build a baby obstacle course, please remember to do so safely. Do not choose anything that would be dangerous for baby, including things with long cords or items that could entrap your baby. You should also do this only when you are with your baby—never leave him alone.

Crawling for play is hard work but your baby is up to the challenge. The more things he tries at this point, the sturdier he will be later.

WEEK 42

Eat

When bottle-feeding your baby, remember a few simple rules:

- Never let your baby lie down with a bottle.
- Do not prop a baby's bottle

Bottle-feeding your baby still requires attention, even as she gets older. As with any feeding method, your baby benefits more from switching sides. Be sure to remember to switch from one side to the other rather than using your dominant hand only.

Hold your baby and snuggle and comfort him while he is eating from a bottle. Your baby still needs that snuggle time with you. If your baby is feeling active and wants to get down to play around, be sure to let him; just remove the bottle. He will have to make a choice—eat or play.

Sleep

Are you upset by your baby's sleep issues? Do you know why? Any chance that it's everyone else telling you what your baby should be doing? Guess what: If it's not bothering you, it's probably not a real issue for anyone else.

Consider how you feel about the way your baby sleeps. Are you and your family doing okay with the way things are going? If the answer is yes, then you should be fine. Ignore your friends and family and their advice. When it is offered, just smile and say, "Thanks." Don't offer too much information, because the more you say, the more others might be tempted to try to tell you what you should do.

MONTH
10

HELPFUL HINTS: BE REASSURED

Sometimes you might worry that your baby is not developing normally, or at least not at the same pace as other babies you know. This can be stressful. If you have concerns, the first thing you should do is make a list of what your baby can do, even if he has only done it once. Then make up a list of questions and concerns you have about your baby's development. This should also include a list of things you think your baby should be doing at this point.

Once you have compiled all of this, make an appointment to see your pediatrician. Do so as soon as you become worried. It is difficult to add these sorts of discussions to a well-child visit in some pediatric practices. Either way, it should not wait. Developmental concerns can be very serious. If your baby is delayed in some area, early intervention gives him the best chance at a full recovery. It also helps to save you from worry.

At a visit of this sort, your pediatrician will listen to your concerns, and then observe your baby. This observation might include normal screenings like you would see at a well-baby checkup. It might also include other testing, like a hearing screen, visits with other health professionals, or observation logs you and other care providers maintain.

If your intuition is telling you that something is not right, you should seek help. Chances are you are picking up on something, even if someone else can't see it immediately. If your pediatrician does not find anything, ask for a second opinion. You might be asked to watch more closely or to follow up in a certain period of time. If you are not satisfied with the answer you receive, do not hesitate to say so.

Eventually your baby will sleep without needing you in the middle of the night. It might seem like these night wakings will never end, especially when you are cranky from being awakened. But remember, your baby will not always need to eat in the late-night hours. You will get sleep again. In the meantime, do what is best for your family.

Play

If you and your family are avid swimmers, you might consider starting swimming lessons for your baby. This is usually best done in a class setting. Here they will teach you the best way to get your baby used to the water. Classes will also include information on infant safety and use of items like life jackets.

There are many baby and toddler swim classes. Consider taking your baby to one. It's great fun for you as well as your baby.

If your family spends time near natural water, like lakes or rivers, you will want to invest not only in swim lessons but in safety equipment as well. This can help prevent disasters. Talk to your pediatrician before taking your baby in lake or river water. Your baby still has an immature immune system and could get ill from contaminated water.

WEEK 43

Eat

If your baby is eating table food, do not be too worried about spices and flavors. In the United States, parents spend a lot of time trying to make baby food bland, thinking that babies will enjoy it more. The truth is, your baby has a very sensitive palate and can thoroughly enjoy the different tastes of foods, the very same ones that you do.

Hold the hot sauce, though—don't go overboard and drown your child with wild spices that you wouldn't eat yourself. Just be reasonable. Garlic isn't going to hurt your baby. Many babies love spicy foods or foods that their parents wouldn't imagine they'd ever eat. Babies also seem to love tastes of foods that you ate while pregnant or nursing—they are familiar to them.

Think about what a great food hummus would be for a baby. By considering new food, you also make feeding your baby easier. Just watch for hidden ingredients, particularly when

MONTH
10

purchasing food out of your home, in case they contain foods baby should not eat yet, such as eggs, milk, and other dairy. Let your baby's taste buds guide you!

Sleep

Now that you are closing in on your baby's first year, he or she might still be eating at night. For the vast majority of babies, this is not medically or nutritionally necessary. However, in some cases it is necessary, and if you have questions about whether or not your baby falls into this category, be sure to ask your pediatrician.

So the question comes, when and how do you night wean? When you night wean is a personal matter. If your baby's middle-of-the-night eating is not bothersome to you, then it is not a problem, as long as you are following safety precautions when using baby bottles. This is namely not letting your baby fall asleep with a bottle or sleep in the crib with a bottle.

Nighttime nursing does not have the same problems as using baby bottles in cribs. Babies who nurse in bed at night have a very different set of circumstances than their bottle-feeding counterparts. When a breastfed baby stops nursing, the milk stops flowing. Breast milk, because of the anatomy, is also not collecting in the baby's mouth because it enters the mouth very far back near the throat, not in the front where it passes all the teeth.

If you have decided that you and your baby are ready for night weaning, determine how you would like to move forward. You can go the cold turkey route and just stop. Most parents report that this is the more painful way to go, and involves lots of crying on everyone's part. It can be effective for many families, sometimes even after a few nights. Also be sure to feed the baby right before bed. And even if you go cold turkey with night weaning, be sure to be there to comfort your baby in a different way if he wakes up for food in the middle of the night. Patting can work really well to help him go back to sleep. If he already has a pacifier or sucks his thumb, you might encourage this in place of eating as well, but do not introduce those habits at this point if they are not already being used as a comfort method.

The key is to comfort and soothe your baby without food and without stimulating him into believing that it is time to wake up. Let this principle guide what you are doing for your baby in the middle of the night. Patting, humming, shhhing, and snuggling are all great ways to comfort your baby. Sometimes it can be better if the person who was feeding him in the middle of the night is not involved in the comforting, if possible.

If your baby is nursing in the middle of the night, you can try moving places to be further away from your baby. So if your baby sleeps right next to you, put your husband in between you and the

HELPFUL HINTS: PICK-UP GAME

Your baby is beginning to understand the idea of cause and effect. At one point, he had no idea why things happened—food appeared, lights came on, and life went on seamlessly. Now that your baby is aware of the details of his surroundings, he is beginning to understand that if you do one thing, something else happens.

If they drop something from the high chair, it will fall and someone will pick it up. Your baby is learning that he has some say in the matter as well—namely the reaction that you will pick up his toy or food. This recognition gives him great pride and joy. And so the accidental dropping stops, and intentional dropping begins.

This "game" is also known as "Pick it up, Mommy." You and your baby are the only ones who can determine how long or if this game is played. Some parents really dislike the idea, while others think it is fun. It is your call.

The good news is that this simple understanding of cause and effect spreads much further. Your baby began with learning that if he called, you would come. Now he knows that if it's morning, you will wake up to get him, then comes breakfast, and so on. This is a whole new idea in his life.

baby. Sometimes this works on the out-of-sight, out-of-mind principle. Another option is to wear less nursing-friendly nightclothes.

If your baby is eating more than once in the middle of the night, this process might take longer.

You should try removing one feeding at a time in the beginning. Then feed your baby as close to bedtime as possible and even consider waking up slightly earlier if needed to help reduce the nighttime feedings.

MONTH
10

Play

Outdoor playgrounds can be a lot of fun for the whole family, and babies this age begin to love the idea of playing at the playground. The problem is that many playgrounds are not baby friendly. This does not mean that you can't play at all, but it does give you more to watch for when your baby is playing. Consider finding a baby-friendly playground, even if you have to travel further to use it.

Playing outside is loads of fun for your baby, but don't let it be a source of stress for you. Be sure to choose age-appropriate playgrounds for your baby, and go at nonpeak play times.

If you are making do with what is in your neighborhood, be sure to give it the once-over for safety issues. Do this every single time you go to the playground. If you let your baby crawl on bridges and the like, be sure small fingers cannot get pinched in between slats or in corners. Be sure that you carry your baby on slides and swings that are not designed for her.

Baby-friendly playgrounds can vary widely. Some may have a simple baby swing among the regular swings. Some playgrounds have a small climbing structure meant for little ones. This might or might not have small slides safe for your toddler. Other things to look for include:

- Fenced-in area
- Softer surfaces such as padding or mulch
- Proximity to bathrooms and changing surfaces
- Access for older children
- Proximity to other playgrounds

Keep your baby safe by watching for older children at playgrounds. You might even have to consider leaving if older children insist on playing on structures meant for babies and toddlers, and their parents will not enforce the rules. Baby and toddler playgrounds are not safe when older children are around.

What to Watch For Explained

Does your baby **react when you call her name?** At this point, most babies know their name when you call it. Be sure you say it often. It's hard for some parents to remember this, but many parents fall into the habit of calling their baby by a nickname or simply calling them "baby." Be sure that you are addressing your baby by name. If your baby isn't responding to her name, try to increase the number of times you use it. If that doesn't seem to help, discuss it with your health care provider.

Letting you know when he is happy or sad is an idea that your baby is getting very good at these days. You may notice facial expressions and even large body movements that say happy and sad. There are other more subtle emotions that your baby is learning, as well. It's often hard to wrap a young mind around them. This may result in your baby being sad instead of scared or happy. These emotions will come with time.

The **ability to make multiple consonant sounds** is a task you are probably hearing a lot of this month. Your baby may sit, play with toys, and have a verbal discussion with them.

These tend to be consonants repeated over and over. So you might get a lot of verbal play with the sounds of *b*, *p*, and *m* to start. This is an important verbal milestone. Try to encourage it by repeating the vocalizations that your baby is making. This will thrill him.

Understanding the meaning of "no" is a concept that we are anxious for our baby to establish for their own safety and protection. The problem is that at first you say "no" and your baby may cry. They typically do not like being told "no." This simply isn't in their plan. The trick is that once they get really good at understanding "no," they turn the tables and quickly start telling others "no." "No" to eating their dinner. "No" to taking a bath. Sometimes it's hard not to laugh at a very serious baby telling you that dinner is not happening. How you handle these early tests of will is decidedly at the core of your parenting philosophies.

MONTH
10

MONTH ELEVEN

Week 44–47

Enjoy Your Baby

✓ Checklist for Month Eleven

- ☐ Learn how to praise your baby.
- ☐ Teach empathy.
- ☐ Avoid food battles.
- ☐ Cope with unusual nursing behavior.
- ☐ Understand how comfort items work for your family
- ☐ Be prepared for a baby meltdown.

What to Watch For in the Eleventh Month

- ☐ The joy of bouncing to music
- ☐ Sleep problems
- ☐ Progress with self-feeding
- ☐ Ability to bear full weight on legs or stand alone
- ☐ Able to play alone

Be Sure to:

- ☐ Let your baby play with a spoon during feeding times.
- ☐ Make your baby's twelve-month appointment.
- ☐ Let your baby eat at the table with you.

Baby Skills:

In the eleventh month, your baby:

- ☐ Sits well
- ☐ Might stack toys
- ☐ Might have teeth on top
- ☐ Might pull up
- ☐ Crawls
- ☐ Can make silly noises, like "raspberries"
- ☐ Puts everything in his mouth
- ☐ Might take first steps

BABY DATA

Having fun is a good thing for baby! Now that he has more control over his body and his movements, he has more opportunities to play. He can stack toys on top of each other—just give him something stackable, like blocks or books. But don't be surprised if he likes knocking the toys back down more than stacking them!

You might see him take first steps this month, but don't worry if he's not there yet. Some babies do not walk until they are eighteen months old. He will find other ways to be mobile.

Your baby still loves to eat everything. This continues to include food items as well as nonfood items. Watch what is in your baby's immediate vicinity, as it will be in his mouth if he can grab it. While he wants to play alone, he still needs supervision.

Teeth might be an issue this month, which could mean some nighttime waking and some clinginess during the day. All the same rules apply, so you should be well prepared by now.

LEARN HOW TO PRAISE YOUR BABY

Being praised is something we all like. Your baby is tickled when you praise her. Her face lights up and she smiles. She knows that you are happy, and that it is related to her.

You praise your baby by giving her a smile when she smiles at you. You greet her positively when she wakes up. You tell her you like that she's eaten her food. This type of praise comes naturally.

To be effective, consider that praise should be:

- Immediate, when possible
- Truthful
- Specific

When you are overly praiseful, it can lose its meaning and effectiveness. By keeping the above three rules in your mind, you can prevent that from happening. Think about it this way: Would you really go on and on about how your child was the best crawler in the world? Or would a simple "good job!" suffice?

MONTH ELEVEN: Bringing Up Baby

Your three goals this month are simple:

- Learn the benefits of baby praise.
- Watch for food battles.
- Know what your philosophy is on comfort items.

Encouraging your baby to walk is only natural. She will be so excited to see you become enthusiastic that she might fall when clapping or laughing back at you.

MONTH
11

You can praise your baby by using positive phrases, like "Good job!" You can also praise her physically by smiling and giving physical attention like hugs and pats on the back. Your time and attention is the best reward your baby can have. Avoid using food, toys, and other bribes for your baby. This sets a bad example for later in life.

TEACH EMPATHY

Empathy is an important quality that everyone should have. Teaching it from the beginning of your baby's life gives her a head start. It is important to remember that empathy is not a one-time lesson, but rather many lessons spread over a lifetime.

The very foundations of teaching your baby empathy help him to recognize how other people are feeling. But before he can do that, your baby must first be able to put words and thoughts toward that feeling. To do this, you must teach him what different emotions are, including:

- Happy
- Sad
- Angry
- Scared

Start slowly. When you see that your baby is happy, say so. "I see you're happy today! I love your smile!" When you say this, you are defining the emotion with a word, "happy," and connecting it with the physical descriptor, "smile." Do the same as you see other emotions from your baby.

From here, start to point out emotions in others close to your baby, including yourself. Come home, pick your baby up, and tell him, "Mommy is sad. She had a hard day at work today."

This sounds simplistic, and to some extent basic, but it is just the start of a lifelong skill. Being able to tell what others are feeling is the first step toward understanding that feeling, offering support and help, and sharing the joys.

Being kind is the best way to teach kindness. Be the person you want your child to be.

Hot Mama for Month Eleven

When dressing up, wear the little black dress only if you want to. Being a mom might make you feel like livening up the place a bit. Be bold and go for a fashion statement!

AVOID FOOD BATTLES

Mealtimes should be pleasant affairs that are meant to nourish your baby's body. Sometimes babies can have their own ideas about what they want and don't want. This can be tiresome for you and your family.

If your baby is refusing to eat solids, do not panic. Think about common reasons why that might be happening. Is your baby feeling healthy? Is your baby teething? Does your baby have a stuffy nose? Any changes in your baby's eating habits can usually be attributed to one of these issues.

When we don't feel well, we tend not to eat well. If your baby is ill, you might notice that he prefers to nurse or drink from a baby bottle. This can be because his stomach is upset or because he needs comfort as well as nourishment.

You might also notice specific changes in eating behaviors when your baby isn't feeling well. For example, if you baby has an earache or sore throat, he might not want to lie down to nurse.

Feeding your baby when he is happy is usually a better way to avoid food problems than to waiting until it's too late.

When babies are teething, their mouths hurt. You might find that other than nursing or a baby bottle, your baby wants only cold foods or hard foods that require biting down. This feels good on her sore gums.

You might be surprised that a stuffy nose can cause a baby to reject once-loved foods quickly. The truth of the matter is that much of what we think about eating and enjoying food is derived from our sense of smell. This means that if we like a food, we know so originally by the smell, before we even taste it. So when a baby has a stuffy nose, he cannot taste as well.

Remember to feed your baby what he will eat. Nurse him to comfort and to keep him hydrated. The illness or teething will pass. Simply offer your baby his food and move on. If your baby does not seem to be feeling better in a reasonable amount of time given his ailment, talk to your pediatrician. Also call your pediatrician if your baby shows signs of dehydration (see page 218 for more details).

COPE WITH UNUSUAL NURSING BEHAVIORS

Nursing your baby might sometimes feel like a circus because babies often want to nurse in a variety of odd positions at this age. This can be because your baby is teething or because she is testing out her new physical skills. You might be nursing when suddenly she is standing up on your lap. Your baby might try to dance or wiggle during the entire nursing session. None of this is unusual, although it might seem crazy to mommy when it happens!

MONTH
11

These changes in position should not make your nipples sore or in any way uncomfortable. (If baby is twisting and turning so much that it's painful, then say "no" firmly and cut the nursing session short. Try again later when he calms down.) If you are in public, these antics might make it harder to nurse discreetly. A blanket or nursing cover might help.

You might be able to predict when your baby will nurse in creative positions. For example, your baby might only nurse this way in the mornings or after lunch. Some babies will only dance or move around when they are sleepy. Once you can predict the behavior, you can try to plan ahead and nurse in a more private location.

If baby is prone to keeping your breast uncovered while you nurse, you can simply insist your shirt stays down. This might be something you revisit, particularly when your baby is sleepy.

You might also notice your baby is once again distracted and is looking away a lot while nursing. She might be nursing and then look off to see what's going on, only to latch right back on. This is also normal. You can encourage your baby by ending the feeding for a bit if she refuses to eat and would rather play. This can be a battle of the wills, but your baby will figure that you mean business if you are consistent.

If your baby is teething, you might notice that she holds her head at an odd angle when nursing. The temporary change usually ceases once the new tooth has broken through. Sometimes odd latches due to teething can increase the chances of some nipple tenderness. If you feel like your baby is nursing in such a manner, do your best to encourage better latch and positioning.

You might even have a return to the nip and nap of earlier baby days. This often happens when your baby has played a lot and is tired from all of that work. Your baby might latch on and then fall asleep, then wakes up. The cycle repeats itself. If you really need your baby to eat, you can make sure that you catch baby to nurse before things go this far. If not, simply encourage a nap instead of a meal.

FIGURE OUT HOW COMFORT ITEMS WORK FOR YOUR FAMILY

Your baby might become attached to a comforting object at this point. She might drag it around and sleep with it, play with it, and eat with it. She might even refuse to go anywhere without it. Most babies choose a blanket or a special soft toy.

If your baby has trouble sleeping without a favorite object, you might need to ensure you have more than one on hand in case you lose his favorite and then have one very cranky baby.

If you find that your child has developed an affinity for an object, buy another one. Having a spare is always a good thing when it is time to wash the item or if it were to become lost. The best advice is to keep both items in play at the same time; this way, should your baby lose her favorite stuffed animal, you aren't pulling out a perfect, brand-new animal that will be glaringly different.

Ensure that your baby has chosen something safe as a special comfort toy. Watch for buttons or small pieces. Routinely check to see that your baby's special toy is not falling apart or becoming frayed to the point of being dangerous.

This attachment to a special item is normal. It is something your baby will do as she's learning to detach from you. Most kids carry this object as a way to get through these first couple of years.

BE PREPARED FOR A BABY MELTDOWN

Your baby will inevitably have meltdowns. It is completely normal and natural. Depending on your baby and your baby's personality, her meltdown can look very different from another baby's meltdown. A baby meltdown can include:

- Crying uncontrollably
- Hitting
- Biting
- Not wanting to play
- Stiffening the body
- Lying on the floor
- Pulling away

Babies have meltdowns for many reasons, but mainly because their needs are not being met. Your baby is most likely to exhibit these negative behaviors when he is tired, unable to communicate, overstimulated, hungry, or otherwise not satisfied. It is much less likely to happen because he simply wants something like a toy that is not being given to him. This type of meltdown or temper tantrum will come as your child is older.

MONTH
11

To prevent your baby from entering meltdown mode, figure out what his most-likely triggers are. If you know that this will occur when tired, be sure to give him a nap before he gets to that point. If being hungry triggers your baby's crying, bring a snack for trips away from home. Being prepared can really decrease the number of meltdowns your baby has and how many you have to deal with.

WEEK 44

Eat

During this month you will not see drastic differences in your baby's food intake. Most babies will remain stable in these later months of the first year. This is particularly true of the quantity of food and drink they consume.

Babies melt down. It's a fact of life. Try to keep your cool when it happens, as it will be easier to calm your baby if you stay calm.

What can and will change are which foods you give to your baby and what consistency they are when you feed them. If your baby is still eating pureed foods, consider chunky food as your baby prepares for table foods.

If your baby is eating table foods, continue to add new foods. Simply be aware of the dangers of adding new foods and watch for allergic reactions.

You can continue to keep a food journal if it is beneficial to you. It is also a good idea to continue the journal if you have found more than a food or two that your baby has a reaction to. Food journals are good communication tool for when you see your pediatrician at the one-year well-baby check.

Sleep

Some babies have been perfectly happy sleeping in their cribs or in your bed, and all of a sudden they want to do something totally different.

You might find that your baby sleeps well for naps in the crib, but not at bedtime. Or perhaps your baby no longer wishes to sleep with you in your bed. Sleeping poorly, fussing at bedtime, and not falling asleep as easily as before can be signs that your baby wants a change of nighttime place.

If you are seeing these behaviors, you can certainly try to overcome the issue by making a change that suits your family. For example, take your baby who once preferred your bed and try him out in the crib or portable crib for a few nights. Or try to see if your baby who once slept in the crib contentedly now needs more nighttime snuggles.

Mama Moment

Are you still wearing sweatpants or pajama bottoms every day to go to the grocery store? If the answer is yes, you need some help. Consider going to a larger department store and asking about a personal shopper. Do not be dissuaded that you are not the weight you want to be or that your body is different now that you are a mother; simply work on looking great. This will help you to feel better about life in general.

Either way, if medical issues are not causing nighttime sleep issues and naps generally go well, look at the nighttime routine. What's different? What could be easily changed? What seems to make baby happy? Do we all get sleep? Remember, the right answer is the one that is safe and fits your family.

Play

You and your baby have grown to really enjoy playing. You might have a routine of games that you play with your baby. But there is a secret about being a good parent—sometimes your baby needs to play alone.

MONTH
11

Now, this alone time doesn't have to be for long and it doesn't even have to occur every day. But by letting her play alone now, you are helping your baby learn to entertain herself. Later, this might prevent a few hundred rounds of "I'm bored!"

Playing alone is not difficult, and you should not be far away. Provide your baby with a safe place to play, perhaps in her portable crib, in her high chair, or on a clean section of the floor. Give her a few age-appropriate toys. Then back away, but not too far away. Be close enough so that you can watch her to ensure she is not in any danger, but not close enough to readily engage in her activities.

As you have backed away, listen to your baby. Listen to the sounds that she makes. Watch her play on her own, and see the ingenuity that can come of it. Realize that she is learning by leaps and bounds, because you have given her the freedom. Do not be overeager to step in if she cries. She may express upset or frustration, but give her time to work it out for herself.

TIP

Help! I Can't Get Down

Sometimes your baby might cry because she is stuck in the standing position. Once a baby learns to get up, the skill for bending her knees to get down comes later. This leaves her unable to get anywhere until you come to the rescue.

WEEK 45

Eat

You might find that your baby is still not interested in solid foods. This is not very common, but it does happen. As long as your baby is receiving adequate amounts of breast milk (which is quite attainable for most mothers) or infant formula, you do not have a nutritional issue.

Talk to your pediatrician about what might be causing the refusal of solid foods. Sometimes it is a sensory issue that can be helped with therapy. It can often simply be your baby's preference, and they might need some coaxing to eat solid foods.

The first rule is not to panic. If your baby is eating liquids and growing well, there is typically not a problem. Your pediatrician and other therapists can help you figure out if you need help or just patience to resolve this issue.

Your baby is still not used to a variety of foods. This is typically not a problem, but if you are concerned about him becoming a picky eater, talk to your pediatrician.

HELPFUL HINTS: CARRY ON

If you are a fan of baby carriers, you might notice you need to make a change. Sometimes, as your baby grows, your original baby carrier is no longer adequate for your needs. This can be because it has become unsafe for your baby or because it has become uncomfortable for you, your partner, or your baby.

Should this be the case, you might want to look into a different type of carrier. It could be that a new carrier will solve your problem. For example, if you have been using a front carrier, a back-based infant/toddler carrier may be perfect for your family.

Sometimes your baby carrier is designed to go to a higher weight, but the specific hold that you are using is not working. If this is the case, look at the manual or go online for more advice on specific types of holds that you can use with an older baby who is quickly becoming a toddler. Some of the hip, side, and back holds are perfect for babies who are transitioning. They are also very comfortable for parents, as they accommodate the growing weight of a baby as well as the way the baby can move at this point

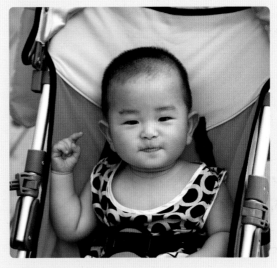

Try a stroller for walks and shopping. It's convenient for you and it gives your baby a whole new view of the world around her.

Some babies also decide that they do not want to be in slings or baby carriers at all. They want to use their newfound motor skills to get down from the carrier. If this is the case, perhaps it is time to retire the baby carrier. A stroller can be helpful for those times when your baby is tired from crawling, walking, or running.

MONTH
11

Sleep

Were you blessed with a non-napper? Sometimes babies give up naps really early. This is usually not a problem for your baby, though it might be an issue for you, particularly if that downtime was your nap time or the time when you got things done at home.

Every baby will have a slightly different sleep schedule, non-napping babies tend to be children who require less sleep. Skipping the nap does not necessarily translate into a longer sleep at night. In fact, you might also have a baby who sleeps less at night, though he sleeps it in one stretch.

Talk to your pediatrician if you are concerned about your baby's sleep habits. If your baby is healthy and developmentally doing everything within a normal time frame, all is well. The good news is that the problem is not a physical one for your baby, merely a scheduling issue on your part.

Your baby will love to play and explore. Don't worry if he wants to use the toys for something other than what they were made for. Thinking creatively is a good thing.

Play

While it may be difficult to believe your baby is already nearing the end of her first year, that time is coming quickly. Your baby still loves when you hold and rock her. Loving your baby in this manner feels good to you and to your child. Nevertheless, as this first year is ending you might notice a shift in your baby's behavior when it comes to wanting to be held.

Your baby might wish to be held less frequently. You might find that she only wants to be held when she is hurting or sleepy. Since she is developing the ability to get down and move around on her own, she's eager to try out all of her newfound skills. Sitting in someone's lap to play or do just about anything is not in her plans.

Do not fear. Your baby still loves you. The desire to move and be down might override the desire to be held and cuddled, but it doesn't mean you will never have any cuddle time. The difference is, you are now on baby's cuddle time schedule. Hang in there.

Affirmation for Month Eleven

I learn from my baby every day.

WEEK 46

Eat

Mealtimes are meant to be social occasions. Have you brought your baby to the family table yet? This can be a really great way to increase your social interaction with your baby.

If you have been feeding your baby before or after the family eats, consider trying a meal together. This can be any meal of the day, though dinner is usually the most common. Breakfast can also work well, as long as you have others sharing the meal with you.

Your baby will learn what mealtime looks like with other people. He will see how you take turns, how you talk, eat, and behave. This is a positive setting for your baby. It might take you a bit more time to eat your food and to feed your baby, but the interaction and teaching moments are worth this exchange.

HELPFUL HINTS: KEY TO COMMUNICATION

Your baby is starting to understand simple commands. He should be able to follow one-word directives. This can be something simple, like "stop."

As your baby begins to understand the one-word command, progress into multiple words with one direction. An example of that would be, "come here." Your baby will take a while to understand. First he needs to recognize that you are talking to him, then he will need to learn how to follow the command.

Once one-word and simple commands are understood, you can move forward. This can involve multiple simple commands. These are given either at one time or in succession. So you might say, "Stop playing and come here." Or you could break a command into parts, for example: "Put the toy down." Once accomplished, you can give the next part of the command: "Now, come to Mommy."

You can also use signs to help your baby understand you. The signs for "stop" and "no" are some parents' favorites. Not only are they easy for your baby to recognize, but you can use them to correct or communicate with your child in a crowded area, without publicly calling your child out.

MONTH
11

If your baby is fussy and has a hard time coming to the table, try giving him a snack before the meal. This can help to ease any cranky behavior that is caused by hunger. You might also consider giving him some smaller bits of food to self-feed to help you bide your time. Try various things to help make this time work for your family.

Play

You might have seen or even inherited a baby walker. These were toys that you put your baby into, and with the help of the wheels, the baby could pretend to walk and be mobile. But baby walkers were found to be very dangerous due to falls and injuries, and have become difficult to find. Many have been taken off the market, but some stores continue to sell them. Even if you do see baby walkers for sale at your local retailer, do not assume they are safe—avoid them.

Some babies have a different tolerances for being held.

If you have one, carefully consider what to do with it. Do you want to use it? If so, be sure to go over all the safety risks in your mind. It should not be used anywhere near stairs (up or down), and you should always be right near your baby. It should also not be used if your baby walks on her own.

Some toys are designed to help your baby walk and develop some standing skills. These are mostly push toys. They also have their dangers, but unlike the baby walkers, they do not hold your baby inside, and they often have wheel devices that prevent them from rolling away too quickly while baby holds on. Some examples of these toys are push-play vacuum cleaners or walker wagons. Your baby will probably enjoy this type of toy, but again, follow all the safety precautions.

Sleep

Nap time may happen in a variety of places with your baby. Now that she is moving around a lot more, she might be more frequently tired. This can mean that she drops off to sleep nearly anywhere she is when the urge strikes.

Sometimes you may find her asleep in her car seat, even after a short drive. You may also find her asleep in her high chair during her meals. Your baby might even fall asleep in the middle of playing on the floor. These impromptu naps can really mess with her sleep schedule.

On the one hand, you want her to sleep because she's tired, but on the other hand, a planned nap in an approved location can be much more restful.

Try to catch your baby's tired state before it becomes a full-blown nap. You might see her head bobbing in the high chair and quickly move her to her bed for a nap. This might signal a need to alter the nap routine just a bit. But if your baby is tired, skipping over some of the pre-nap activities might be welcome.

WEEK 47

Eat

When you give your baby new foods, she might shiver. This is not a reaction to the temperature of the food, but merely how she responds physically to the new taste. You might find your baby only does this with certain types of food, like spicy foods or bitter foods. Some babies do it with nearly every new food.

HELPFUL HINTS: CLEANUP ROUTINE

It is time to teach your baby a new game: "Clean up!" If you expect your baby to keep her things neatly put away, then you need to teach her this behavior early on. As soon as your baby can begin to play with toys alone, start a cleanup routine.

At the end of each play session, be sure to leave a bit of time to put everything away. Help him to pick up each toy and put it where it goes.

At first you will be the one who does the majority of the cleanup. In fact, it will probably take longer to "help" him clean up than if you did it yourself. Resist the urge to do that, because you are teaching him how to put away his toys. As he gets older, he will do more. Don't be dismayed if your baby doesn't really catch on for a long while. Just consider this a foundation for what will come in time!

Be sure to share mealtimes with your baby. The social aspects are important and will teach your baby to try new foods as she watches you eat.

MONTH
11

The good news is that the shiver is normal and not a bad allergic reaction. The shivering also does not necessarily correlate to whether or not your baby will like the food. Keep offering the food, and if she keeps eating, she likes it, despite the shiver.

Sleep

Babies experience rapid eye movement sleep, or REM sleep. This leads most scientists to infer that babies do dream, and it agrees with what most parents would tell you about observing their baby while sleeping.

This is about as far as the science can go when talking about babies and dreaming. Now, you can walk into the room where your baby is sleeping and watch his eyes moving while he sleeps. But what is he dreaming about? No one knows.

Some parents will say that their babies appear to be distressed, while most just note quiet sleep. It can be unsettling to see your baby distressed while sleeping. It is best to talk to your pediatrician for advice on handling the dreams and sleep issues.

Play

Books are a favorite plaything for your baby. You can find a wide variety of titles and book styles in your baby's age range.

Some books are made for bathtub play and are plastic. They can also be really good if your baby is all about chewing right now. There are also hard board books. These are nice and sturdy. The pages of board books are easier for babies to turn as well.

TIP

SCAREDY CAT?

Fear of animals is not uncommon in babies of this age, particularly if they have never really been around animals. While it is a great idea to expose your baby to some kid-friendly animals, you need to do so in a safe and gentle manner.

Cloth books are a good alternative to paper books simply because the pages are hard to tear out, even when baby is trying to turn the page vigorously.

Your baby probably enjoys being read to, but at this age, simple text with single, large-print words also work well. You can imagine a farm book with great photos of animals and one-word descriptions. Read this to baby and add your own comments like, "Oh a cow! We saw a cow last week driving to Grandma's. Cows say 'Moooo!'"

Be sure to read to your baby. Sometimes allow baby to pick out the book, even if it's the same book, every night for weeks. Also be sure to give your baby some time alone to look at books.

What to Watch For Explained

The **joy of bouncing to music** is one that is universally shared. These beginning dance moves are fun to watch as your baby moves rhythmically. This shows that physically she is paying attention to her environment. Don't go sign her up for ballet class just yet, but you should ensure that she is exposed to different varieties of music. If your baby seems indifferent to the music you play, see if you can switch the type of music to find something your little one responds to. If your baby seems to ignore music completely, mention this at next month's well check.

Sleep problems may not be a thing of the past. While everyone has different sleep habits, you may still be having more restless nights than you would like. You may see a return to restless nights after months of great sleeping habits. This can be disconcerting for both of you. Check for physical issues first. Is your baby healthy? Is he running a fever? Does he have a runny nose? Is he experiencing pain anywhere? If the answer to all these questions is "no," then turn to ways of calming. Sometimes experiencing all the milestones that happen in these last few months is enough to induce some sleepless nights. Think of it as the excitement you feel after a big day at work for you.

Progress with self-feeding should be evident by now. Your baby may even be a bit neater—or maybe not! But, if you have a baby who was not interested in self-feeding up to this point, perhaps now you will find that he is more interested in feeding himself. This may also go in the opposite direction, when he will only allow self-feeding. You still need to be mindful of the foods he is eating. Safety is the main thing to watch for, particularly choking hazards while perfecting this new skill.

Your baby should now have the **ability to bear full weight on legs or stand alone**. This doesn't mean that she is doing it consistently, but that you have at least seen it once or twice. Your baby will tend to do something and then it won't happen again for a short while. If you haven't seen this, mention it to your practitioner. Your baby may have issues with hip clicks or other issues that prevent her from wanting to stand. Or, she simply doesn't want to do it yet.

By now, your baby should also be **able to play alone** for a short while. If you are unable to walk away from your baby and hand her a toy, then you may want to think about time she spends alone. Is she able to calm herself? Do you always help her in every situation? Even babies need some alone time, when happy and safe. Try to provide her with that time.

MONTH
11

MONTH TWELVE

Week 48–52

Prepare for Toddlerhood

✓ Checklist for Month Twelve

- ☐ Plan your baby's first birthday party.
- ☐ Re-evaluate your playgroup.
- ☐ Check your car seat.
- ☐ Prepare to take away the baby bottle or pacifier.
- ☐ Lay the groundwork for potty training.
- ☐ Recheck your baby proofing.

What to Watch For in the Twelfth Month

- ☐ Interest in walking
- ☐ Waving and gesturing
- ☐ Use of sound to get your attention
- ☐ Adverse reactions to shots
- ☐ Developing vocabulary

Be Sure to:

- ☐ Have your baby's one-year photos taken
- ☐ Save memorabilia from the first birthday party.
- ☐ Restock your first-aid kit, throwing out expired items.

Baby Skills:

In the twelfth month, your baby:

- ☐ Enjoys imitating sounds
- ☐ Has visual acuity of about 20/30
- ☐ Says a few words
- ☐ Can follow simple commands (No. Stop. Come here.)
- ☐ Solves simple puzzles and problems
- ☐ Understands many words
- ☐ Can crawl. Might walk
- ☐ Might have teeth on top
- ☐ Enjoys books and pictures
- ☐ Knows many signs
- ☐ Is able to show frustration
- ☐ Plays alone for a few minutes

BABY DATA

The end of the first year is upon you. When you look back at everything that your baby has learned to do from the first days of life until now, you are probably pretty amazed. Sometimes it can be easy to forget just how much has happened this first year. There will never be another year like it.

Your baby is quickly moving into toddlerhood. She is most likely able to get around by herself by crawling or scooting, if not by walking. This gives her a sense of independence. It can also increase your fears, not only for safety but because your baby is growing up. It can be hard to acknowledge that each stage has wonderful things about it and remember not to look too far ahead. Enjoy where your baby is right now.

Making noise, singing, and talking are all ways that your baby likes to communicate. You will hear lots of different sounds and possibly even some words in there. The first words are usually things like "mama" and "dada," followed quickly with "hi" and "bye-bye." But soon you've got "dog" or "cow" mixed in. "No" is also a word that might creep into your baby's vocabulary right away. For words your baby is not yet able to say, she might be able to use sign language to help both of you decrease your communication frustrations.

Her independence also gives her the ability to play alone now, even if only for a few minutes. At dinnertime you might be able to sit her down with a book while you are in the same room, and she doesn't need your involvement. However, when she is not able to do something, she is quickly frustrated. She is also probably sleeping alone easily as well as self-feeding. You are still very much needed in her life, however; do not let her foray into alone time fool you.

Keeping your baby close by while you do your chores is a great way to let him have some independent time without really being alone. Being near you is comforting to him while at play.

MONTH TWELVE:
Bringing Up Baby

Your three goals this month are simple:

- Learn to love toddlers.
- Watch for signs of frustration.
- Know your parenting style.

PLAN YOUR BABY'S BIRTHDAY PARTY

It is finally time for your baby's first birthday! Most families will choose to celebrate with a party. But the word *party* looks very different to different people.

- The child will not remember the party.
- Lots of one-year-olds in a room is chaos.
- Your baby is the shining star of the event.
- This is a great photo opportunity for baby, friends, and family.

Once you have some realistic expectations about planning a party for a one-year-old, you are bound to have an easier time planning. Just remember who this party is really for—you, the parents. You should plan the party accordingly. Consider these points.

Time of Day

You should plan your party at a time when your baby is normally awake and ready to play. Be mindful of nap times and times that your baby normally

MONTH
12

eats. You will want to ensure that your baby has his best chance to participate in the festivities as much as possible.

Birthday Party Theme

Your party theme does not have to be wild; simply focusing on this first-year milestone is enough. Nevertheless, if you are inclined, you could go with a theme such as the zoo, primary-colored blocks, or something that you feel represents your baby or this first year. Once you have a theme, you can plan other things around it.

Number of Guests

How many guests you invite will affect many of the following categories, so make this one of your first considerations when planning. You might keep your party really simple, and invite just your immediate family. Or you might decide to open it to family and selected friends. Some families choose to do a bigger party open-house style, where guests simply drop in whenever during a chunk of the day.

Food Served

You will want to have a wide variety of foods that appeal to all of your guests, particularly your guest of honor—your child. So in addition to normal party food that meets with your theme, include some toddler- and baby-friendly food for the younger crowd as well.

Games and Activities

Your baby is most likely not ready for a piñata. But if your baby is walking, Pin the Tail on the Donkey can be a cute game. If your baby likes to crawl and be chased, consider "Pin the Diaper on the Baby" using paper images of diapers and tape. It's pretty funny to watch a three-year-old trying to catch a fast crawler. Think major parental supervision no matter which games you play.

Will you or won't you? Baby's first cake is to be enjoyed. How messy will you let your baby be? Your baby's first birthday is a once-in-a-lifetime photo opportunity.

Decorations

These can be very simple, like streamers and Mylar balloons. Be leery of latex balloons because of the increased risk of choking for small children. Some families enjoy hanging fun quotes about their baby under pictures lining a wall. Think of pictures spanning the year with some saying simply what was going on at the time ("Vacation with Grandma") or a fast fact (Baby weighed 7 pounds [3.2 kg] at birth and 14 pounds [6.4 kg] at six months!).

Presents

At this age, your baby has no clue about presents. In fact, presents can be overwhelming for such a young child. Nevertheless, some gifts are likely to be involved, so help your baby open them, and do not be offended if he prefers the ribbons, paper, and boxes. If you're having a large party, consider asking for donations to a charity or for something specific, like books or clothes.

Cake!

No birthday party would be complete without birthday cake. While you can certainly serve some to your guests, a cake is typically made just for your baby, sometimes called a smash cake for fairly obvious reasons. Consider putting your baby down on a plastic-backed, disposable tablecloth, dressed only in a diaper, before you hand him the cake. Then start the video rolling and the cameras a-clicking for the reactions!

Just remember that there is no one right formula for your baby's first birthday bash. Like parenting, how you choose to celebrate your baby's first birthday is personal. The party should fit your family's style and your baby's needs.

Mama Moment

As your baby has gotten bigger, learned skills, and mastered tasks that are all a part of growing up, you might find yourself missing the baby stage. This is a normal feeling to have as a parent. Some families use this feeling as the signal to have another baby. Others recognize the feeling as the change in relationship from baby to toddler. No matter how you cope with it, choose to move forward in a positive manner.

Some families feel the opposite way. They feel that they are able to read their baby a bit better. This is more comfortable, and they feel like they have more skills to parent a child who is more communicative. This means that the end of the first year signals a big upswing in their relationship.

MONTH
12

RE-EVALUATE YOUR PLAYGROUP

Now that your baby is older and you have grown as a parent, it might be time to re-evaluate your playgroup. You will want to have a playgroup that meets the baby's needs as well as your own.

So how do you decide if your current playgroup is working for your baby? Does she seem to enjoy the time you are there? Does she "play" nicely with others? Are the other children near her age? If not, are they younger or older? Some playgroups do well with a mixture of ages, while others tend to be better balanced with kids who are the same age. Does your baby have the skills needed to keep up?

Your playgroup may be made up of a bunch of friends. This might be great for you. But how does it work for your baby? If you are good friends with other members of the playgroup, you might have a harder time leaving it than you think. But if it is

not the right playgroup for you and your baby, then staying is not doing anyone any good. If your baby is having an okay time and it's not terribly problematic, consider adding a second playgroup that meets her needs so that you can still have social time with your friends. This can save some hurt feelings.

If you do not have the entanglement of friends in the playgroup and your baby is having a good time, consider whether the playgroup works for you. Does it still fit your schedule? Perhaps now you have to wake your baby up early from a nap to get there on time. Or maybe the playground location is farther away than where you originally lived. Do you get along with the others in the playgroup?

While it is not essential to have the exact same opinions as everyone else in playgroup, some similarities do help. For example, if you are the only one in playgroup who thinks that a certain parenting style is beneficial, you might feel left out, hurt, or worse when discussions come up about this topic or others.

Ensuring that you, your baby, and your schedule are still fine is the best way to ensure that your playgroup is a good match. Periodically re-evaluate your playgroup for these factors. Your own needs will change as your baby grows and matures. Don't hesitate to make the switch if need be.

Your playgroup should be a joy to go to every time. If you wonder or worry, let that be a sign that something is up and discuss it with the other members of the group.

CHECK YOUR CAR SEAT

The car seat is your baby's best defense in an accident. The problem is that the vast majority of parents use the car seat incorrectly. Parents often make mistakes with both the installation and use of the car seat. For instance, the straps might not be tight enough or the car seat might not be strapped into the seat tightly enough. But there is also the issue of the wrong car seat for the wrong kid.

As your baby is growing, re-evaluate your car seat for a proper fit. Babies are usually best served by a car seat designed for an infant. These are only rear-facing car seats and are designed to fit infants from about five pounds (2.3 kg) to about twenty-plus pounds (9.1 kg). As your baby reaches this weight limit, or their height is such that their feet are bent in the car seat from touching the back of the vehicle's seat, you will want to consider moving your baby to the convertible car seat.

The convertible car seat is the combination car seat. It can hold weights from five pounds (2.3 kg) to forty or fifty pounds (18.1 or 22.3 kg). It can also be rear or front facing. Remember, your baby is safest in a rear-facing position for as long as possible. Babies should not switch to facing forward until they are at least one year old AND weigh at least twenty pounds (9.1 kg). Some car seats are meant for babies/toddlers over twenty pounds (9.1 kg), but they face forward only.

When shopping for a convertible car seat, keep safety features in mind. The car seat you choose should include a five-point harness for the safest fit and accident protection. By now you will also know how your baby uses a car seat. Does your baby take a lot of naps in the seat? If so, look for a car seat with sides that are big enough and padded for your baby's napping comfort. You will also want to determine that the car seat will fit, rear facing, in your vehicle.

Most babies will be fine with switching car seats. You can make a big deal out of it and tell your baby that he is getting so big, or you can simply make the switch and see if he even notices. Many babies will not notice or care. You know your baby best and can determine which car seat makes most sense for him.

GEAR UP TO TAKE AWAY THE BABY BOTTLE OR PACIFIER

Weaning from the baby bottle or pacifier is typically not easy, but it should be done around the end of the first year. After the end of the first year your baby does not need a bottle or pacifier, even if she wants one or both. Most pediatricians and pediatric dentists agree that this should be the age of weaning from these items.

This weaning process can be accomplished in a couple of ways. The most obvious and potentially most painful is to go cold turkey. No baby bottles,

MONTH
12

no pacifiers again. Ever. You pick a date and you do it. It's only cups and snuggles from there on out.

This method can be quite a shock to your baby. You can tell her that it is coming, but she is probably too young to understand. Some parents even go as far as to have a party to say good-bye to "baby items" and have their child gift a new baby with their favorite baby bottle or pacifier. (Just be sure to warn the other parents first.)

The hardest part is that you may feel the urge to give in when your baby cries for the bottle or pacifier. This will only mean you have to do it again, and will not help to break the habit. Try to be firm and stick to your mission of removing the bottles and pacifiers.

If you prefer a more gentle approach, you can slowly start by removing one feeding a day out of a baby bottle—so you would put any breast milk or infant formula in a cup for your baby. Since many babies enjoy walking around with their bottles, if you remove that ability and only allow your baby to sit in the high chair, their desire for the bottle can decrease.

Remember, your baby has been using the bottle or pacifier for comfort. You should try to offer more hugs and snuggles as your baby is going through this difficult transition. It is also wise to try to keep other life issues and changes at a minimum if possible. For example, do not get rid of these items just as you are moving to a new house.

BENEFITS OF NURSING BEYOND ONE YEAR

As mentioned above, weaning off bottles is recommended by age one. Weaning from the breast is a completely different process. Because your baby still gets nutrition as well as comfort from nursing, there is no need to stop nursing at one year. The vast majority of babies will continue to nurse and eventually wean on their own, in a slow and gentle process, although it rarely occurs prior to one year. Occasionally a baby might wean suddenly if there is

Breastfeeding a one-year-old is vastly different than feeding the newborn that you nursed just twelve months ago. Enjoy the relaxation of the few sessions that you have each day.

some major occurrence like a pregnancy, which can cause an abrupt and noticeable change in the milk's taste or quantity of milk supply. In most cases, however, babies wean gradually over a long period of time. This is a perfectly normal and natural process.

Remember that breastfeeding your baby past the first year is completely supported by the American Academy of Pediatrics and the World Health Organization. Your baby is still getting antibodies from your breast milk as well as a variety of different levels of protein and fats throughout the day that match with your baby's growth and development. As your baby grows and begins to develop and test his emerging independence, he will also gain a sense of emotional reassurance from continued nursing.

By about a year, your baby will be able to let you know when he wants and needs to nurse. Respond as seems reasonable, and nurse according to his cues. Your nursing relationship will continue to evolve as you learn to set appropriate limits and teach your young toddler to become mindful of others' needs. (For instance, you probably wouldn't rush out of the grocery store to nurse a fourteen-month-old as you would with a two-month-old. A fourteen-month-old can begin to understand that he can wait a few minutes to nurse!) As always with nursing, continue to follow your baby's lead during this next phase of the relationship—your baby's individual personality and style will help to guide you.

FIRST STEPS TOWARD POTTY TRAINING

Most parents dread potty training. Eventually, however, you'll have had enough of diapering your baby, and you'll start to dream about the day when she won't ever need to wear diapers again.

Some parents actually start potty training surprisingly early, with something called elimination communication (EC). In fact, this process is often started when a baby is first born. Parents who use the EC method watch for natural signs that their baby is eliminating waste. By following those signs, they can help their baby to use the toilet or a special toilet designed for babies and toddlers. Some of these families rarely change dirty diapers, enough so that the babies are diaper free very shortly, many by six months of age.

Hot Mama for Month Twelve

Celebrate thriving in a year of new motherhood by getting some spa treatments. Consider a manicure and pedicure, facial, or even a massage. Go all out—you deserve it, Hot Mama!

MONTH
12

While the vast majority of people do not use elimination communication (EC) at such a young age, it does work. Even when you begin to think about potty training, you need to start with the EC thought process first. Observe your baby. Can you tell when your baby is eliminating waste? When she is having a bowel movement, you might notice that your baby grunts or stops moving, and her face concentrates. Likewise, you might notice that your baby releases her shoulders or shivers when urinating.

You will also need to be able to find the pattern to your baby's bowel and urine habits. For instance, how long does it take your baby to wet her diaper when she first wakes up in the morning? Do you notice that your baby has a bowel movement at

The first step toward potty readiness is the purchase of a potty. This is great fun, but don't expect a lot of potty progress at this young age.

certain times before or after she eats? These cues will help to remind you when you need to get her to the potty.

Don't worry if all of this sounds daunting to you at first. With EC, parents have to do all of the potty work for their babies by reading their signs. If left to their own developmental readiness, however, most babies are not ready to use the potty on their own until well after a year old.

You can start thinking about potty training for your baby when she has longer periods of dryness, can follow simple directions, can pull her bottom clothes on and off alone, can play alone or concentrate for a few minutes, recognizes that she is eliminating waste, and has a desire to use the potty. For most babies, this is not until well into the second year or later (eighteen months plus). Use this time to observe your baby's habits and form your own thoughts, so that when your baby is ready for potty training, you are ready as well.

RECHECK YOUR BABY PROOFING

The more skills your baby gains, the more baby proofing you need to do. For every new skill, you should spend some time replicating that skill yourself, to see the world from your baby's eyes. This can help you spot dangers you might have missed before.

Once again, as she begins to walk and pull up, you should watch for toppling dangers. These don't just include small pieces of furniture, but large pieces as well. A good example would be a dresser with drawers. If your baby can open a drawer and climb in, she could accidentally pull the whole thing over on herself. This can be very dangerous and even deadly.

Think of all the new things your baby is doing and head out to check those areas. Crawling, walking, and climbing mean securing the stairs at the tops and bottoms. It also means ensuring that the drapes and cords are kept away from baby's reach. Recheck that no medicines or poisons have gotten out of their hiding spots. And be sure to turn pot handles in on the stove to prevent your baby from pulling something over on her head.

Messy eating is a part of the experience. Clean baby off in the tub or the sink after a meal as needed.

WEEK 48

Eat

Messy is the name of the eating game for most babies of this age. Self-feeding is a good skill to encourage, but the learning curve is sharp when it comes to keeping the food in your baby's mouth and off her face and the floor. Never fear—that's what cleanup is for.

As mentioned in earlier sections, to preserve clothes, you can strip your baby down to a diaper before meals. You can also stick him in the kitchen sink for an impromptu bath if needed. Big bibs are another option. If your baby resists being cleaned off, switch the type of cloth you are using. If it's a rough washcloth meant to grab food particles, try a smoother cloth like a baby washcloth. Sometimes a regular baby wipe will also work. Or you can just use your wet hands and then wash yourself.

Food in the hair is another issue. Your baby might not intend to get food in her hair, but it happens. Encouraging her not to do this might not be as effective. You can try to get her not to put food in her hair all you like, but it's only a benefit to you—she won't care, because she's having fun. You can also put an old hat on her, which she might really like. For babies who resist these measures and hate to be cleaned up, use a small comb and dip it in water to get the food out of the hair without washing!

Sleep

Now that you've made it to the one-year mark, you might wonder if it is time to ditch the baby crib. Most likely there is no need. If you are doing this simply because you feel like it is expected, you might want to reconsider.

MONTH
12

Most babies move from their crib to a bed near the time when they are potty training. This allows them some freedom to go to the bathroom at night without the confines of the crib. Getting rid of the crib at this point has few benefits for most families. If you are having issues with the crib, address those before making a final decision.

Play

Pucker up! Now might be a good time to teach your baby to blow kisses. Kissing is very similar to waving, which many babies pick up on their own.

Start by blowing kisses to your baby as you leave the room. Then as you are near baby and someone else is leaving the room, help him to blow a kiss as well. Take his arm and fold his hand near his mouth. From here say, "Blow a kiss!" Make a big kissing sound as you "throw" the kiss to whoever is leaving. If both parties praise baby and this gets repeated, your baby will be throwing kisses to everyone!

HELPFUL HINTS: COMFORT ZONE

Do not be concerned by "bad" habits that your baby might have developed, like thumb sucking or using a pacifier. While you may want encourage her to give up the habit, remember, these are comforts for your child. Quite often, your baby is not even aware that she is doing the thumb sucking or whatever habit it is.

Give your baby time. Most of these habits go away on their own. If they do not go away in the toddler years, going to school can often help children stop these habits because of peer relationships. A child does not want to suck his thumb around friends at school and so begins to impose his own checks and measures to prevent the habit from lingering.

WEEK 49

Eat

You might have to pack a lunch for your baby for a variety of reasons. It could be that you and baby are off for an outing. Some child care centers or nannies require that you bring your baby's meals every day.

When considering what to pack, think about what your baby likes to eat. Is the meal you are planning well-balanced? Can you easily make it transportable without it being breakable? What items will be available for you where you are going? Will you need to pack utensils? Will you be able to heat it up or will you need to keep it cold?

Test out a few meals to see how your baby responds. Some families use prepackaged baby foods for a long while simply because they are convenient and ready to go. It might take a while to get into the planning mode, but once you figure things out, you can pack your baby's meals with no issues whatsoever.

Play

Parallel play is a term used to describe what most people believe happens when you put two burgeoning toddlers on the ground with toys next to one another. They play with the toys, but not with each other. However, some experts believe that this is not exactly what is happening; that as adults, we are missing the interactions babies have while playing with each other.

When two babies are together, what parents see is one baby taking the toy from another baby. Another baby might shove food into her friend's mouth. These are all forms of play, albeit not what we would call friendly play. But look at things from your baby's perspective—that toy she has never had any interest in is suddenly interesting simply because someone else is interacting with it.

Babies at this age often "parallel play." This means your baby plays while sitting next to another baby. Often, this means very little interaction occurs, if any. This is perfectly normal at this age.

Rather than worry that your baby is antisocial or a bully, simply use these times as a chance to tell your baby how you want her to act. Label the feelings her friend has—"See, Sarah is sad that you took the toy. You can have it in a minute. We will share the toy." The truth is that you cannot simply plop two babies down to play. Babies need help initiating play with another person at this point.

Try to find things that the two playmates can do together. Block stacking and placing items in a basket can be great dual fun. So can removing items from a basket. You can sit with them and show them what you have in mind.

To make the most out of baby playdates, be sure your baby is well rested and not hungry. Babies get cranky, just like adults. To have a successful playdate, try to do this more frequently so that your baby learns what is expected and how to behave.

Sleep

There might be times when you need your baby to sleep away from home or away from your normal child-care setting. This can wreak havoc on your baby. Any time a baby's normal routine is disrupted, you run the risk of a meltdown. Keep in mind, however, that this might also depend on the baby and his individual personality.

To minimize the disruption, try to keep the times of sleep periods fairly consistent with what your baby would find at home. Make his sleep environment similar. To do this you can bring a blanket or sheet set from home. Consider bringing music your baby might listen to as well.

Safe sleep needs to be a priority when sleeping away from home. If you are cosleeping, be sure to use the same precautions you would observe in your own bed. Be sure to look around the sleeping area for safety hazards no matter where your baby is sleeping.

You might have brought your own portable crib or portable play yard for your baby to sleep in. This is probably the best option. However, borrowing a portable bed from family, friends, or even a hotel might also be an option. Be sure that if you borrow an infant bed, it is up to current safety standards and is clean.

WEEK 50

Eat

Teaching your baby to use a straw for drinks can be handy. If your baby can use a straw, she can drink just about anywhere you are, even if you do not have a sippy cup. Keep in mind that a straw is very different from nursing, so it might take a while before your baby gets a real grasp on the skill. Though all babies are different, if your baby seems to do better with a straw, there is no reason to go to a sippy cup.

Infant and toddler cups are sold with straws, though this might defeat the purpose of figuring out how to travel lightly and without special cups. However, they are more kid-friendly in size and might be better for teaching your baby to use the straw than a regular-size straw would be.

Straws are not without danger. Since they are long, they can poke your baby's sensitive mouth and gums fairly easily. This can be quite painful, even if not a lot of damage is done. For this reason, make sure your baby is sitting down while drinking.

In the learning phase be prepared for lots of mess. Your baby will probably dump the cup over a few times, making that covered sippy cup/straw combination a really good thing. Your baby is also likely to dribble and spit liquid from his mouth, simply because it is easy for him to get a lot fluid at once, and that can be overwhelming.

Play

In case you haven't noticed yet, babies love telephones and are fascinated with telephone conversations. Perhaps your baby already tries to pull the phone away from you when you're using it, or maybe he tries to give the phone to you, in hopes you will make a call. Make the most of this fascination and

Your twelve-month-old finds fascination in your everyday things. He wants to be just like you!

play telephone with your baby. This is always a fun game. You can use either an old phone or a play phone to start with. Even making a fake phone using your fingers will do. As you are playing or talking to your baby, imitate the sound of a ringing phone.

"Hello?" you ask in a very friendly voice on your pretend phone. "You want to speak to baby?" Smile and hand over the phone to your little one. Her face will light up and she will learn to imitate you. Your baby might even have fun phone conversations and practice all her newfound talking skills.

Sleep

Crib issues can creep up at this stage. One concern might be that your baby is trying to get out of the crib. This first thing you need to do is to ensure a safe sleep environment. Make sure there is nothing in the crib that your baby could climb on. This means no pillows, bumper pads, toys, stuffed animals—nothing.

Also ensure that your crib mattress is in the correct location. The vast majority of cribs have settings that allow you to move the mattress up and down. The mattress should be as low as it can possibly go. This will help your baby to stay put in the crib.

Devices have also been designed to keep your baby in the crib. Think of these as tent toppers—a mesh canopy you attach to the top of the crib. You zip and unzip your baby out of the crib. These are very dangerous and should be avoided. Babies have even been known to die from pulling these devices down on themselves in the middle of the night and suffocating. Be sure that you talk to your child's

MONTH
12

pediatrician about this issue before making any decisions about preventing your baby from climbing out of the crib.

WEEK 51

Eat

Have you let your baby try a spoon or fork yet? This is a very important skill for your baby to learn, although it can be very frustrating, particularly when your baby knows that fingers work much better than utensils.

Try to decrease that frustration in a couple of ways. One is to use baby- and toddler-friendly utensils. This will give your baby a better shot at actually getting food into her mouth. You might also employ two utensils at a time, taking turns with "filling" the utensil with food to speed the process along.

Blowing kisses is a fun skill for babies to learn. Not only is it fun for them, but it's a real crowd pleaser.

HELPFUL HINTS: NO WAY

"No!" You might find your baby using that word a lot these days. And if you are not hearing it yet, you soon will be hearing it. *No* is such an easy thing to say. It means stop. It means your baby wants something she can't have. It means you have got a NO maniac on your hands.

Since *no* is an easy word to say and it carries with it so much force and meaning, your baby will pick it up quickly. From there, your baby will use it often. Sometimes your baby will say no, even when doing whatever you have asked him to do. This defiance is a verbal issue and not usually physical, at this age anyway.

This is where redirection really comes in handy. Try your best to focus on the positive and minimize the no's that come out of your mouth. This might help in the long run, but until then, remember this is just a phase.

Remember that practice and patience will make this skill a lasting one. Try to smile—enjoy the peas on the floor and applesauce in baby's hair. Just be sure to snap a few pictures along the way for blackmail later in life.

Sleep

If you are still cosleeping, you might be perfectly happy with the arrangement. If you are ready to start the moving process from your bed to a crib or other sleeping arrangement, you should do so gently, as with any drastic change in your baby's life. Your first step will be to decide where you will move your baby.

You might decide to move your baby to a crib. This is probably the safest solution. It might also be the easiest solution, because your baby has likely seen a crib someplace, even if not in his own home. If your baby has experience in a crib, it might be less frightening or stressful for him.

MONTH
12

Other options that parents moving from a family bed sometimes choose include:

- Portable crib
- Toddler bed
- Mattress on the floor

A portable crib is less expensive and more movable than a traditional crib. It might also provide less space for your baby, which is not always a bad thing. A toddler bed is less expensive, but can be problematic. Once your baby can get out of bed, you need to find a way to prevent midnight wandering, which can often lead to trouble like falling, getting into things that baby shouldn't, or even coming back to your bed. A mattress on the floor has some similar issues, but is less expensive and certainly grows with your baby. You will also want to ensure that the mattress is nowhere near a wall or other piece of furniture to prevent entrapment.

Play

Homemade toys are so wonderful! Consider this sensory toy for your little one: a tactile board. You can take a piece of cardboard and divide it into sections. In each section you can add a different texture. You might glue down a piece of sandpaper on one part, silky cloth on another part, burlap for another section, and so on.

Have your baby feel each section. Watch her reaction as she touches the various areas. Tell her what she is feeling. "Isn't that burlap scratchy and rough?" "Oooh, the silk is so soft." Using tactile play helps to stimulate your baby's largest sensory organ: the skin.

WEEK 52

Eat

As the end of the first year comes, some parents feel that they are done with watching what baby eats. This is far from the truth. Concerns still exist about foods and how they are eaten.

The amount of control you need to keep over foods will depend on your baby. Has your baby had any allergic reactions or sensitivities to any food in the first year? If the answer is yes, continuing a good watch is probably best. Talk to your pediatrician and perhaps a nutritionist. There are some general guidelines about foods like honey (after a year) or peanut butter (after three years). But will your baby need something specific?

Also keep encouraging self-feeding. But pay particular attention to choking hazards. This part continues for quite a while, even past the second year of life as your baby gets more teeth.

Sleep

Your baby might decide that nightclothes are for the birds. Or perhaps your baby has ditched the blanket, no matter where you put it in bed with him. As your baby gets older, he will be able to tell you his likes and dislikes. Though he can't use words, he can let you know that he prefers not to be covered at night.

This worries many a mom. After all, part of our job is to keep our children warm, particularly at night. But think back to good old human differences. Some babies are simply hot-natured. You might notice this if your baby sweats a lot at night.

If this is the case, your baby might really prefer to have fewer clothes on at night to prevent him from getting hot or sweaty.

Try to give your baby some breathing room, so to speak. Consider alternatives to the nightclothes you are currently using. Is there a way to keep your baby covered but not as hot? The most obvious answer is to try a different, lighter material. Nightclothes made of breathable cottons can be very relieving. This might solve the struggle of both the pajamas and the blanket.

Since blankets are not a good idea anyway, try to skip the blanket, even as your baby is becoming a toddler. You can use footed pajamas or sleep sacks made for older babies, if your baby will tolerate them. The most mobile babies of this age do not deal well with their legs being "trapped" in the bag. See if you can borrow one before investing. If your baby will tolerate it, problem solved!

Sometimes your baby simply falls asleep while playing. Maybe it's time to re-evaluate nap time.

HELPFUL HINTS: GROWTH SPURT

Babies grow at different rates. Some babies grow quickly in the beginning of the first year and simply do not gain much weight from about four months on. Other babies slowly and steadily move up the growth chart as they plot their own growth pattern.

All of this data can be confusing. Your pediatrician will have a record of your baby's growth, and you should discuss that information at routine checkups.

The larger issue is what your baby looks like when he is growing. You might one day wake up and notice that your thin baby has gotten a bit chubby. Then, a few weeks later, your baby grows lengthwise and slims down. This might be your baby's pattern of growing. You might also notice that your baby, who was normally a bit on the heavier side, slims down. Then later that month he has outgrown new outfits lengthwise. These are both normal patterns and are not of any concern as long as your baby stays on his own individual growth curve. Discuss any concerns you have with your pediatrician.

MONTH
12

HELPFUL HINTS: CARE TO SHARE

You'll want your baby to have many qualities as she grows up. You have taught her to be so many things this first year. Now that she is older, she is ready to learn about generosity and sharing.

To help encourage that, be sure that she sees you sharing. It might feel silly, but announce, "Here, Daddy, you can push the stroller for a turn." Or, when holding the snack out, say, "You can choose your snack first, Mommy." This shows your child what sharing and generosity look like.

Then ask her to do the same. As you go to play a game, say, "May I go first, Baby?" Take your turn and then thank her for waiting. Do this as often as possible to show her the qualities that you want her to demonstrate in life. Sharing and taking turns are great skills that she will take with her everywhere.

If the change in pajamas does not work for you, ask yourself what other options you have available. Can you control the room temperature easily? If so, consider letting your little one sleep with just a diaper on. This might solve that problem, though do watch for diapers being removed. (Hint: Put it on backward; it confuses baby for at least a few nights!)

Play

Your baby is likely to have amassed a sizable number of toys over the period of this first year. You will need to find a place and a way to store these toys reasonably. This place should be easily accessible for your baby. It should be safe and clean.

For many families, this is a toy box. It should be of a reasonable height so that your child can reach in easily to grab most toys. It should be fitted with safety features such as a non-locking, non-slamming lid, and airholes should your child get stuck inside.

You can also use the toy box as a way to promote cleaning up. At the end of a play session, announce it's cleanup time. Help your baby march the toys over to the toy chest, and put them away.

Affirmation for Month Twelve

There is more to learn and love as we enter our second year together.

What to Watch For Explained

Your baby is on the move! There are so many developmental milestones being reached. You will begin to notice that your baby is **interested in walking**. This can be as basic as watching others walk with great intent, or trying to succeed in those first steps. This means that your baby will also begin to have spills and falls. This can means lots of love and kisses from mom and dad. Don't be too tempted to stop your baby from being mobile for fear of falls, just make the environment safe and be watchful.

Waving and gesturing is fun for your baby. He will notice your coming and going and tell you physically "hello" and "goodbye". There may also be some kisses being blown. If you don't notice these skills, you should ask your practitioner if there is a reason.

Your baby will be **using sound to try to get your attention**. The more body movements she has, the better able she is to do that. Use of sound to get your attention is one of their favorites. Think of it as verbal peek-a-boo. Baby makes a noise, and you peek over the newspaper or look to where she is playing and respond. What a fun game!

Along with this skill will be a **developing vocabulary**. This will involve small words at first that get used a lot—hi, bye, mom, milk, no. At first you may just hear the mutterings, but soon you can realize that your baby is actually saying something—all of a sudden it clicks and you realize he's saying "bye-bye." This makes both of you very proud and happy. If you're not seeing any signs of this, then you need to discuss this with your baby's practitioner.

Adverse reaction to shots is something else you may see this month after your one-year check up. If your baby has had reactions to shots in the past, be mindful—you may see similar reactions, though your baby may be getting different vaccines at this age. These immunizations may include chicken pox, or measles, mumps and rubella (MMR). Ask your practitioner for a list of potential adverse reactions and what you should watch for and how to take care of your baby in the event that one may occur.

MONTH
12

APPENDIX I: BABY SUPPLIES

When you are pregnant, it's tempting to go out and buy everything under the sun. Many of the important supplies you'll need for your baby can be purchased after the birth, however. Sometimes you may spend more money than you need to because you buy things you later realize you have no use for. Save yourself the headache and the heartache—wait a bit.

That said, much of what your baby needs does not need to be brand new. Many families prefer that a few items be new, or some items are safer if they are new. Those would include:

- Car seat
- Breast pump
- Feeding supplies
- Crib

The car seat is an important consideration for a few reasons, the first of which is that the safety requirements change so frequently. A five-year-old car seat, while in good condition, is probably not up to current standards. If you are getting the car seat from someone you do not know, you have no idea about the history of the seat. If it has been in a car accident, you might not be able to tell, but hidden damage could make it unsafe for your baby.

Breast pumps are, for the most part, single-user items. The one exception would be breast pumps that are hospital grade. However, these are usually extremely expensive. The single-user ones, in the $400 (£252) range, are not designed to be shared according to the Food and Drug Administration. The reason is that they do not have closed systems, and impurities can get into the motor. Do not be fooled and think that because you can change the tubing you are safe from contamination. The other practical reason is that the motors in these breast pumps are fairly limited. A used pump might sound the same, but not have the actual power you need. This can lead to low milk supply or a pump that stops functioning shortly after purchase.

Feeding supplies for your baby, toddler items like fancy plates that have been sanitized well and do not break down, can be acceptable. But smaller items, like breast-pump parts, nipples, collars, valves, and the like can actually break down quite easily. This makes them more expensive to repair than if you had purchased them new.

Your crib falls into an unusual category. For one thing, not every family will have a crib, ever. Secondly, a crib might be a very symbolic piece of furniture for a family, and they really want it to be new for their baby. This is particularly true if this is a first baby. So as long as the crib is up to safety codes as far as slat placement and paint are concerned, used cribs can be safe, particularly if you know where the crib is coming from before it comes to you. The same is also true of other baby beds, such as cosleepers, bassinets, and cradles.

WHAT YOU NEED FOR BABY

Basic List

This basic list, or baby layette, is a good place to start. Consider these the things that you should have before the baby is born. You can also add or subtract from this list as needed, according to your family needs or preferences.

- Car seat
- Place for baby to sleep safely (crib, cradle, bassinet, cosleeper, family bed)
- Sheets and bedding for sleep location
- Baby carrier (sling, wrap, front carrier, etc.)
- Coming-home outfit
- Six side-snap T-shirts (for newborn period when umbilical cord is present)
- Two to four baby hats (depending on the season)
- Ten bodysuits (short sleeve)
- Two bodysuits (long sleeve)
- Two baby gowns (elastic bottoms)
- Four outfits (sleeve length based on season, can be footed)
- Ten pairs baby socks
- Four baby blankets (two lightweight, two heavyweight)
- Burp cloths
- Bathing suit (summer)
- Car-seat cover or snow suit (winter)
- Thermometer (digital, variable location)
- Nail clippers
- First-aid kit
- Ibuprofen, acetaminophen
- Bulb syringe
- Diaper bag

Extended List

These items can be added after your baby is born. You might wait for your baby to show a need or preference for items on this list.

You will also add items from this list as your baby grows. An example might be a new car seat if your baby outgrows the first car seat within a year. Sometimes you will add items because a previous item broke or did not perform up to the standards you were expecting.

- Dresser
- Diaper-changing table
- Baby monitor
- Additional outfits of various sizes (number depends on season and growth pattern)
- Diaper bag
- Stroller
- Mobile
- Baby gym
- Various toys (rattles, etc.)
- Books
- Exersaucer or stationary jumper seat (not the type that hang from doorways, as those are more dangerous)
- Bouncy chair
- Infant swing
- Second car seat or car-seat base

- Baby food grinder or baby food processor/steamer
- Portable play yard

DIAPERS

Cloth Diapering Supplies

Supplies for cloth diapering your baby can vary widely. What you need will depend largely on which type of cloth diapers you use. For example, some diapers require covers or fasteners. This might alter your list. If you use a variety of cloth diapers, you might need smaller amounts, but a wider variety than if you used only one type.

- Cloth diapers of your choice (twelve to eighteen diapers)
- Diaper covers (if needed, six to twelve)
- Cloth-diaper fasteners (pins, plastic hooks, etc., depending on brand of diaper)
- Baby wipes (cloth or disposable)
- Baby diaper liner (cloth or disposable, optional)
- Baby wipes warmer (optional)
- Baby diaper rash cream (optional)
- Baby diaper barrier cream (optional)
- Diaper pail (optional)
- Diaper-pail liners (depends on type of pail)

Disposable Diapering Supplies

This list should be fairly simple and straightforward. You can add or subtract the extras as needed:

- Two dozen baby diapers in the correct size for your baby

- Baby wipes
- Baby wipes warmer (optional)
- Baby diaper rash cream (optional)
- Baby diaper barrier cream (optional)
- Diaper pail (optional)
- Diaper-pail liners (depends on type of pail)

BREASTFEEDING SUPPLIES

Breastfeeding should require minimal supplies. That's one of the great benefits—it's portable and easy. But some nicer items can make it easier or faster for you. Some of these might be useful or recommended if you are having difficulties breast-feeding.

- Nursing bras (three)
- Breast pads (washable or disposable)
- Nipple cream
- Breastfeeding pillow
- Breastfeeding reference book, such as *Complete Illustrated Breastfeeding Companion* (Weiss) or *Breastfeeding Made Simple* (Mohbacher and Kendall-Tackett)
- Breast pump (There are various types, from hand pumps to electric pumps to hospital-grade pumps, depending on your level of need.)
- Breast-milk storage bags or bottles
- Breast-milk feeding devices (syringe, cup, finger feeder, bottle)
- Sterilizing equipment for breast pump parts and feeding equipment

BOTTLE-FEEDING SUPPLIES (WITH OR WITHOUT INFANT FORMULA)

Your needs will depend on how frequently your baby requires a bottle or alternate feeder.

- Eight to ten baby bottles and appropriate parts
- Nipples for each stage (usually 0, 1, 2, 3)
- Sterilizing equipment for the baby bottles
- Tongs for handling hot bottles
- Bottle drying rack
- Baby bottle brush
- Nipple brush
- Dishwasher parts holder for dishwashing
- Baby bottle warmer
- Storage containers
- Breast milk or infant formula for the feedings

BABY GEAR SAFETY CHECKS

Baby proofing and baby-gear safety are important parts of ensuring that your baby is in a safe environment. Unfortunately, things happen and manufacturers have issues with their products. If you purchase something that has a warranty card to return for product registration, it is important that you do so. This ensures that the company will contact you should they discover a problem or issue a recall on a part or product. Otherwise, you are left to find out on your own through various websites such as those listed below or through news outlets. However, the news outlets usually report only the larger recalls, often leaving out smaller warnings.

Consumer Product Safety Commission

http://cpsc.gov

Seat Check

This site is dedicated to helping parents find local safety inspectors to ensure that their car seat is correctly installed. It also offers other tips and tricks related to car seats and infant safety.

http://seatcheck.org

APPENDIX II: RESOURCES

BABY GEAR

About Baby Products
This site offers user reviews and forums to discuss products, as well as information on recalls.
www.babyproducts.about.com

Consumer Product Safety Commission Recall List
This site features an up-to-date listing of recalls from the United States government.
www.cpsc.gov/cpscpub/prerel/category/child.html

Baby 411 by Denise and Alan Fields
This no-nonsense guide to baby gear gives you the scoop on hundreds of products related to babies, including the contact info for the manufacturers and other safety information.

BABY TRACKING

Trixie Tracker
This site gives you a way to track your baby's diapers, feedings, breast milk pumping and storage, medication, sleep, and much more. Free full two-week trial.
www.trixietracker.com

BOTTLE FEEDING

About Formula Feeding
Step-by-step instructions on how to prepare various types of infant formulas.
http://pregnancy.about.com/od/formula

Bottle Feeding
A physician talks about how to choose baby bottles and use breast milk or infant formula.
www.askdrsears.com/html/0/T000100.asp

BREASTFEEDING

About Breastfeeding
The latest news and informative articles on breastfeeding written by a board-certified lactation consultant (IBCLC) and mother
http://breastfeeding.about.com

Best for Babes
A non-profit organization whose goal is to help moms beat the "booby traps" associated with breastfeeding
http://Bestforbabes.org

International Lactation Consultants Association (ILCA)
You can use ILCA's site to find an IBCLC.
www.ilca.org

La Leche League International

This service organization is dedicated to helping mothers breastfeed, whether for a day, a month, a year, or longer. They are trained, certified volunteers who have help lines and Internet resources as well as local chapters with meetings and other help.
http://llli.org

Low Milk Supply

A site that helps mothers who have low milk supplies for various reasons, including breastfeeding after a breast reduction and more.
www.lowmilksupply.org

Kelly Mom

KellyMom site is written by IBCLCs for mothers. It includes lots of great information on breastfeeding, addressing the simple and the not-so-simple issues alike.
www.kellymom.com

Breastfeeding Made Simple by Nancy Morebacher and Kathleen Kendall-Tackett

This guide to breastfeeding has simple steps and guidelines to help you understand how breastfeeding works and how to get off to a good start.

The Complete Illustrated Guide to Breastfeeding by Robin Elise Weiss, LCCE, CLC

This is a step-by-step, photo-illustrated guide to breastfeeding from the beginning to end. You will find helpful tips to navigate potential complications and information on living a breastfeeding lifestyle, from fashion to fun.

Making More Milk by Diana West, IBCLC, and Lisa Marasco, MA, IBCLC

An in-depth look at what can cause low breast-milk supply and how to overcome it

The Nursing Mother's Companion by Kathleen Huggins

This handy guide is a great resource for mothers who want to nurse. You'll get targeted information on getting started and continuing to breastfeed.

BREAST PUMPS

Ameda
www.ameda.com

Hygeia
www.hygeiababy.com

Medela
www.medela.com

PumpMoms

This group is dedicated to women who pump full- or part-time for their babies. It is an open group for mothers who fit into this category, and it is a very supportive community.
http://groups.yahoo.com/group/pumpmoms

CESAREAN RECOVERY

International Cesarean Awareness Network (ICAN)

ICAN offers online and local support groups for those who have had a cesarean birth.
www.ican-online.org

DAY CARE

About Day Care

Informational articles on choosing a day care and working with your provider.

http://daycare.about.com

RESOURCES FOR FATHERS

About Fathers

A place for just dads to come and hang out: You can read articles that pertain to fatherhood as well as talk to other dads on the forums.

http://fatherhood.about.com/

MEDICAL CARE

American Academy of Family Physicians

This helpful website has a lot of useful patient information for families from newborns on.

http://familydoctor.org

American Academy of Pediatrics

The official organization of United States pediatricians: Here you can find their recommendations.

http://aap.org

MOTHERS

About Pregnancy

Meet with other mothers to chat about babies, breastfeeding, raising kids, and life in general.

http://pregnancy.about.com

American College of Nurse Midwifery

Nurse midwifery providers who give care to expectant and postpartum women and their families

http://mymidwife.org

American College of Obstetricians and Gynecologists

Obstetrical providers who provide care to expectant and postpartum women and their families

http://acog.org

The Birth Survey

Once you have given birth, log on to The Birth Survey for a chance to talk about your labor and birth. You can also rate the care you received prenatally and during birth. This is a free service.

http://thebirthsurvey.com

Midwives Alliance of North American

A listing of midwifery providers who offer care to expectant and postpartum women and their families

http://mana.org

Mothering Magazine

All about mothering and parenting in general. Written in a more holistic style than most parenting magazines.

http://mothering.com

Stay-at-Home Moms

Join other stay-at-home mothers to discuss life as well as read informative articles on everything from managing your home to raising your kids.

http://stayathomemoms.about.com

Work-at-Home Moms

Informative site about topics pertaining to running a business from home while managing the kids.

http://workathomemoms.about.com

About Multiples

Looking at life with twins or more? This site has informative articles as well as a discussion area meant to help parents support each other in the journey.
http://multiples.about.com

National Organization for Mothers of Twins Clubs

This organization is designed to help mothers of twins and other multiples find and support each other. You can search for local clubs as well as look through the numerous resources.
http://nomotc.org

Mothering Multiples **by Karen Kerkhoff Gromada**

A great look at the last days of pregnancy, early parenting, and life with multiple babies. This is the most informative book on realistically feeding your babies and getting by without being overwhelmed.

POSTPARTUM

DONA International (Formerly Doulas of North America)

Interested in finding a postpartum doula for some help at home? This is the largest certifying agency for postpartum doulas. Their online site can give you a list of postpartum doulas in your area.
http://dona.org

International Cesarean Awareness Network (ICAN)

ICAN provides local and online support groups for women recovering from cesarean section as well as those planning for a future vaginal birth.
http://ican-online.org

Laughter and Tears: The Emotional Life of New Mothers **by Elisabeth Bing and Libby Coleman**

A gentle look at how life after having a baby can be amazing and frightening all at once.

This Isn't What I Expected **by Karen Kleiman and Valerie Raskin**

A realistic look at life as a new parent

Guide to Mother's First Year **by Robin Elise Weiss, LCCE**

A month-by-month resource for finding yourself as a mother

Eat Well, Lose Weight While Breastfeeding **by Eileen Behan**

Learn how to lose weight safely while breastfeeding.

Everything Guide to Postpartum Care **by Meagan Francis**

A detailed guide to helping you get back on your feet after having a baby, from the physical to the emotional, vaginal to cesarean.

Essential Exercises for the Childbearing Year **by Elizabeth Noble**

A guide to physical exercise to ensure a healthy pregnancy, delivery, and faster recovery.

POSTPARTUM DEPRESSION

Postpartum Support International

Provides you with information on the signs and symptoms of postpartum mood disorders as well as how to get in touch with local resources.
www.postpartum.net

SAFETY

Consumer Product Safety Commission

This governmental agency's sole responsibility is to help consumers ensure product safety. In addition to recalls, you will find the current safety standards for various items including cribs and car seats.

www.cpsc.gov

Seat Check

This website is dedicated to helping parents find local safety inspectors to ensure that their car seat is correctly installed. It also offers other tips and tricks related to car seats and infant safety.

www.seatcheck.org

SINGLE PARENTING

About Single Parenting

Looking for good resources on what it takes to be a good single parent and how to deal with some of the issues that can come up? Between the expert articles and the discussion forums, you can get support from many single parents.

http://singleparents.about.com

SLEEP

The No-Cry Sleep Solution
by Elizabeth Pantley

A favorite of new parents, this book discusses methods to help you and your baby get more sleep in the gentlest approach possible. Includes stories from families with a variety of sleeping arrangements.

Helping Baby Sleep
by Anni Gethin and Beth Macgregor

This book marries current research with a practical approach to helping your baby sleep. Gone are the days of simply being told what to do. Here is a way to understand why things work and don't work for infants.

SUDDEN INFANT DEATH SYNDROME (SIDS) / INFANT LOSS

First Candle

An informative website that also includes ways to contact local providers for information on support and fundraising to help with SIDS research

www.firstcandle.org

VAGINAL BIRTH AFTER CESAREAN (VBAC)

International Cesarean Awareness Network (ICAN)

ICAN offers local meetings, Internet discussions, and other resources for those looking forward to having a VBAC as well as cesarean recovery.

www.ican-online.org

Vaginal Birth after Cesarean

This factual site will offer you insight on the medical and emotional side of VBAC. This is also a great site for recovery after a cesarean or VBAC birth.

www.vbac.com

PHOTOGRAPHER CREDITS

Absodels/gettyimages.com, 166

altrendo images/gettyimages.com, 236

© Bartomeu Amengual/agefotostock.com, 32

Tony Anderson/gettyimages.com, 100

Bruce Ayres/gettyimages.com, 220

Bambu Productions/gettyimages.com, 91; 139

Liz Banfield/gettyimages.com, 208

Ben Bloom/gettyimages.com, 285

© blueduck/agefotostock.com, 159

Brand New Images/gettyimages.com, 87

© Liane Cary/agefotostock.com, 14; 212; 157

© Stewart Cohen/agefotostock.com, 187

Comstock Images/gettyimages.com, 56

John Cumming/gettyimages.com, 262

Vanessa Davies/gettyimages.com, 241

Ghislain & Marie David de Lossy/gettyimages.com, 153

© Fabre Florence/agefotostock.com, 140

fotolia.com, 116; 147; 206

Courtesy of Daryl Gammon-Jones, 36

© Glowimages/agefotostock.com, 205

Charles Gullung/gettyimages.com, 20

Gary Houlder/gettyimages.com, 99

John Howard/gettyimages.com, 154

© Mirko Iannace/agefotostock.com, 199

Image Source/agefotostock.com, 8–9

iStockphoto.com, 6; 10; 13; 22; 23; 27; 29; 30; 38; 49; 50; 51; 60; 65; 67; 71; 72; 78; 79; 81; 83; 96; 97; 104; 106; 110; 112; 113; 120; 122; 123; 125; 129; 130; 132; 136; 137; 142; 144; 148; 150; 155; 161; 162; 163; 164; 171; 179; 181; 183; 184; 190; 195; 200; 204; 210; 214; 222; 224; 231; 232; 245; 248; 254; 255; 260; 261; 264; 265; 272; 274; 278; 283; 284; 287

JGI/gettyimages.com, 201

Ruth Jenkinson/gettyimages.com, 156

© Joseph/agefotostock.com, 84

Jupiterimages/getttyimages.com, 107; 194; 237

Courtesy of William Kiester, 40

Carol Kohen/gettyimages.com, 180

Jaime Kowal/gettyimages.com, 279

Elyse Lewin/gettyimages.com, 268

Ryan McVay/gettyimages.com, 258

© Marcus Mok/agefotostock.com, 198; 226

© Monkey Business–LBR/agefotostock.com, 34; 59

Laurence Monneret/gettyimages.com, 41

© Moodboard/agefotostock.com, 52; 62

Mooney Green Photography/gettyimages.com, 250

© Roy Morsch/agefotostock.com, 2

Nancy Ney/DK Stock/gettyimages.com, 54; 82

© Lucianne Pashley/agefotostock.com, 135

© Picture Partners/agefotostock.com, 257

© Martin Plöb/agefotostock.com, 234

© Nicole Plöb/agefotostock.com, 281

© Piotr Powietrzynski/agefotostock.com, 182

Ben Welsh Premium/Alamy.com, 276

© Marina Raith/agefotostock.com, 102; 114; 128; 168

Christa Renee/gettyimages.com, 68

Marc Romanelli/gettyimages.com, 238

Andersen Ross/gettyimages.com, 271

Science Photo Library, 93

© Science Photo Library/agefotostock.com, 228

shutterstock.com, 86; 92; 117; 173; 177; 186; 192; 217; 223; 239; 257

© Juan Manuel Silva/agefotostock.com, 243

Ariel Skelley/gettyimages.com, 196

Zia Soleil/gettyimages.com, 253

© SuperStock/gettyimages.com, 108

Jerome Tisne/gettyimages.com, 240

Titus/gettyimages.com, 188

Camille Tokerud/gettyimages.com, 76; 170

Michal Venera/gettyimages.com, 90

Courtesy of Robin Elise Weiss, 5

Ross Whitaker/gettyimages.com, 26

© Wilmar/agefotostock.com, 15

Yellow Dog Productions/gettyimages.com, 46

INDEX